W9-COM-991

"The state of Camden Public Schools when I was young left my parents fearful for my future and my safety. They jumped at the chance to send me to LEAP Academy University Charter School, a place they knew had the potential to provide me with a better quality education. I entered at 3rd grade and continued to grow with the school till I graduated my senior year of high school after being accepted to Brown University. My parents were right and I would not be in the position I am now without the opportunities that LEAP offered me."

JULIANNA PEREZ,
LEAP Academy Graduate, Class of 2007

"My visit to the LEAP Academy Camden was inspiring. The school is achieving amazing results academically, emotionally and socially because they have involved the community to join together to raise the children. They have been able to provide life opportunities for the students and something from which we can learn."

ANNIE FOGARTY,
President and Chair of the Fogarty Foundation,
West Australia

"Dr. Gloria Bonilla-Santiago has written an engrossing memoir that describes the personal journey from her modest beginnings in Puerto Rico to the highest honors of academic excellence. Hers is a story of outstanding leadership. Her ability to implement innovative and effective practices continues to provide environments of educational excellence for students, where failure and despair are too often the norm. A must read for educators and for everyone who enjoys an inspiring story well told."

DOROTHY S. STRICKLAND, PH.D.,
Distinguished Research Fellow National Institute for Early Education
Research, Rutgers, the State University of New Jersey

"One woman's vision, many people's hands joined together to build a future for a community's children. It is a story to inspire and encourage others never to lose sight of what can be done when you know it is the right thing to do."

CAROLE LELAND, PH.D.,
Honorary Fellow, Center for Creative Leadership and Co-Author Women of Influence, Women of Vision

"There are times we find people like Gloria Bonilla Santiago, who provide us with extraordinary insight and perspective that make us realize who we are and what we stand for as a people and as a nation. She has captured the essence of public service and what it means to be part of a community."

BOB MENENDEZ,
US Senator for New Jersey

Dr. Gloria Bonilla-Santiago fulfilled her vision of the egalitarianism in educational opportunity for underserved students of all backgrounds. Through her dedication and courage, she has worked with her associates to create a remarkable institution that has enabled disadvantaged, minority young people to achieve academically, and thereby become more productive citizens. This book shares her experiences and wisdom, and her program sets a fine example for all educators. It teaches us how we might strive to improve educational opportunity for all Americans through dedicated public service."

S. ALLEN COUNTER, D.M. S.c., PH.D.
Professor and Director of the Harvard Foundation

From her impoverished beginnings to the highest ranks in academia, Dr. Bonilla-Santiago's remarkable journey illustrates how she overcame adversity and transformed an entire urban community by creating one of today's most successful charter schools …a must read.

FORMER U.S. SENATOR BILL BRADLEY

The Miracle on Cooper Street

The Miracle on Cooper Street

Lessons from an Inner City

Gloria Bonilla-Santiago, PhD

ARCHWAY
PUBLISHING

Copyright © 2014 Gloria Bonilla-Santiago, PhD.

All rights reserved. No part of this book may be used or reproduced by any means, graphic, electronic, or mechanical, including photocopying, recording, taping or by any information storage retrieval system without the written permission of the publisher except in the case of brief quotations embodied in critical articles and reviews.

Archway Publishing books may be ordered through booksellers or by contacting:

Archway Publishing
1663 Liberty Drive
Bloomington, IN 47403
www.archwaypublishing.com
1-(888)-242-5904

Because of the dynamic nature of the Internet, any web addresses or links contained in this book may have changed since publication and may no longer be valid. The views expressed in this work are solely those of the author and do not necessarily reflect the views of the publisher, and the publisher hereby disclaims any responsibility for them.

Any people depicted in stock imagery provided by Thinkstock are models, and such images are being used for illustrative purposes only. Certain stock imagery © Thinkstock.

ISBN: 978-1-4808-0623-8 (sc)
ISBN: 978-1-4808-0625-2 (hc)
ISBN: 978-1-4808-0624-5 (e)

Library of Congress Control Number: 2014904722

Printed in the United States of America

Archway Publishing rev. date: 03/21/2014

*To om
with love
Dr Santiago*

This book is dedicated to the children
and families of LEAP Academy.

CONTENTS

FOREWORD

The LEAP Academy Charter School in Camden, New Jersey is one of the most impressive schools in the urban United States. It currently has an enrollment of thirteen hundred students from K through 12. For the last several years its high school has realized a 100 percent rate in graduation as well as admission into higher education. In this book, its founder, Dr. Gloria Bonilla-Santiago shares the challenges and obstacles, the potential resources, and the support of fellow professionals in higher education, the private sector, and elected officials that moved LEAP Academy from a small charter school in 1997 to today, where it includes an elementary to high school pipeline, nurtured by comprehensive supportive services for students and their families. This book describes and analyzes the establishment, and accomplishments, of LEAP Academy in what many consider among the poorest and most economically distressed cities in America.

But this is also a story of Dr. Bonilla-Santiago's personal and professional struggles as a Latina—*puertorriqueña*—from an impoverished and working-class background, surviving and fighting for respect in an academic world that many times did not value racial or ethnic diversity. Dr. Bonilla-Santiago realized at some point in her life that the struggles she was engaged as a person were parcel to the everyday struggles of children and youth living in impoverished communities across the nation. And she believed that education represents a critical venue for people to fight poverty and enhance opportunities for the growth and enrichment of their children. This vision and the work accompanying it have propelled the school into national and international prominence.

She founded LEAP Academy Charter School not to weaken or dismantle public schools in the city of Camden but rather to strengthen the proposition that every single child is a potential genius. This proposition also reflects the belief that all children can be nurtured to love learning, and very important, to develop a commitment to give back to his or her community. This is a standing feature of LEAP Academy. What also is highlighted here is Dr. Bonilla-Santiago's work with the parents of children. Parents have been continually assisted in becoming important learning partners with the teachers of their children and with their own children after school hours. It would not be a boast that LEAP Academy has made an enormous contribution in strengthening families in Camden and raising the stock of social capital and civic engagement on the part of youth and parents. Alas, while the story of LEAP Academy is unique, it has important lessons for many other communities and cities in this country. This is a book that should be read by anyone concerned about ensuring that all children, regardless of race or ethnicity or language background or economic status or where they happen to live, can enjoy the fruits of quality and empowering educational experiences as part of their foundation for a productive future.

JAMES JENNINGS, PhD
Tufts University

PROLOGUE

Validation and Acceptance at Last!

For decades I had prepared for this moment. All my hard work had come down to this one warm evening in June 2006 when the LEAP Academy University Charter School graduation was held in the most unlikely place for a Camden public high school—a spanking-new amphitheater on the Rutgers University campus in the poverty- and crime-ridden New Jersey city.

Nearly one thousand people, mostly black and Latino, filled the amphitheater, hugging and high-fiving each other as they waited for the ceremony to begin. They were the parents, families, and friends gathered for this graduation of the students of LEAP, which stands for Learning Education and Partnership. The fact that the audience far outnumbered the thirty-five graduating students was an indication of how important this event was in their lives.

Their faces, shining with joy and pride, brought a flush to my face that had nothing to do with the steamy weather. At age fifty and regarded as a tough, no-nonsense Latino academician and social activist, I am not someone who cries easily. That night, however, my tears began with the first strains of "Pomp and Circumstance" and continued throughout the ceremony. And, unlike many other times in my life, these were tears of joy, for this graduation represented both a major milestone in my life's work and the validation of my belief that poor, urban communities can be transformed through education.

This was, after all, Camden, New Jersey—one of the nation's poorest, most depressed, and most violent cities. It is located directly across the Delaware River from the penultimate American city of Philadelphia. But with its average annual family income of $24,000, Camden exists outside the American strata and miles away from the American dream. Nearly half the city's children live below the poverty line and have only a 50 percent chance of graduating from one of its subpar public high schools. Those who do graduate usually lack the financial resources or grades to attend college. Instead they find their options are limited to low-paying jobs with no access to careers that can break the cycle of poverty that grips their lives.

With little hope of prosperous futures, many Camden teens just hang out on street corners in front of dilapidated and abandoned buildings. Some will turn to illegal activities to make their livings, and whether they are perpetrators of violence or victims, the bulk of their time will be spent on merely surviving.

But that was not the case for these LEAP graduates or for the hundreds who have followed them since—all students who were lucky enough to be chosen in an annual lottery, an often cruel and disheartening practice charter schools must conduct to fill their classrooms. These

LEAP students achieve a 100 percent graduation rate and will earn 100 percent admission into college, where they will maintain a 90 percent retention rate.

Every LEAP graduating class since the first in 2005 has achieved that remarkable record. I don't know of a public or charter school anywhere that can match those outcomes over the same length of time.

When the US Department of Education revised its formula for determining public-school graduation rates in early 2012, reducing the schools with perfect 100 percent records in New Jersey from several hundred to seven, the LEAP Academy survived as the only charter school on the list. More importantly, those numbers tell me LEAP has given its students the skills and social capital to succeed in society, truly transforming their lives and futures.

But serious thoughts of the future were not on anyone's mind in the Rutgers amphitheater that night in 2006. It was actually the second graduation of LEAP students. The first, held the year before in the LEAP high school's gym, had been a validation of LEAP's mission and program. The second graduation, in 2006, was both validation and acceptance of LEAP's students and their families on the Rutgers campus and into the world of the university.

Each LEAP graduation, wherever it's held, is all about the students and the very human stories they represent—overcoming unimaginable poverty and crushing violence in their neighborhoods and conquering language and comprehension barriers to earn, in most cases, what no one else in their families ever have: diplomas and opportunities to continue their educations.

On graduation night in 2006, the Rutgers auditorium was overflowing with balloons, banners, stuffed animals, and flowers, to the point that

Rutgers security interrupted the ceremony and, for "safety reasons," required that all the decorations be moved to a covered entryway to the auditorium. The audience moved swiftly to comply, and even though this delayed the ceremony by thirty minutes, it didn't dampen anyone's enthusiasm. Everyone in the room knew these graduating students had beaten the odds, and they'd come to celebrate accordingly, with passion and noise and shouts of "Olé," *"Felicidades,"* "We love you," and "You go, gal!"

The cheers grew louder as each graduate appeared in a maroon robe and mortarboard at the rear of the auditorium. Each strolled down the aisle with a distinctive swagger of self-confidence toward the elevated stage. Many in the audience smiled, noticing the huge platforms and stiletto high heels worn by the female students, personal touches that have become graduation traditions. I have always believed each person has his or her own unique talents, gifts, and personality, and these fashion statements are small but powerful reminders that LEAP has successfully instilled this credo in its students. For many this graduation is the first time in their lives they are being honored both individually and as part of a cohesive community.

Indeed this is an evening of many firsts. For most in the room, it is the first time anyone in their family has graduated from high school. It is also the first time most of the families and relatives have been on the Rutgers campus for the simple reason that they have never been welcomed.

For decades the Rutgers campus had stood in stark relief against the decay, violence, and abject poverty of Camden as the university had ignored any responsibility or connection to the community in which it is located. One might think Rutgers's beautiful buildings and rigorous academics would serve as inspirations for the community. Instead they have stood for vast social inequalities.

Like a castle with a moat, signs in Spanish when I first had come to Rutgers Camden read *"PROHIBIDO EL PASO,"* which the university administration thought meant "keep off the grass" instead of "keep out"—a reminder to the people of Camden that they did not belong. I was stunned and angered by the signs, which to me represented a lot of what was broken with our education and immigration systems. Getting rid of them became my first order of business at Rutgers.

Seeing so many community people there for the LEAP graduation was vindication; I felt not just for me or for Camden but for all those who have been marginalized in our society. That night it felt as though the "keep out" signs had vanished from Rutgers for good.

The tone for LEAP graduations was actually set at the first, a year earlier, when the keynote speakers—US Representative Rob Andrews and Rutgers Camden Provost Roger Dennis—both commented on the significance of the event in a city like Camden. In fact it was Dennis's remarks urging students to "define yourself as a kid from Camden" that drew the loudest applause.

Two students graduating that night—Sylvia Vasquez, the class valedictorian, who had come to LEAP as a shy, reclusive young girl from Guatemala; and Julio Atenco, the class salutatorian, who had come to LEAP as a seven-year-old from Mexico—were in many ways typical of their classmates. Sylvia and Julio had overcome poverty, language barriers, and uncertain immigration statuses as well as learning challenges and social handicaps to graduate with honors from LEAP and go on to excel in college. Sylvia earned advanced degrees in engineering from Villanova and could have landed a professorship at any prestigious university. Instead she returned to LEAP to teach math to third- and fourth-graders because that's the age she believes students are most receptive to math concepts. Julio, whose dream of becoming a doctor was nearly shattered when Brown University withdrew financial aid when it discovered he was an undocumented immigrant, returned to Camden to complete his undergraduate work at Rutgers. He is now applying for medical school in the hope of reaching his dream.

When they had enrolled at LEAP, many if not all of the students graduating in 2005 had been fourth-graders reading at low-grade levels, to say nothing of their poor writing and critical-thinking skills. In short they had fallen through the cracks in both the public education system in Camden and in society.

What these remarkable children, and every child who came to LEAP after them, did have was a passionate desire to learn, which I believe is the most important ingredient for success in education and in life.

No, I thought, as I moved through the auditorium on those graduation nights, the children were never the obstacles to the work. The obstacles were the adults—the politicians, administrators, and even teachers who lacked the sensitivity, training, and compassion to engage these bright young minds. The most difficult aspect of my work over the past twenty-five years has been convincing those adults that educating Camden's children would uplift not only them and their families but their community and our society as a whole.

I tell these graduation stories as an introduction to *The Miracle on Cooper Street* because they were pivotal events in the story of my life and the development of LEAP, which essentially is a story of dreams and realities. These LEAP graduations could have been the culminations of those dreams, times to pause and reflect, relax, and regroup. They could have been capstones to my career as an educator and social entrepreneur. In reality they were just the beginning of a story that gets better and better as each year passes.

The Miracle on Cooper Street tells the story of my life—the life of a destitute Puerto Rican child of migrant farm workers who defied family, tradition, and expectations to reach the highest ranks of academia and overcame monumental obstacles to create one of the nation's best charter schools in, arguably, America's poorest and most violent city.

It is a story about the American dream come true for one of its most disadvantaged and challenged citizens. There is heart-wrenching drama in my life. There are life-changing tragedies. There is a murder. And there are contentious political and decades-long bureaucratic struggles to achieve my goal of transforming a poor, urban community through education.

My personal journey began on a dirt-poor mountain farm in Puerto Rico and led to desolate and gritty migrant-worker camps in New Jersey and Florida; to treks by the age of eighteen to Mexico, to Russia, and to work in the Cuban brigades; to the crime and poverty on the streets and in the barrios of Camden; then to becoming a Board of Governors Distinguished Service Professor and the Community Leadership Center director at Rutgers Camden.

My education journey has earned me multiple advanced degrees and has taken me to the pinnacle of academia. The list of people who have guided me, mentored me, and helped me achieve my dream reads like a modern history of social activism and education policy, from Saul Alinsky to Cesar Chavez, from Delores Huerta to Joe Nathan and Joe Fernandez. There are the many political leaders, from nearly every governor of New Jersey to the Clintons in Washington, DC, who have helped me along the way.

I might still have been picking asparagus in the migrant-worker fields today if not for a woman named Marta Benavides, a mysterious Salvadoran revolutionary, social activist, and ordained minister who mentored me for nearly twenty years, nurturing my intellect and independence as a woman. It was Marta who made me realize I did not have to spend my life as a migrant worker or, for that matter, as a wife and mother—which were at the time radical notions in the Puerto Rican community.

Those experiences forged my dream of transforming a poor, urban community through education. It led me to found the LEAP Academy, the miracle on Cooper Street in Camden, which today is not just a single school in one building but a complex of five schools creating an education pipeline from birth to college. It teaches 15 percent of Camden's schoolchildren and provides an essential comprehensive, holistic model with wraparound social services and health care to LEAP families through six LEAP Academy Centers of Excellence.

Those centers, operated by contract with Rutgers and other institutions, are an essential component of my concept of a community school. We have created:

1. A health and wellness clinic for LEAP families, most of whom have no health insurance

2. A parents' academy that instructs parents on how to support their children's educations and includes job and leadership trainings

3. A legal clinic for LEAP families, maintained by the Rutgers Camden School of Law

4. A professional-development teacher education center, which provides ongoing training for LEAP's faculty and staff

5. A college-access office, which advises LEAP parents and students from birth to preschool and onward to get them ready for the college experience

6. A health and human services center to provide healing and counseling for the children and families of LEAP

In the process we have transformed Cooper Street from a series of dilapidated, abandoned, and boarded-up buildings into a vibrant, emerging education corridor attracting new construction by two universities, a county college, and support businesses. As a result, the local media has dubbed me the patron saint of Cooper Street.

The LEAP complex on Cooper Street consists of a STEM (science, technology, engineering, and math) elementary school and high school, a traditional elementary school and high school, and an early learning research academy (ELRA) that admits children from birth to pre-K and allows researchers to study the benefits of early learning. A LEAP environmental-science school is under development on a protected wetlands tract adjacent to the Cramer Hill Camden neighborhood, which will offer inner-city kids the unique opportunity to study and experience their natural environment.

I paid for the construction and operation of these state-of-the-art schools mostly with the $50 million in capital support I raised through grants and fund-raising activities since LEAP opened its doors in 1996. Scholarship funds I created to assist LEAP graduates in college now total more than $1.3 million.

Along the way LEAP as a charter school has established a longer school year and longer school days and negotiated New Jersey's first pay-for-performance contract with its teachers union, leading Governor Chris Christie's administration in 2013 to approve LEAP's teacher-evaluation performance pay tool as a model for all schools in New Jersey.

At the same time, the State Department of Education has supported LEAP's enrollment growth and revenue projections as well as its expansion.

This means in the next few years, LEAP can grow its education pipeline to 2,340 students—fully more than one-fifth of Camden's public-school population. That truly is a miracle.

In chapter 8 I will present an extensive case study of the LEAP experience that will detail the background and history of LEAP, the City of Camden, and the charter movement; discuss the key strategies and methodology used in creating LEAP; provide quantitative student and teacher performance results from 1997 to present; and, importantly, detail the lessons learned and the best practices of the LEAP experience.

To think, all this sprung from the mind of an idealistic young girl who dared to believe that an education would take her out of the migrant-worker fields. My experiences have only cemented my belief that education must be the centerpiece of any comprehensive strategy to overcome obstacles facing children in poor communities.

If the American dream is the ability to achieve success regardless of one's birthplace and economic status, then LEAP is that dream in action. I believe implicitly that safe, prosperous communities are the right of every individual, and a quality education is the right of every child.

My next step, and a central reason for this book, is hopefully to inspire other educators, parents, and community leaders to adapt the LEAP model in other impoverished areas throughout the country and, eventually, around the globe.

Since the beginning of LEAP, I have visited, lectured at, and consulted in more than thirty countries, from Australia to Brazil to South and West Africa. I initiated an innovative exchange program between Rutgers and the University of Havana that takes Rutgers students and me annually to Cuba. And I am currently advising the governments and NGOs of Brazil and Ghana on education policy; I also advise the administration of Puerto Rican Governor Alejandro Garcia Padilla on transforming the island's school system to the LEAP model.

Whenever I speak about my work at LEAP, someone inevitably asks, "Dr. Santiago, how have you been able to do it?" After all these years, I don't have to think about the answer. I tell my audiences that before taking each step, before making every decision, I simply ask myself two questions: "How will this benefit children?" and, "Will it help them grow and learn and acquire the social capital they need to survive and excel?"

I've had tremendous help and support along the long road to answering those questions in a positive way and while creating this remarkable enterprise of LEAP through struggles and setbacks—all of which I have overcome.

That road may have been unimaginably bumpy at times. But, oh my God, what a ride it has been!

CHAPTER 1

. . . .

The Beginning: A Road Map
of My Life in Education

I sit wedged between my mother and father in the front seat of our battered blue 1950s Chevy station wagon, reading a carefully marked road map for my father. He is driving the Bonilla family on our annual trek from a migrant worker camp in New Jersey to a camp in Florida. It is 1962, and this is my first trip. I am eight years old.

My father has given me the job as his navigator, because I have learned English faster than anyone else in our family since we migrated from Puerto Rico to work in the big agribusiness farms of New Jersey and Florida. The map is in English, while everything else in our migrant world and life is still in Spanish. But I also suspect that as the youngest and smallest of the six Bonillas—my father, Pedro; my mother, Nuncia;

my older sisters, Milagros and Irma; my brother, Pedro Jr.; and our dog, Lobo—all of whom are in the car—I take up less room in the front seat.

This is a trip we make twice a year, according to the picking season for crops. We spend March to September in New Jersey and September to March in Florida. We drive straight through, stopping only for bathroom and rest breaks and to eat the sandwiches and fruit my mother has packed for the trip. Even Lobo adheres to our scheduled stops, never offering so much as a whimper if the time between breaks is long. There are no hotels or motels marked on our maps. The car is our home.

"Don" Pedro Bonilla, Gloria Bonilla-Santiago's father

My father is the sole driver. He is a very quiet and disciplined man. He does not smoke or drink (not even the wine offered as a holy sacrament in church), although my mother, Nuncia, insists he must taste it if he is to honor the sacrament. He eats only half the food he is ever served, dividing his rice and beans on his plate and eating only one portion. It is a peculiarity that keeps him trim, and one he will continue, even when his children are grown.

His remarkable endurance behind the wheel is built on years of eighteen- to twenty-hour workdays in the fields. In the 1960s, it takes more than thirty hours of steady driving to make the trip between the migrant camps, because the interstate highway system is not yet complete, and the route we must travel is circuitous.

There are many exits and turns in Virginia, the Carolinas, and Georgia, and they must be carefully monitored on the map. My father has marked in detail every road we plan to take and every gas and rest stop we plan to make. This increases the importance of my job as the map reader. At night, when the dashboard light is insufficient, my father gives me a small pocket flashlight to illuminate the map and to keep us on the right route. My endurance grows along with his.

Under the map on my lap, I carry my school records in a folder. Even at this young age, I consider it my most prized possession. My school year conforms to the migrant seasons and is spent partly in New Jersey and partly in Florida. I learn early that without the records of what I have accomplished to show new teachers in new schools, my schooling can be interrupted and inconsistent. Every year I am either the new kid in class or the kid who will be leaving soon.

I carry the records on my lap, instead of leaving them in the box my mother has for our birth certificates and other important family documents. I do this because I want to make sure that everything is in order for my new school. In a sense, I am already taking charge of my education.

I share the front bench seat in the car with my father and mother. I am cradled between my parents for the few hours I do sleep—usually at the urging of my father, who tells me to pass the map and flashlight to my mother for a while. My two older sisters sit side by side in the backseat, and my brother shares the rear of the station wagon with our dog—and the occasional cat that tags along for the trip. Pedro is the only one who can actually lie down to sleep, curled up with Lobo.

All our family possessions are firmly tied to the roof of the car in boxes and crates. My mother, who cooks for the migrants my father recruits to work on the farms, leaves her utensils and her pots and pans behind in New Jersey, because she knows we will return to the camp six months later. Everything else we own—mostly well-worn clothes—is carried with us or tied to the roof of our home on wheels. There are no unnecessary items. There are no dolls or toys. We are not going on vacation. I have managed to bring a few books to sate my thirst for learning. I sometimes read them instead of the map, often by flashlight in the middle of the night, when there are long stretches of road or highway that don't need attention.

I made that trip for eight years, twice a year, until I rebelled. I'd learned almost every twist and turn and rest stop by heart on our route to Florida and back again to New Jersey. I can still feel the bumps and vibrations of the road and, when I close my eyes, experience the sheer joy of stretching, after hours of sitting cramped in the car. But at fifteen, my education had become too important to me to interrupt again, and I refused to make another trip to Florida.

I was taken in that year by Marta Benavides, the woman who would become my intellectual mentor. That separation from my family marked the beginning of not only an avid pursuit of education but also my life as a strongly independent Latina woman. Just as meaningful was the fact that I broke the cycle of life as a migrant.

It was years later when I realized how much I had benefited from the many practical life lessons learned on the annual jaunts to Florida and back—not the least of which was the road map as a way to plan for the future and assure success. The road map became the metaphor for my life in education and the discipline of planning it represented. Knowing where I wanted to go and what I wanted to do became the greatest part of my success in creating LEAP.

I also learned endurance on those more-than-thirty-hour trips, emulating my father and his steady focus on the task at hand. Years later, as a young Puerto Rican activist, I drove long distances and long hours to Canada and points west in America. To this day, I can stay awake for long periods of time and get by on only several hours of sleep a night. Often, my most productive time is late at night, when others are sleeping.

Perhaps the most valuable lesson gleaned from our trips, however, was the realization that learning comes quickest and easiest at an early age—the earlier the better. My father saw how fast I, the youngest in the family, learned to read English when we migrated from Puerto Rico, and he arranged for me to be tutored in English and to have help with my schoolwork. He took me for tutoring to a nearby camp in Woodstown, New Jersey, where a migrant cousin who had married a girl from New York City lived. She gave me special instruction and, as untrained as she was, instilled in me the first yearning and passion for teaching.

My father took me—not my brother or sisters—for tutoring. It wasn't that he didn't value education for them, but they were old enough to work in the fields. I was not. Back then, farmers required children of migrants to begin working in the fields at age fourteen—sometimes earlier, if families wanted to stay in the camps. I was the inquisitive one in the family, and I learned English the fastest. I was always asking questions, always talking with the farmers and translating for the workers. I was the one my mother sent on errands.

Gloria Bonilla-Santiago and godparents Fautino Mercado and Isabel Ayala when she was one year old, Sabana Grande, Puerto Rico

Years later, my firsthand experience with early learning would benefit literally hundreds and hundreds of LEAP Academy students. In a reversal of my experience, Spanish instruction three days a week begins in preschool for LEAP students and assures that everyone who graduates is bilingual. I have also applied early learning to science and math at LEAP, with specialized STEM education starting in the elementary grades and continuing through high school. I learned that the sooner interest in a subject is sparked, the greater the probability the student will succeed.

Life for me began on January 17, 1954, far from any city, on my grandfather's farm in the small town of Molinas, which is in the region known as Sabana Grande in the southwest corner of Puerto Rico. I was delivered by a midwife, as were my sisters and brother, because no hospital or doctor was nearby. I was born into a world ruled by men but in many ways silently dominated by strong-willed women.

At that time, Puerto Rican culture was filled with contradictions. It was a world where devout Catholicism coexisted with an even more deeply held belief in *Espiritismo*, the very well defined Caribbean form of spiritualism that embraced old wives' tales and family legends in everyday life.

My grandfather's farm sat on the side of a hill in a green valley that was divided by a *quebrada*, a rocky creek that ran through the valley and overflowed several times a year in the rainy season. The creek separated the farm from a dirt road that led to a small Catholic church, a one-room schoolhouse, and then into the town of Molinas. There was no bridge, so the only access to the farm was by fording the creek, which slowed to a trickle most of the year.

An abundance of fruits and produce—mangoes, avocados, guavas, tamarinds, bananas, beans, corn, and yucca for making *cassava* bread—were grown and harvested on the farm. Coffee and sugarcane in nearby fields provided income for the Bonillas who worked those fields. There were horses and a cow on the farm, and pigs and chickens roamed free. Fresh vegetables such as lettuce, yams, potatoes, and other greens were grown, although many poor Puerto Ricans did not eat salads or vegetables. We lived on a diet of rice and beans and meat.

Despite its lush appearance, the farm could barely sustain the generations of Bonillas and extended family who lived there. My grandfather, Abelino Bonilla, had twelve children with two wives. And his children, including my father, had families of their own. Everyone had many aunts and uncles and cousins, and some aunts and uncles and nieces and nephews were the same age and grew up together. At times more than thirty people were living on the farm. Everyone thought we were poor, but we didn't know that.

My grandfather's house was very big with many rooms. My father, who was the oldest of the twelve brothers and sisters, was allowed to build his own smaller house nearby, where I spent the first seven years of my life. I remember my grandfather, for the most part, as a frightening figure, always with a big hat and often on horseback. He was much darker skinned, almost Indian-like, than most of the Bonillas, who, like my mother and father, were fairer in complexion. It was much later in life that I came to realize that lighter-skinned Latinos had an easier time of getting along in the world. I should have realized sooner, perhaps, because my father's oldest sister, my aunt, who was very fair, married a man of means and moved away from the farm at a young age while another aunt who was dark like my grandfather didn't marry until late in life and never left the farm.

My most enduring memory of my grandfather is a prophetic chant he would utter after chasing me down, grabbing me, and lifting me to his face: "Gory! Gory! Gory!" he would shout. *Gory* is my nickname to this day. "Gory! Gory! Gory! *Héchale tierra al pobre!*" ("Gory! Gory! Gory! Throw earth to the poor!") he would incant over and over. I was frightened every time he said it. But my Bonilla aunts, who were deep into spiritualism, assured me it meant I would grow up to do something important in my life to help poor people.

My mother had named me Gloria because, she said, it meant "glorious." It is the only name I have, unlike most Latinos who are christened with two or three names. My sisters and brother and I have only single names because my father, despite his strong religious beliefs, did not believe in the Catholic practice of bestowing multiple names.

Gloria Bonilla-Santiago's birthday celebration at three years old

My grandfather's first wife, Samona Mojica, was fair skinned and had Asian features because, as the family legend goes, she was descended from Japanese adventurers who had searched the western mountains of Puerto Rico for gold. Many of us in the Bonilla family, including me, inherited those traits. I met Samona only once in my life, after my grandfather died. She had fled the Bonilla farm before I was born and disappeared for years after my grandfather took one of her daughters from a previous marriage, Alejandrina Cintrón, just twelve or thirteen years old at the time, as his second wife. It was many years later when I met Samona at a reunion, after several of her sons had tracked her down in San Juan, where she had lived alone and worked hard for years supporting herself as a housekeeper. It was a very brief and sad reunion. And, as much as I may have wanted

Alejandrina Cintron and Abelino Bonilla Grandparents

to, I never learned a lot about her struggles to survive because her life story was such a closely held family secret.

As bizarre and shocking as my grandfather's marriages may seem, we were told as children that in those days in rural Puerto Rico, marriage was often less a legal or religious rite than a matter of self-indulgence and convenience in a world where men ruled absolutely. In this instance, my grandfather made the arbitrary decision to take Alejandrina as his wife, and no one was there to object.

My mother and father married in their teens, without a religious ceremony or wedding celebration, by obtaining a license in town from a local magistrate and later having a local priest consecrate their union.

They have endured as partners for more than sixty years. And they did not celebrate their marriage until I gave them a fiftieth-anniversary party in 1997.

Nuncia and Pedro Bonilla at their 50th wedding anniversary

The story of how my mother and father met is a wonderful one that I, as a child, would ask my mother to retell over and over again. Their meeting was very typical of how couples came together in rural Puerto Rico at that time. And the fact they have endured together for so long despite their different personalities and backgrounds is a testament, I believe, to the way they have always worked hard together, placing family and traditional values above all else. It is a trait I've seen many times in the Latino families and parents who came together to help me create LEAP.

My father's family, the Bonillas, lived on a big farm and were very conservative in their personalities and politics, and very socially active. My mother's family, the Rodriquezes, lived on the other side of the island, on a small farm many miles away. She inherited the outgoing, socially active nature of her family, which was very involved in the Puerto Rican Democratic Party where they lived.

My mother and father met at a dance party in Sabana Grande. My mother often went to the dances, which many times followed political rallies for the Democratic candidate she was supporting at the time. The campaigning consisted of riding the countryside in big open trucks and singing songs and shouting slogans for their candidate. At night there would be parties, and my mother, who loved to dance and have fun, would always go.

At one of the parties, she saw my father. He never had learned how to dance, but he was there with his brothers because it was the only place rural farm boys could meet young girls socially. My mother said she and my father exchanged fervent glances before they struck up a conversation that lasted the entire night. They talked and talked, she said, and their feelings of mutual affection immediately grew. Their dates consisted of my mother telling my father which dance party she would be at, and they would meet there. But he would never dance.

Soon they were engaged, to the great satisfaction of the Bonilla and Rodriquez families, but the fact my father did not dance almost ended their relationship. My mother loved to dance, so much so that at one of the parties she asked my father for permission to dance with other men. When she started dancing, her mother, Dona Luisa—who had a special affection for my father because he had asked for her daughter's hand and visiting privileges in the very strict and traditional Latino way—took a palette of palm fronds and began to hit my mother, driving her from the dance floor, exclaiming, "You should be ashamed of yourself. You are engaged, and you should not be doing that. A good woman does not do that." Then she took her home.

To my father it was okay for his Nuncia to dance. It didn't bother him because he knew she was just enjoying the dance. He was way ahead of his time in thinking that way, but it bothered my Dona Luisa because it violated her standards of how she believed an engaged couple should behave.

My mother said she was so upset and humiliated by her dance-floor expulsion that she broke up with my father, maintaining the incident was entirely his fault, that he was too fearful of confrontation with her mother and didn't do anything to defend her or prevent her public embarrassment at her mother's hand.

It was at this point in the story that I would always ask my mother, "So how did you get back together?" And she would tell me how my father won her back by writing her letters nearly every day and dropping them in her mailbox. His persistence reminded my mother of the quiet strength she had come to love, and their reconciliation marked the beginning of the sixty-year partnership that continues today.

The lesson I took from the story was the way my father handled his problem. He always believed and taught us Bonilla children that there are ways to achieve justice without confrontation. Many times I saw him, as a migrant crew and union leader, apply that wisdom in his dealings with the workers and farmers who employed him, and I was reminded of how he had wooed and won my mother.

My grandfather's second wife, Alejandrina, is the woman I came to know and love as my grandmother. She nurtured me as a child and singled me out among all the Bonilla children on the farm for special attention and affection. She lived to be one hundred; she passed away in 2007. I visited her often in Puerto Rico, where she still lived as the matriarch on the Bonilla farm. As her oldest son, my father inherited portions of the Bonilla farm, and knowing I was Alejandrina's favorite, he asked my advice on what to do with it. Considering the displacement of the Bonillas who still lived there and the fact that absentee management of a farm like that is not possible, I sadly told him just to let it go.

Most of my memories of life on the farm in Puerto Rico are wonderful, interspersed with a number of traumatic experiences and incidents I seem to recall most vividly of all. As a small child, most of my days were spent barefoot, roaming the farm, playing games I no longer recall, tagging along to help pick fruit in the fields or help with menial chores. My grandmother often gave me sandals to wear, but as soon as I was out of sight they would be discarded. When I was five or six, I began to attend the one-room schoolhouse across the *quebrada* and down the dirt road with my sisters, brother and cousins, and even an aunt or uncle or two. The school housed grades one through eight. I do not recall much of my time there because I only attended for a year or two before we left for the States. I do know it was not the place where my passionate pursuit of learning began.

One of my favorite pastimes on the farm was sitting on the rocks by the quebrada as my mother and aunts did their laundry in the creek and gossiped and told stories, mostly about the family and the Bonilla men. Several times a year the creek would overflow, and the Bonilla children would gather on the banks to throw stones and watch the raging waters rush by. For as long as the rapids flowed, we were isolated on the farm and could not get to the road to go to church or to the one-room schoolhouse that all the Bonilla children attended. I can attest to the fact that it was the only time in my life I was glad I didn't have to go to school.

Several times a year, hurricanes would sweep across our part of Puerto Rico, and all the Bonillas would take cover, sometimes for several days, in a makeshift storm shelter and take turns peeking through slats to survey the wind and havoc of the passing storm. It was frightening to a young child, and I often wondered if anything would be left standing when we emerged. But whatever was happening, life on the farm, in good times and bad, was always very communal, a sense of feeling we were all in it together. It was certainly an experience and a concept that stayed with me through my career in education and at LEAP.

One of the near tragedies in my early childhood involved my older sister, Milagros, when I was five or six years old. The cooking for my family was done in a *fogón*, an earth oven carved out of a mound near our house and fueled by wood. Milagros had gathered wood for a fire and was trying to ignite it; I took several matches and playfully lit them and tossed them into the oven. One of them missed its target and struck my sister on her back, instantly igniting her thin cotton dress in a sheet of flames. She was severely burned and to this day bears the scars on her back. I cried uncontrollably for days—one of the first times in my life, but certainly not the last, that I shed tears of pain and sorrow. I felt responsible for the near tragedy and still do fifty years later. I remember it so vividly not only out of guilt but because of the terrifying realization that a moment's turn of fate could lead to disaster.

Another near tragedy occurred when, at three years old, I was stricken with a mysterious stomach and intestinal illness that almost cost me my life. When I wasn't vomiting, I was fading in and out of consciousness. My mother, who was suffering from severe depression after a recent miscarriage, was unable to care for me. I was so thin and small, and the situation got so serious, that my father, who had begun migrating to the States to work, returned home and began to treat me with a steady diet of pear juice. Every day he gave me pear juice until I slowly got better and better. Whatever the illness actually was, to this day he says he saved me with pear juice. In the end, nearly everyone attributed the mysterious illness to bad meat, and as a result I have lived most of my life as a vegetarian.

Perhaps the early childhood experience that made the most enduring impression on me was the influence of so many strong-willed and strong-minded women, though not always in positive or pleasant ways as witnessed by the long-running contentious relationship and test of wills between my mother and grandmother. When I was three, my father left Puerto Rico to begin working as a migrant in the States, first under a contract program with the Puerto Rican government and then through the Operation Bootstrap program for migrants initiated by President Kennedy. He took all five of his brothers with him to the States, leaving behind their wives to work the farm and raise their children. Years later my grandfather committed suicide, hanging himself from the limb of a mango tree, utterly despondent, it was said, that none of his sons had ever returned to the farm in Puerto Rico.

The Bonilla women, who proved to be the most influential on my early childhood, scraped by the best they could on the farm. But it was a hard and poor life for them. At one point my mother embroidered edges of handkerchiefs on consignment, working well into the night after the day's chores were done. It didn't pay much, but it was her first job involving

Mother Nuncia Bonilla, sisters Milagros, Irma and Gloria Bonilla

piecework—an experience that would be replicated many times over in the migrant fields of New Jersey and Florida.

Much of the tension between my mother and grandmother, both stubborn and single-minded women, stemmed from the circumstances of my grandparents' marriage. My mother, who had come from a distant town to marry my father, never accepted or felt comfortable with the very nontraditional arrangement or, for that matter, fully warmed to many of the Bonilla women. But, I also believe part of the difficulty between them was my mother's resentment over the extra attention and affection my grandmother showed me. It's almost as if my mother felt she was losing me.

The catalyst for the showdown between my mother and grandmother seemed innocuous enough—a doll my grandmother gave me as a Christmas gift when I was five years old. My parents never celebrated Christmas with gift giving. Instead we would begin each New Year a few days later with a ritual cleansing shower or bath and then celebrate Three

Kings Day on January 6, when my father would give us candy or take us for an ice cream treat, a practice that continued even when we moved to the migrant farms in the States. It wasn't until many years later, when I was married, that my husband, Alfie, and I began to exchange gifts at Christmas.

My grandmother would give small gifts to the Bonilla children during the holidays against the objections of my mother, who insisted she did not want her children spoiled, although I now suspect some of my mother's resentment had to do with her rivalry with my grandmother. One year my grandmother gave my sisters ribbons and barrettes for their hair, and because I was her favorite she gave me a beautiful doll with a long ponytail. I loved the doll, but my mother would not let me keep it. She would not even let my sisters keep the trinkets for their hair. It triggered a series of arguments and screaming matches between my mother and me until she grabbed the doll and tossed it behind my bed, ordering me to return it.

I retrieved the doll and tearfully brought it to my grandmother, telling her of the bitter fight I'd had with my mother. My grandmother told me to keep the doll, but the arguments over it continued. I finally decided to settle the issue; I took a machete that hung near the fogón earth oven to chop food and wood and hacked the beautiful doll to pieces, believing I had ended the source of all the anger in our family. Crying, I took the pieces to my grandmother to show her I had gotten rid of the problem that caused such anger in our family. She consoled me but said, "You should not have done that. This was not about you or the doll!" Then she took one last look at the broken doll and said, "I'll get you another one." The following year she did, and it was even prettier than the first.

It was the first time I had ever defied my mother. And even at that young age, it was the first time I had exhibited many of the traits I inherited from my mother—*sagacidad, tenacidad, y resolución,* or willfullness, tenacity, and resoluteness. Coupled with a healthy dose of *obstinación*—stubbornness, which I also shared with my mother—these later led to years of alienation with no communication between us.

Soon after I turned seven, my father sent for his family to join him in the States. He had become a crew leader, organizing migrant workers for one of the major farm conglomerates in Salem County, New Jersey, which allowed him to bring his family to the camp. It all happened very suddenly and quickly. One day my mother simply told us to pack everything we owned, which was not much, and say good-bye to our family and friends because we were moving. The next day we left. My mother arranged for a car, with money my father had sent for our transportation, to take us on the long trip to the airport in San Juan. We really did not have much time to get too emotional about what was happening.

In fact, besides the anxiety over where we were going, the saddest part of leaving the farm and Puerto Rico was leaving our family dog behind. We always had a dog not as a pet but as a protector against animals or poachers or anyone who might threaten us. That was the dog's job. He was a member of the family but had a job just like everyone else. As we carried our bags across the quebrada to the car that would take us to the airport, Lobo followed us. After we packed up and drove off, the dog ran after the car for miles and miles until he could no longer keep up. My grandmother wrote us that he disappeared for nearly a year but eventually returned to the farm. Although he ate the food she gave him, she said he never left our house until the day he died, no doubt waiting for his family to return.

It was February, the middle of winter, when our Eastern Airlines flight from San Juan landed in Philadelphia. I had never flown or experienced cold weather before, and it was bitterly cold. As we descended the stairs from the plane, which was parked some distance from the terminal, and started our walk across the tarmac, I began to shiver uncontrollably. My sisters and I wore only thin cotton dresses. We did not own winter clothes. My mother, seeing me shake, took a sweater from her bag and wrapped it around me, and I don't think I have ever worn anything as warm.

My father picked us up at the airport in the old blue Chevy station wagon for the forty-mile drive, most of it through nearly endless fields of crops, to our new home in a South Jersey migrant camp. The landscape was mostly flat with vast fields of crops, unlike the green hills and valley where we had lived in Puerto Rico. The shock of cold air turned out to be mild compared to the shock of seeing our new home, a bare wooden barracks where the whitewash had long ago peeled or faded, isolated in a field of brown on a single-lane rural road. There were no curtains, no lawn, no greenery, no plants or flowers, again unlike the home we had left in Puerto Rico. It wasn't until years later that I realized the barracks bore a striking resemblance to military-camp barracks I had seen in pictures.

Forty years later I visited the migrant camp on the farm where I had grown up and was surprised to see our barracks home was still standing though virtually unrecognizable, having been converted into a ranch-like residence. It had a driveway, a birdbath on the front lawn, greenery and flowers around the house, and window treatments. It was painted a reddish-brown earth tone with white trim and showed no evidence of its history.

The barracks we moved into in New Jersey was our home for the next eight years. On the one end were two bedrooms—one for my mother and father and the other shared by my sisters, my brother, and me—as well as a sizeable bathroom with a big shower but no bathtub. After a day in the fields, the shower ran nonstop seemingly for hours. In the middle of the barracks were the kitchen and a big dining area with a long, wooden table and benches. At the other end were sleeping quarters, with bunks stacked three and four high, for the crew of migrants my father recruited to stay for a couple days or weeks to work in the fields.

Everything was bare bones. There was little furniture and, although we had electricity, no TV. Several years later my father bought a small black-and-white set, but I don't recall watching it. Even then my pastime was reading. Only two pictures were in the house, hanging in my parents' bedroom: one of Jesus Christ and the other of President John F. Kennedy because he was the first Catholic president and had supported economic progress for the island.

There was no privacy in our barracks home until I discovered the one place that I, as the smallest Bonilla, could be alone: under my bunk bed. All my life I have been a dreamer, and the dark seclusion under my bed was the perfect spot to crawl into to dream of the future and fantasize about the people and things I had read about in books. I took to writing my hopes and wishes on small slips of paper. I would write: "I want to have a big house. I want to go to school. I want to be a teacher." Anything I wanted to do in my life, I would jot down. I had little notion of reality in my dreams.

I would hide the little slips of paper under the mattress on my bed. Periodically my mother would find them and tease me about the things I wished for. It wasn't until years later that she acknowledged the power of this childhood practice, saying, "I used to think it was ridiculous when you hid under your bed and wrote those things down. But you did everything you said you were going to do!"

In Florida the living conditions were better because the camp we migrated to was set up differently. It was actually a fenced and gated compound with individual cottage-like houses for crew leaders and their families, located in central Florida between West Palm Beach and Boca Raton. The migrant workers were trucked, sometimes many miles, to the fields to work. And migrant children were bused to schools near West Palm Beach.

The camp was run by Polish people who contracted with big farmers to house migrants. They also operated several small stores in a central area of the camp to meet the everyday needs of the migrants so no one had to leave the compound. While the conditions and community atmosphere were better in Florida, the fenced and guarded compound certainly reinforced the sense that we were confined and different from people outside the gates. Because of that I actually preferred living in the harsher conditions in New Jersey, where there were no fences, and we were free to come and go as we pleased.

Soon after we moved into our barracks home in New Jersey, we got another dog, also named Lobo. And because I had cried the hardest over leaving our first Lobo behind in Puerto Rico, my parents gave me a cat. It was the first pet I had ever owned. In fact it wasn't until many years later that I had a dog that didn't have a job to do. Today I have two shih tzus, Tilin and Atachi, who are perhaps the most loved and pampered pets in dogdom. It is my job to protect them, not the other way around.

Every day in the migrant camp was essentially the same, filled with hard work and a routine that didn't change. Most days began before dawn, when my father either drove his crew of migrants to the fields that had to be worked or drove to a holding camp in Woodstown where all the migrants had to register before being recruited. Nearly all the migrants were Puerto Ricans or Mexicans who had come to the States under government contracts.

Because my English was best, I would often go with my father to Woodstown to help with translation when necessary. Out of respect for his fairness as a crew leader, the migrants called him Don Pedro, and because he had that reputation he never had a problem recruiting the best workers for his farms. My father never carried a gun or other weapon, as did many of the crew leaders in the camps to intimidate and control their workers. There were always stories of beatings and violence, even murders, in other camps. And years later, after we had left the migrant camps, there was a nationally publicized incident involving a New Jersey state legislator and a news reporter who were brutally beaten with baseball bats when they tried to inspect conditions in a migrant camp. The incident led to significant legislative reforms for migrants.

My father ran a very clean camp. He never drank or smoked and would not allow alcohol in his camp. He treated everyone, the farmers and migrant workers alike, with dignity and justice, and they regarded him with mutual respect. I admired his integrity and the way he stuck to his principles. On the weekends life in the migrant camps could be depressing. There was little to do. No TV. No recreation. So, many of the crew leaders would allow road vendors into their camps on Saturdays and Sundays to sell just about anything—beer, drugs, and even prostitutes. My father would allow only vendors who sold clothes—shoes and socks and blue jeans, shirts and pants and dresses. He told us we could never allow our camp to become like many of the others where fights and drunkenness were the norm on weekends, because the farmers would lose faith in us, and we would lose our jobs.

I wrote my doctoral dissertation on the plight of migrant workers. It was published in 1988, titled *Organizing Puerto Rican Migrant Farmworkers: The Experience of Puerto Ricans in New Jersey*, by Peter Lang Publishing Inc., New York, London. It too led to migrant reforms.

I think my father made a big difference in my life and in the lives of the farmers he worked for, the migrants who worked for him, and everyone who was around him because he treated everyone so equally and so well. I learned the values of fairness and social justice firsthand at my father's side. He would take me to meetings and rallies he attended as a migrant crew leader and then as a union organizer in a South Jersey steel mill, often carrying me on his shoulders when I was younger so I could see what was going on and tell him what was happening. When there were protests, he would tell me when to raise my sign and when to pull it down. He would tell me in Spanish what to say, and I would shout it in English. I saw that his quiet but assured demeanor and his leadership by example were more effective in confrontations than the loud and bullying tactics of some of the other migrant or union leaders. Those values of fairness and social justice served me well later in the distressed Latino community in Camden, particularly in organizing poor, urban parents to work for the creation of LEAP Academy.

My father was a reflective man with a lot of patience and an incredible sense of justice that gave him the strength and courage to stand up for his migrant workers. He never lost in disputes with farmers over individual workers or camp conditions because he had a way about him, an air of confidence and sincerity, that was not confrontational. He always did his homework and always had the facts in a dispute. He played his role well, and as a result the workers trusted him; the farmers too trusted him and never viewed him as threatening their control.

He developed an incredible network of social capital and resources—churches, priests, ministers, social service agencies, legal services, and farm worker agencies. He knew the people at the Migrant Farm Workers Agency in Vineland, which had units all over the area, and the lawyers at Legal Services in Glassboro.

It was this network that proved particularly effective in my father's efforts to combat one of the most abhorrent practices on the migrant farms: dumping on the roadways of South Jersey workers who were being evicted or replaced by other migrants who might be younger or faster in the fields. The fired workers were literally left by the roadside with their bags, sometimes in the middle of the night, with nowhere to go. My father was always picking them up, sometimes driving the farm roads to look for them. He became their advocate, trying to get them placed at other farms where they would be treated better or taking them to an agency where he knew they would get help. This was no doubt the main reason migrant workers bestowed the title of don on him.

Dumping wasn't the only abuse inflicted on migrant workers. Living conditions were barely tolerable back then. There was no health care. No health insurance. If workers got sick, they had to work no matter how ill they were or face expulsion from the camp. Worst of all, there was no recourse for the injustices. Whatever the farmers said was the law. Whatever they told workers to do had to be done.

By the time I was ten, I knew there were things that were not right. I knew that migrants were treated differently and not always fairly. But we adjusted to that kind of life, and at times I thought that was the way it was always going to be. My father, being the introspective and nonconfrontational man he was, didn't want us, his family, to question anything in a way that would anger or displease the farmers. He would question conditions when he was with his workers, and he would advocate on their behalf with the farmers. But we women—my mother, my sisters, and I—were not supposed to question or get involved. That changed for me as I got older and wanted to speak out more openly about the migrant-worker conditions and injustices.

While my mother continued to tell me not to get involved, my father's objections turned to tacit approval and, eventually, support.

Whatever the conditions or dire circumstances we faced as a family, my mother and father never complained. Every time I think about it, I realize they were phenomenal people to have lived the way they did and not have anything and yet keep working, working, working. For me it was to become a cycle of sameness and poverty that had to be broken. As a young girl, the vision I had of our life was New Jersey to Florida, Florida to New Jersey. The seasons changed, but other than that nothing new happened.

For as long as we lived in migrant camps in New Jersey or in Florida, I was never kept out of school to work in the fields. My sisters and brother were kept out when they reached the mandatory age for migrant children to work: fourteen, though in many camps it was earlier. When school was not in session, which for me meant the summer months in New Jersey, everyone worked. Because my English was so good, and I could best translate their instructions, the farmers told my father to put me in the truck at their side and assigned me the job of collecting and keeping an accounting of the tickets the migrants were issued for their piecework. Those tickets were the most valuable commodity to the migrants because without them, the workers would not get paid. There were often reports of crew leaders who cheated their workers or were sloppy and careless in their accounting. Occasionally a worker would question why such an important task was in the hands of a small girl. But in all the years I collected tickets for my father, I'm proud to say I never once made a mistake or lost a single ticket.

At the age of twelve, I learned to drive the truck that was used to transport the workers to and from and across the huge fields they worked. It was a large and unwieldy stick-shift truck with a canopied flatbed in back where the workers sat. Because my legs were too short, my father would tie wood blocks to the pedals—the gas, the clutch, and the brake—so my feet could reach them. From all accounts I was a good driver. And I loved to drive the truck if for no other reason than the cab provided some shelter from the unrelenting heat and blistering sun in the wide-open fields. Needless to say, the ability to drive just about any vehicle for long hours and distances was an asset later as a community organizer and Latina activist on many cross-country trips.

The crops we primarily harvested in New Jersey were tomatoes, peppers, beans, blueberries, and asparagus. In Florida it was mostly tomatoes, peppers, and cut flowers for the floral industry. The picking was hard, hot, and dirty work. Gloves had to be worn even on the hottest days to pick most of the produce. In particular the tomatoes would ooze a sticky juice that could produce an irritating rash after too much contact. To this day I hate the smell of tomatoes and peppers. And the blueberries—I don't eat them now because I ate so many when I was working in the fields.

The asparagus was actually magical to me as a young girl because they grew so quickly. It seemed to grow not by minutes or hours but by seconds, and migrants had to work in lines, one behind the other, down the rows of asparagus plants, each worker in turn slicing off a stalk with a metal cutter. If you glanced back down the row over your shoulder, you would see the asparagus sprouting again. So I never really liked it because there was so much of it, and when cut in such large quantities it gave off a very bad smell. It is easy to understand why migrants didn't eat a lot of what they picked.

My mother did all the cooking: three meals a day for our family and my father's migrant crew, which sometimes numbered more than twenty men. Our diet consisted mostly of meat and rice and beans, cheese and meat sandwiches to take to the fields, and occasionally fruit or other vegetables that were being picked at the time. Our family ate first at night, and then the migrant crew would be fed. Immediately after our meal, I would be sent to my room. My two older sisters would stay behind to help my mother serve the men, but as soon as that task was done they were also sent to the room we shared. My mother did not want her daughters mingling too much with the men, although they found time during the day to tease me a lot, especially about snakes. They knew I was terrified of snakes and had me convinced the small stand of woods across the road from our barracks home was infested by huge ones. I never went into the woods and lived in terror that someday the snakes would get our dog, my cat, or me.

I drank milk mostly until I fell deathly sick with an illness that was attributed to drinking raw milk. That time my father took me immediately for medical care in Woodstown, which no doubt was the reason I got better so quickly. But my mother, still adhering to the ways of rural Puerto Rico, insisted I also had to see a spiritualist if I were to be cured. She took me to a spiritualist in Vineland, about thirty miles away, who many of the Puerto Rican migrants in our camp visited and recommended. And while there may have been potions and herb poultices involved, all I recall about the visit was a prediction the spiritualist made about my future. She told me I would have three men in my life: a dark man, a man with green eyes, and a man with light hair and a fair complexion. I recall it so vividly because I think it came true. My first serious involvement was with a dark-haired Latino in Philadelphia. The man I married, my beloved Alfie, had green eyes. And now Michele, the man I am seeing fifteen years after Alfie's death, is a light-haired, fair-complexioned Northern Italian.

Since I did not eat meat as a result of my childhood illness in Puerto Rico and no longer could drink milk, my diet consisted mostly of small portions of rice and beans supplemented by vitamins my mother would make me take and large quantities of cod-liver oil she would force me to drink. The cod-liver oil was horrible, and I shiver today even to think about it. The vitamins and oil were my mother's way of trying to give me energy and nutrition. I'm not sure it worked, though. I remained very thin—the thinnest of all the Bonillas because, I believe, I never ate properly.

The best part of my life was school. It opened the world to me beyond the migrant camps and the farm in Puerto Rico. I soon developed a passion for learning, and reading everything I could get my hands on became my way to gain knowledge. I was the most inquisitive one in my family and always talked to the farmers, other migrants, and just about anyone else my family would meet.

Whatever the subject, math or history or civics, I wanted to learn as much as I could about it. And since every subject was taught in English, I concentrated hardest on learning my new language. My thirst for knowledge soon became a continuous quest to learn something new. That's why I carefully carried my school records from New Jersey to Florida and back again. Migrant children, who often attended two or three different schools in a school year, were treated differently by most teachers and often were made to repeat subject matter they had learned before. I did not want that to happen to me.

In New Jersey I would walk nearly a half mile to an intersection to get on a school bus that would take me to an elementary school in nearby Pedricktown. I would do the same in Florida, walking a distance from the compound gate to catch the bus to school in West Palm Beach. My father often chastised me for the practice, saying the buses would come directly to our house to pick me up, but I would make up some excuse or other for not asking them to do it. I did not want the other children to see where I lived, although I'm sure they knew I was a migrant child. But because I suspected they did, it spurred me on to do the best I could in school.

Every day I went to school, my pet cat would follow me down the road to the bus stop. And, quite astonishingly, the cat would be waiting at the stop when the bus dropped me off at the end of the school day. But one day when I stepped off the bus, the cat was not there. I was devastated when my parents told me the cat had been killed, run over by an earlier school bus after darting out into the roadway. I cried for days and days over the loss.

If school was my favorite place to be, then Cowtown, a huge flea market and rodeo several miles away on State Route 40 in Pilesgrove, New Jersey, was not far behind. It's difficult to describe Cowtown and what it meant to migrants and their families. It was the one place migrants could go after long, hard days in the fields to shop and socialize. It was loud and raucous. And it was always exciting. A thirty-foot statue of a cowboy and an equally large statue of a steer stood alongside the highway, beckoning and welcoming visitors to Cowtown, a huge complex of red-painted barns and wooden buildings that housed stables and a flea market and a rodeo arena. The flea market, open year round several days during the week and on Saturdays, stretched for row upon row through several long, red barns with booths and tables for hundreds of vendors. It advertised that "everything imaginable" was for sale in Cowtown, and for migrants and their families it was the place to go for anything they might need. For years all my clothes and shoes were bought in Cowtown.

Every Saturday during the summer months, a rodeo was staged in a big, stadium-like arena with wooden bleachers. It was a professional rodeo with bull riding, steer wrestling, bronco riding, and barrel racing. My father loved the rodeo, and it was where he would go while the rest of the Bonilla family shopped or found amusement elsewhere in Cowtown.

About a half mile down the road to the left of Cowtown was a large ice cream factory. As out of place as it might have seemed in rural farm country, the Richman Ice Cream Co. had been located at the isolated Salem County crossroads since 1894. The factory had a small window in front to sell ice cream cones and cups to passersby, and it was my favorite destination when the Bonilla family went to Cowtown. I was saddened to learn in 2009 that the ice cream factory had closed.

A half mile to the right of Cowtown was a place none of the Bonillas ever went—a big tavern with music and dancing that catered to the rodeo cowboys and migrant workers. Located behind the tavern was a house where women were brought in from Philadelphia on the weekends to entertain migrant men. As youngsters, we were not supposed to know about that. But we did.

Cowtown is significant in my memory because it was where I met Marta Benavides, one of the most important people in my life. She was a Salvadoran exile and social activist who recruited young Latinos to her causes at Cowtown. She became my intellectual mentor and the key supporter of my pursuit of higher education. I had just turned fifteen, and she enabled me to defy my parents and refuse to make another trip to Florida because I did not want to interrupt my education again. She let me move into a small house she rented with her sister, and, having met my parents earlier, assured them she would see to my schooling and take care of me while they were working in Florida.

As it turned out, that trip to Florida was the last one my family would make because my father got a job in a steel mill in Swedesboro, a gritty manufacturing town in South Jersey. When they returned, he bought a house in Penns Grove, a small, equally gritty town near Swedesboro. Penns Grove was nestled between steel mills, oil refineries, and canneries in an industrial corner of New Jersey on the Delaware River, across from Wilmington, Delaware, and just south of Philadelphia. The house, a small cottage on a quiet residential street several blocks from the river, is where my parents still live today.

Through her contacts, Marta had helped my father find his new job and buy the house. As a teenager who still had the best command of English in the family, I translated for my parents with the lawyers who handled the purchase of the house. It had a rose-trellis portico and a picket fence and hedges in the front, and in back a big vegetable and flower garden that my parents carefully tended. My father worked very hard as a laborer in the steel mill and, later, in a Del Monte cannery. It wasn't long before he became a supervisor and union organizer recognized for his ability to deal with both management and workers.

In her new house, my mother had only to cook and care for her family, which meant she had more time to be involved in the daily lives of her son and daughters, a situation that would soon have ominous repercussions for my relationship with her. She had already lost her two older daughters to bad marriages to migrants, and her son was about to follow the same path. It meant she had more time and more reason to try to make sure that I, her youngest daughter, followed a traditional Latino path to a good marriage and raising a family. Unfortunately I was as strong-willed and stubborn as my mother and was looking only for the independence to pursue my quest for education and the opportunity to do something socially meaningful with my life.

The best part of the move to Penns Grove for me was the opportunity to attend the regional high school, a very large, sprawling, one-story quadrangle building that had just been built. I loved school, and my school life was filled with reading and study. I did not date or have a boyfriend. I didn't go to parties or to the movies. I devoted nearly all my time to class work. And I read, mostly schoolbooks and books that Marta Benavides recommended on social issues and political history. Under her tutelage I was becoming aware of the inequalities that existed in society and the unfair treatment many Latinos faced in America.

The only problem I encountered in my four years at Penns Grove High School was a stereotypical bias against migrant schoolchildren, who were often pigeonholed as difficult or impossible to educate. I faced that problem when my guidance counselors refused to schedule me for college-preparatory courses because they summarily deemed I was not college material. I had an after-school job in the principal's office at the time, and the secretaries there urged me not to listen to the counselors.

When my father learned about it, he was angry. He had taken a special interest in my education since we had migrated from Puerto Rico, arranging for tutoring in English, never keeping me out of school to work in the fields, and supporting my quest for education. In Penns Grove he would drive me to the library anytime I wanted to borrow a book or had a term paper due and needed to do research. And he would not pick me up until he felt assured I had spent enough time researching a subject.

Now, with his sense of fairness aroused, he came to the high school with my records from elementary and middle school that I had held carried so carefully on my lap during our migrations to Florida and back. He aimed to prove to the counselors that I was more than capable of doing the necessary college prep work and to insist they give me a chance. It worked. The counselors relented. And I went on to graduate with a straight A average.

Twenty years after I graduated, after I had earned my doctorate and achieved the highest status as a Board of Governors Distinguished Service Professor at Rutgers Camden, I was inducted into the Penns Grove High School Hall of Fame along with a more famous classmate, the actor Bruce Willis. In school I had known Bruce from a distance as a very popular student and playful prankster who was attractive to a lot of girls. Now our pictures hang side by side among the plaques and photos that comprise the hall of fame on a wall across from the principal's office.

At the installation ceremony, Bruce announced a multimillion-dollar economic revitalization program for Penns Grove, which had suffered severe depression and deterioration when major industries—the steel mills and several other big manufacturers—shut down. It was a remarkably generous gesture. But as noble as his motives were, the program was never implemented because of local bureaucratic obstinacy, bickering, and red tape. At the urging of my husband, Alfie, who accompanied me to the ceremony, I also announced a small scholarship program to assist Penns Grove graduates who would attend Rutgers Camden.

My graduation from high school and intention to go to college led to a serious rift between my family—mainly my mother—and me, a separation that lasted nearly ten years. My father had always been supportive of my education, whatever level I aspired to, including college. He was much more introspective than my mother, much more philosophical and respectful of book learning. From an early age, he had instilled in me a philosophy based on independence and freedom of choice, of being respectful to others and truthful to my own ideals and sense of justice. He had taught me how to survive outside the family and had always demanded and expected the best from me. Life is about integrity, he would say, and you should never compromise on that. His only advice when I told him I had decided to go to college was, "You've got to be responsible. And you've got to be on time!"

My mother, on the other hand, was much more the traditionalist, adhering to the values of family and religion that are prevalent in the

Latino culture and had been essential parts of her upbringing in Puerto Rico. Yet she is filled with contradictions. She is very intuitive and very intelligent and always the extrovert in the family. She senses when anyone in the family is ill or in trouble. She can feel when we are not okay. And because she is so smart, I believe she would have been a great lawyer or judge if she had gone to college. She was always more politically aware and astute than my father. She was the Democrat in our family, and my father the conservative Republican.

Yet in practice it was only her family, her children, and her spiritualistic aspirations for them that mattered. She was the controlling parent. My father never punished us. My mother did. She would punish and spank us often, and my father would actually be upset when she did. She dictated to us what we were supposed to do and how we were supposed to behave. She staunchly opposed my going to college. Her plans for me were to marry—hopefully a Latino who shared her traditionalist values—and raise a family. This despite the fact her two older daughters both had eloped in their teens to marry Puerto Rican migrants, marriages that were to end in failure. My brother too soon followed the traditional route. He had been accepted to college on a football scholarship but never attended, instead opting for a marriage that also ended in failure.

In the end I was fortunate to have inherited my values and sense of fairness from my father and my strength and will from my mother. It proved to be a very powerful combination. It gave me the wisdom to decide to go to college and the strength to stand by that decision regardless of the consequences.

With the advice, counsel, and strong support of Marta Benavides, I enrolled in Douglass College, the women's college at Rutgers University in New Brunswick, New Jersey, majoring in political science. It was a big step forward in my quest for education. And, as unwanted as it may have been, it was also a big step away from my family for a long time.

As a result, Marta emerged as the most important influence in my life.

CHAPTER 2

. . . .

Marta and the Seeds of Social Activism

I was thirteen when Marta Benavides came into my life. This mysterious Central American revolutionary and social activist would serve as my mentor and role model for nearly thirty years. She also played a critical role in helping me escape the migrant world, which, for all intents and purposes, had appeared to be my destiny.

I didn't realize it then, but even at that early age I was at a critical point of decision about my future. I could follow the path taken by my older siblings: marriage to a migrant Latino, children, and a life of hard labor in the fields or factories. It was the path my mother had so ardently advocated for all her children, and even after the marriages of my sisters and brother failed miserably she believed that my first priority should be finding a husband.

I saw an alternative. Even at that young age, I instinctively knew that an education was the only way to escape the bleak world of migrant work and intergenerational poverty in which I had grown up. To me the choice was clear: I had to purse my education even if it led to conflict with my mother.

My father, on the other hand, had been quietly assisting me with my education since I had arrived in the United States. Early on he had acknowledged my strong English skills; that was why he had chosen me as the map reader on our trips between New Jersey and Florida. Later he had made me his assistant in the fields while still encouraging me to do my schoolwork. At age thirteen I would have been required under the migrant workers' contract with the farmers to begin full-time work in the fields; however, my dad refused to pull me out of school. He did take me to the fields with him but only on summer breaks. By the age of twelve, I knew how every crop was picked and had learned to drive the stick-shift field truck. But my father would only let me work on tasks that complemented my schooling. I was responsible for the tickets that kept track of the workers' earnings, and I served as a translator for the migrant crews.

Until that point I had grown up with this wonderful combination of both my parents—the *sagacidad, tenacidad, y resolucion* of my mother and the shrewd yet gentle diplomacy of my father. But after years of witnessing life at the migrant camps, I had begun to question everything, and that was when I met Marta. She was the one who instilled in me the sense of purpose and justice. She also showed me that the inequities of the world were far more pervasive than what I had seen even in the migrant camps. I began to see what social justice is and how I could play a role in achieving it. So while Marta Benavides didn't make the decision for me to pursue an academic life, she did serve as a catalyst. She provided opportunities and opened doors, and I eagerly walked through them, for Marta was the first mentor and adviser outside of my immediate family to enter my life.

Marta had been born into a very wealthy, well-educated military family in El Salvador. She had come to the United States to attend the

Philadelphia Bible Study College, and after graduating she'd joined the New Jersey Department of Education's Educational Opportunity Fund (EOF). Her work focused on creating educational opportunities for migrant children. Therefore, Cowtown—a marketplace where migrant workers went to socialize, shop, and forget about life in the fields for a little while—was the perfect place for her to become involved with this otherwise isolated community.

Going to Cowtown was one of the highlights of my childhood. Since there were no TVs or movies at the camp, no recreational activities to speak of, a bustling marketplace seemed like the most exciting place in the world. It was as if Cowtown was a window to the other America, the one I had glimpsed from the front seat of my father's car as we made our biannual trips between the camps in New Jersey and Florida.

Whenever I went to Cowtown, I made sure to stop by the entrance to the barn, where upcoming events and programs were posted on a bulletin board and leaflets were laid out on a table. One day I was reading a flyer seeking tutors for the children of migrant workers when a woman approached and asked if I was interested in the position.

I could instantly tell she was not a migrant or in any way connected to the farm operations. She was impeccably dressed in an outfit that certainly had not been purchased at Cowtown and was petite, although she appeared taller because she was so thin. With her fair skin and short, cropped, light-brown hair, she looked more Caucasian than Hispanic. The fact that she did not wear a stitch of makeup only enhanced her elegant appearance, and she had an air of success I had never felt before but recognized immediately. Her only jewelry was a pair small diamond-earring studs. I would later learn she never wore makeup of any kind, never removed the diamond earrings, and despite her sophisticated appearance, was only about ten years older than I was.

What impressed me most about this woman was the way she spoke. Usually when I met a bilingual person, it was very clear which language had been his or her first. Marta, however, was equally fluent in English and Spanish, with only a trace of Spanish accent. She engaged me in conversation to gauge my interest in tutoring as much as my language skills. After we chatted for a while, she asked if my parents were with me at Cowtown, and if so, whether she could meet them.

The Cowtown encounter with Marta led to a series of visits to our home at the migrant camp. Surprisingly she did not pay much attention to me during her visits but talked at length with my parents about the importance of education as well as Latino politics, particularly the debate around whether Puerto Rico should become a state or be independent from the United States. She also talked about her ideas about improving life for migrant workers, including teaching them new, healthier cooking techniques.

Despite opening her home to Marta, my mother did not like or trust her. From the start she believed this well-dressed intellectual was interested only in recruiting her youngest daughter into a life of social activism and pulling her away from the family and the Catholic Church. I also believe that to some extent my mother was jealous of Marta, and she feared Marta would interfere in the traditional Latina relationship between a mother and daughter. To this day my mother maintains that Marta "stole" her daughter from the family. I, on the other hand, was thrilled by Marta and her offer of a tutoring job. For the first time, I would be earning my own money. More importantly, I believed, it would further my education and language abilities.

From then on Marta became a fixture in my life, and she was heavily involved with the workers at the camp. She worked with my mother to host a cooking class for the ladies, which enabled her to teach them about healthy eating habits while getting to know the worker community.

Suddenly I had a mentor—someone who understood the life I wanted for myself and was going to help me get there. She secured work papers from my school and paid me for tutoring the migrant children. She also got me involved in developing a youth organization, Puerto Rican Youth in Action (PRYA). She worked with PRYA to organize young people, mostly from migrant families, and she wanted me to be the president. I began to feel like I had an identity separate from my parents and the migrant community. So when it came time for the next trip to Florida, I told my parents I wasn't going. Instead, I would stay with Marta and continue to attend my school in New Jersey.

My mother and father were not happy with this, but in the end they gave in. I didn't tell them the whole story: that I had decided never to travel with them again. I figured I would fight that battle when the time came. It would be a moot point, however, because by the following year my father was offered the job in a factory in Swedesboro. For the first time since moving to the United States, my parents would have their own private home.

In the meantime, Marta continued to mentor my education, providing exposure to social and political activism as well as many learning opportunities. Despite her commitment to helping the poor, she wanted to introduce me to the finer things in life. So she taught me about culture and manners, how to set a table, and which utensils to use; for most of my life I had used only a spoon to eat. She took me to stores to show me what to wear and how to dress—like her, impeccably with brand labels. All I knew about were secondhand clothes from the Cowtown flea market, and it was years before I learned what the alligator logo on much of Marta's clothes stood for.

She often drove me and some of the other kids around, even to Philadelphia, showing us the nicer restaurants and saying things such as, "I want you to understand there is another life. You can have things like this. You can go to these restaurants and have good things to eat. You can have quality of life." We would read the restaurant menus in the windows but never go in. She pointed out the museums in Philadelphia, explaining that they were places to learn about art, culture, and even politics, and always emphasizing the point that we could one day have access to them.

Marta's mentoring was all encompassing, much of it about philosophy and life in general. "It's all about the relationships you make and keep," she would say. "It's about how you treat people with respect, kindness, and love." She taught me the difference between respect in American and Latino cultures. In America, she said, it's a sign of respect to make eye contact when being spoken to. "Look into my eyes," she would say when telling me something. In a Latino family, eye contact was actually a sign of disrespect, particularly when being admonished by a parent, which happened to me more and more the older I got.

One of Marta's favorite admonitions, one she often repeated, was about understanding the meaning of events in your life. "If you have an experience and you miss the meaning," she would say, "then you miss the experience!" It was a saying that had a dramatic impact on me. And it wasn't until years later I learned that the saying was not Marta's but actually a paraphrase of a quote from T. S. Eliot. It in no way diminished its importance for me or my belief in Marta's intellect.

She taught me how to read and told me what to read. The first book she gave me soon after we met was *The Little Prince*, by de Saint-Exupéry, a book that changed my life by giving me a sense of purpose and a philosophy of respecting myself. I still use it today at LEAP, reading it regularly to pre-K and grammar-school classes. Most of the books she told me to read were about Latino history, especially the history of Puerto Rico, and biographies of important people such as Abraham Lincoln (because "he stood up for justice"); Marianna Bracetti, a Puerto Rican national heroine; Nelson Mandela; Gloria Steinem; and Eleanor Roosevelt. When I balked at Eleanor Roosevelt, Marta insisted I read about her, saying, "You'll be like her someday because you have her strength."

She taught me how to write, insisting I copy long passages from the books I studied at the library, where, rather than dating or going to the movies, I spent most of my free time when in high school. Marta also worked diligently to improve my self-image and self-esteem. Early on she told me, "You don't have what all the other girls in school have—the jeans, the shoes, all the clothes—because your parents can't afford that. Okay.

But you have other more important things. You're inquisitive. You're smart. You have endurance. You have the ability to do things."

Marta taught me practical things too, introducing me to the writings and principles of Saul Alinsky, a renowned sociologist who wrote the book on community organizing. She taught me how to organize and instructed me on parliamentary procedures, how to run and control meetings, and how to work to a positive outcome. The lessons proved invaluable when, as an eighteen-year-old college student, I served as a board member for the Ministerio Ecuménico de Trabajadores Agrícolas (META), an ecumenical farm workers ministry in Vineland, New Jersey, and later as a board member for the Comité de Apoyo a los Trabajadores Agrícolas (CATA), the farm workers' support committee in South Jersey. I still recall a META meeting in July 1973 that went on for seven and a half hours without a break, trying to make rival factions cooperate.

When I was fifteen, Marta learned of a camp in Tucson, Arizona—the Encampment for Citizenship—and suggested I go. It was sponsored by the American Friends Service Committee, a Philadelphia-based group committed to nonviolent activism. Marta was working with them by that time, and she arranged for me to get a scholarship. In many ways it was like any recreational camp; however, it also had a program designed to foster leadership skills, and she thought it would be an important step in my development.

I was very excited about the idea. I had never been away from my family before and certainly not with a group of kids my age. But when I broached the subject with my mother, it immediately ignited another battle of wills and, eventually, a round of intense negotiations. After much effort on my part, my mother went from "no, no, you are not going" to "if you do this, you can go."

This was a seemingly endless list of chores in addition to those for which I was already responsible. Undeterred, I did more work around the house than I ever had before, and in the end my mother grudgingly honored our agreement. Marta would pick me up and drive me to New

York City, where I would catch the bus to Arizona. However, my mother was not going to give up control over the situation completely. When it was time for me to leave, she insisted on packing my bag, an old-fashioned suitcase like the ones we used to put on top of the car. She also insisted I wear a dress, a flowery frock that completely embarrassed me. Somehow I had to find a way to change clothes before getting on that bus!

Marta knew it was important for me to fit in with the other kids, but she just said, "Don't worry. Go like that. Go with a plan, and I will take care of everything." And she did. When we arrived in the city, she didn't head straight for the Port Authority but to a clothing store. She bought me jeans, T-shirts, sneakers that I changed into right there in the store, and a backpack. Indeed, by the time I boarded the bus I was wearing the uniform of the average American teenager.

That was where the similarities ended, however. The other kids on the bus were from wealthy New York families. They went to private schools, were very liberal, and, although they conversed in English, they still somehow spoke a completely different language from mine. I was the only Latina; everyone else, save one black guy from Georgia, was white.

The two-day bus ride was difficult. I was very shy and had absolutely nothing in common with these kids. My only comfort was studying the map Marta had given me. I traced the route with a pencil, circling the towns we would pass along the way just as my father had done with the map from New Jersey to Florida.

I said very little on the trip, but I did listen to the conversations going on around me. I listened to a tall girl with long hair and a hippie guy talking about smoking (I had no idea what they smoked, for I had led a rather sheltered existence); I listened to the other kids talking about their lives and future plans. The most important thing I learned from all that talking was that everybody on the bus wanted to go to college. Moreover, it was assumed they would have the means to do so.

When we finally arrived in Arizona, the camp directors gave us the schedule of activities as well as our sleeping assignments. I was to room with a bunch of girls, including the one with the long hair. She took an interest in me, perhaps because I was so quiet. She wanted to know where I was from and then, oddly enough, what kind of car my parents drove.

"What?"

"You know," she said. "A Mercedes or what?"

"Well, we do have a station wagon."

It was the same battered, blue Chevy station wagon we had driven every year to Florida and back. I didn't understand she was asking me these questions to find out what my social capital and status were like. In other words, I was poor, different from her, and she knew it. But then she said, "Oh, don't worry. It doesn't matter anyway. I just want you to come with me."

From then on she took me under her wing. She introduced me to the other girls, and when a guy came around with these little cigarettes—marijuana—and wanted me to smoke, she always protected me.

We took our meals in the cafeteria, and there were all these different fruits and vegetables I had never seen before: kiwis, strawberries, salads, an incredible variety. We never ate salads in our family, and I couldn't bear to eat most of the fruits or vegetables we picked. It was the worst thing in the world, but my mother thought it was the best way to get some nutrients into my system. Now, for the first time, I found myself eating fresh produce—salads, fruits, and vegetables. The other kids thought it was odd that I never ate the breads or other items in the cafeteria, but I wasn't interested in those things.

Since the goal of the camp was to introduce kids to leadership, several speakers would lecture us on the qualities of a leader, how we could work on our own development, and the importance of learning to trust our own judgments and abilities. There was also a social component to the camp, but aside from my small circle of friends I was virtually invisible to the others.

Then an amazing thing happened that changed everything for me: Dolores Huerta came to speak. She was very young at the time and so passionate about the plight of farm workers. Suddenly I thought, *Oh my*

God, I know about this. This was the movement my father had been telling me about!

Cesar Chavez also came to speak about the workers' movement. Both he and Huerta taught me it was okay to be proud of who I was as the child of migrant workers. They also reinforced what I had always believed: migrant workers have rights, and I could play a role in advocating for them. When they spoke of the need for workers to organize, I immediately connected it with the workers back home. I knew what pesticides were doing to them, and I understood that consumers could exert pressure on farmers by refusing to purchase certain produce. I sat there mesmerized by these powerful Latino activists; they were speaking about my life and about the lives of my family members and fellow migrants. It was completely random that I was there at this camp with a bunch of rich kids, and yet it felt like it was meant to be.

The next day a bunch of us went to the supermarket and saw workers picketing out front. Everyone else was about to go in, but I told them I wouldn't cross the picket line. When they asked me why, I turned to them in surprise. "Didn't you hear last night's discussion?"

The counselor with us said, "She's right. We don't cross a picket line because we're going to get hurt."

This made me very upset because clearly they had all missed the point of what Chavez and Huerta had been telling us. "It's not about us but about the thousands of workers who are being oppressed. By crossing this line, we're contributing to the oppression of migrant workers. I'm the daughter of a migrant worker!" It was like my shyness had suddenly evaporated; these kids needed to know the truth, and before I knew it, I was delivering it to them.

Before that day I had been just a quiet girl from New Jersey whose clothes weren't quite up to par. After that trip to the market, however, I became an important voice at the camp. They wanted to know how it was at the migrant camps. I began telling them about our barracks home, the lack of privacy, the insanely long hours, the abysmal pay, and finally the practice of dumping of migrant workers against which my father fought so hard. For me it was just a matter of talking about my normal life, but the rich kids were shocked by what they heard. They began offering help—and money. The worst part was they pitied me. I never let them see how that made me feel; I hid my true emotions. I just thanked them and said I had my own money, which, thanks to Marta, was the truth. Every two weeks she sent me a $50 stipend, which seemed like a fortune and added to my growing self-esteem.

My trip to Arizona was a life-changing experience. It exposed me to the world outside the migrant camps and showed me I could contribute in a very real way simply by educating others. That was a realization that shaped my future. When I returned home, I was completely different in both my thinking and my physical appearance. My hair was long, and I was dark from the Arizona sun. I was also stick thin again from a diet of fruits and vegetables. I had a new, positive perspective on life.

I began to study and read about Cesar Chavez and his work. And I soon discovered a quote that gave meaning to my Arizona experience and has shaped my life and work since then. He said:

> Once social change begins, it cannot be reversed. You cannot uneducate the person who has learned to read. You cannot humiliate the person who feels pride. You cannot oppress the people who are not afraid anymore. We have seen the future, and the future is ours! (Chavez, C., 1984)

This was an epiphany for me. Yet the self-esteem and positive perspective it gave me only made it harder to face my mother. In her eyes I had become a rebel, and she believed Marta was the cause. I, on the other hand, knew Marta would help me achieve independence from both my mother and the migrant way of life. It wasn't long before the struggle between us began again, with my mom trying to mold me into a traditional Latina and me fighting for the right to follow my own path.

Cesar Chavez in an interview for Gloria Bonilla-Santiago's
first book: Organizing Puerto Rican Migrant Farmworkers:
the Experience of Puerto Ricans in New Jersey, 1985

My mother also distrusted Marta because of her politics; she believed Marta was trying to convert me to be a Communist or Socialist. However, this was not the case at all. Marta was what I referred to as a "social-justice religious person." At least that's what she conveyed to me during those years. Even when I went to college and became a political-science major and therefore interested in an academic way in the Communist and Socialist ideologies, Marta never pushed them on me. She was interested only in social justice. She had ties to the Quakers and other religious people who advocated independence without following a particular political theory.

At first I simply accepted what she told me; after all, she was my idol. However, as I got older, I began to question her lack of political affiliation. I was learning that without a political ideology, working for independence accomplished nothing. For example, how could we advocate independence for Puerto Rico without any economic base or political system to support it? But whenever I took a political position or questioned her lack of one,

Marta got angry, saying, "We will not talk about the politics of Puerto Rico." Refusing to answer questions about her personal life or politics was a character flaw I noticed with increasing frequency as time went by.

Marta's religious views baffled me as much as her politics did. She had gone to a Baptist college only to become a Quaker and later an ordained minister—either Unitarian or Episcopalian, I wasn't sure which. Having been raised as a Catholic, I never understood how someone could jump so easily from religion to religion, but I simply chalked it up to another of Marta's mysteries.

Whatever her true feelings on spirituality were, this mix of religious contacts was Marta's bread and butter. To me this was the fascinating thing about her: she was able to bring together this religious mix of people. They provided her with grants to move forward with her activism, including the work she was doing with the migrant workers and the Puerto Rican Youth Association.

Despite her considerable influence over me, Marta never preached to me or pushed her religious views. She did take me to some Quaker meetings, but the members discussed only their personal shortcomings and how they could overcome them. Marta participated in this open confession and encouraged me to do the same. When I refused, saying I believed confession was a private matter between a person and his or her priest, she did not force the issue. I think she knew that although I was not the most devout Catholic in the world, I was used to certain traditions and rituals around religion, and she did not challenge them.

While Marta did not overtly control my religious life, she did influence it. Although she respected the Catholic Church as an institution, she did not think highly of the priesthood. She also maintained that institutions were not really religions, which should be about philosophy not rules or bureaucracy. Hearing her views did lead me to begin questioning Catholicism, especially after she told me the church had oppressed so many people throughout the centuries.

Out of respect I never told my very devout father about my religious doubts. However, soon after meeting Marta, I stopped attending Mass. Even when I got married, it was not in a Catholic Church but in the Douglass College chapel on the Rutgers University campus in New Brunswick. Alfie and I were married by Father Michael, who, besides being a Catholic priest, was also a social activist I knew through our work in the Camden community; still this was more for my devout parents and husband than for me.

Marta belonged to many committees and equity coalitions that in addition to being religious also advocated for social justice and equity throughout the world. Through these groups she secured grants that financed her international activism, which often required costly travel. Eventually these monies would also pay for my trips to Cuba, Mexico, and Russia, all of which I visited by the time I was eighteen.

Marta Benavides, March 1991

After I returned from Tucson, Marta got me a summer job with the American Friends Service Committee and even arranged for me to join one of their many youth councils. In 1976 some of the Olympic Games events were held in Varadero Beach, Cuba, and the youth councils were invited to go, essentially to accompany a bunch of wealthy American children who were attending. I was already working with these kids, so Marta knew I would want to go on the trip. She explained that because of the embargo between the United States and Cuba, we would have to fly first to Mexico, just as most Americans traveling to Cuba did in those days. I was young—only seventeen—and didn't even know about the embargo, but even if I had known it wouldn't have mattered because I wanted so badly to go. Besides, I trusted Marta implicitly, so if this was how it had to be done, that was enough for me. I never questioned her judgment or her motives until many years later.

When we arrived in Mexico, there were visas waiting for us just as Marta had said. The next day we flew to Havana, and there on the beach was a youth encampment where thousands of kids were learning about art and politics in a Communist country. Once again it was a bunch of rich kids and me trying to figure out our places in the world.

Gloria Bonilla-Santiago at eighteen years of age; first trip to Varadero, Cuba, in 1972, sponsored by America Friends Committee Philadelphia Youth Conference

I quickly fell in love with Cuba. At first it was because of the guys; after all, I was a teenager, and this was the first time I was traveling with peers. In fact, I met my first love on that trip, an artist named Humberto. He was wonderful, which made it even more difficult because we both knew he would never be able to get out of Cuba. I would keep in touch with him for many years and saved each and every picture he sent me.

I also loved the country itself, so much so that when I was in college I went there every chance I got. It did not matter how complicated the route had to be; I would go through Mexico, Trinidad, even Canada and Jamaica. In the late '70s, I went there with the Brigades, a collection of international—and usually politically motivated—work groups. I was in the sugarcane fields and did work on houses and on other tasks. For me it was a way to get to Cuba and to see a different political system in action, a system I eventually rejected. I also found a way to incorporate my experiences into my formal education by writing about Cuba for my school papers. When all is said and done, I have traveled to Cuba thirty times.

These years would shape my ideologies. I saw the good and the bad of the political system in Cuba, and I appreciated the Cuban way of life and the need for revolution. However, when Socialists came around the migrant camps trying to recruit the workers, I often wondered why they were there; in other words I questioned their motives.

My feelings were reinforced by Marta, who didn't want them recruiting the workers at all, particularly the young people. In fact she seemed determined to protect us from it. When I volunteered to sell the Socialist newspapers, her answer was an emphatic "no way." She said they had a very different agenda from ours: they were looking to spread Socialism, whereas we were advocating social justice irrespective of politics. I think this is why my father respected her work: he also approached social justice from a religious rather than a political perspective. My family never believed in or advocated leftist policies, not even my politically more liberal mother.

It was through this exposure to these varied and often nuanced viewpoints that my political formation emerged. After studying the different schools of thought and systems of government both in books and on my trips abroad, I cultivated a disdain for party politics and concluded I would be part of an establishment only to an extent that would allow me to change it from the inside. I did not want to work for or in government; I simply wanted to impact policy and gradually began to seek out an independent platform from which to do this.

Graduate student in International Women Conference—Brigades Cuba, 1978

It was this very independence that would lead to my estrangement from my family, particularly my mother. The conflict had been building since I had met Marta. My mother, and to some extent my father, feared they were losing me. I was spending every day after school with Marta as well as weekends and was falling more and more under her influence.

I began to walk a very fine line between Marta and my family. When she came to pick me up, my mother would try to assert her control. "I need you back here in an hour. If you are not home in an hour, you are going to be punished. You are not going to be able to go where you want anymore."

My father, who hated conflict, was also on a tightrope: he wanted to encourage my education without upsetting my mother. This would prove to be impossible. When I announced I would be going to college, the conflict that had been building for years came to a head. I left home and would not return for ten years.

Once again I went to stay with Marta. She helped me fill out my college applications and celebrated with me when I got in to every school. She even went to church and other local groups, including the prestigious Rotary Club, to raise money for my graduation present.

When all was said and done, I received $1,000, which Marta arranged to be announced at the graduation. No one had ever done anything like that for me. I had already beaten the odds by graduating from high school and with honors. The fact that people were celebrating it in such a way had me bursting with pride. I was excited to begin my studies at Douglass College, and thanks to Marta I didn't have to worry about tuition. She helped me fill out all the financial aid forms, explaining that as the child of low-income parents I was eligible for full assistance.

I began my freshman year brimming with excitement that the future I had envisioned for so long was now within reach. The school assigned me a "big sister" named Virginia Class, a junior who showed me the ropes. She taught me how to play tennis, how to socialize with the other students, and generally how to survive in college.

Still, it was very lonely without my family. The holidays were the worst. That first Christmas and New Year's, Marta invited me to go with her to her sister's house, but I refused. They were rich—bourgeoisie, in my mind—and I felt like I didn't belong. I told her I had to study anyway, but once she left I began to panic. *What am I doing here?* I thought. Suddenly I desperately wanted to call my parents; but I stopped myself because I knew if I called I would wind up going back, and I knew that would mean leaving school and giving in to my mother's demands that I live a traditional life.

My loneliness was short-lived, however, in part because I willed it to be so, but also because I was so busy with my studies. I was reading everything I could get my hands on about political science and devoured information as voraciously as I had done as a child. I was especially interested in the political systems of the third world, particularly the Caribbean and Latin America. And of course I continued to receive instruction outside of school courtesy of Marta and her social justice work.

Around that time Marta began pushing a leftist agenda—something she had never done before—and encouraged me to take part in her activities. She taught me through the American Friends Service Committee (AFS) to do research on Latin America and Central America, and I traveled with her to Mexico and El Salvador. When I went for an interview with the AFS, they asked me if I believed in using violence to achieve political ends. I would have been surprised by the question had Marta not prepared me for it.

"Tell them it depends," she had said, so even though the interviewer told me AFS was a nonviolent organization, I gave this answer. I explained that where I came from, people—poor people—sometimes had to use violence to defend themselves. The interviewer replied that I had gotten the job because I answered correctly. It had all been a test to see what I was willing to do, and I had passed it thanks to Marta.

During my second year at Douglass, I became involved with student government. It was the 1970s, and everyone was marching about some political issue or other. It was a time of giving back. If you were studying to be a lawyer, it was so you could help your community. Everybody around me—my fellow students, Marta, and the intellectuals she associated with—were telling me that my role was to get educated and go back to help my community. They advocated independence for Puerto Rico. But although I was continuing to develop my interest in politics, I continued to ask questions and never committed myself to one group or another.

I was confused by this shift in Marta's focus. She maintained that her work had religious underpinnings while she was promoting a leftist agenda that I found very contradictory to any sort of religious philosophy. I kept asking her questions, but she dismissed them and never clearly defined her positions.

While in school I was recruited by a theater group; they were doing a political play and looking for actors. I had actually been interested in theater for some time and had even taken a drama course. They were also paying a little bit of money—around ten dollars an hour—so I agreed to do it. The play was about Mariana Bracetti, a leader in the movement for Puerto Rican independence in the 1860s, when the island was trying to free itself from Spain. Bracetti is credited with knitting the first Puerto Rican flag, which was to become the symbol of a sovereign republic.

I was so excited when I found out the theater company needed to fill the role of Bracetti herself, for I already knew her story. I knew it because I had studied the history of my people; I had even written about Bracetti for a course. She had led the whole movement of women when the Americans were going in to take Puerto Rico and the men were all dying. Bracetti organized a candlelit march of thousands of women through San Juan in order to trick the Americans into thinking it was several regiments of troops. When the Americans saw it, they withdrew, and Mariana became a hero in the history of Puerto Rico.

Years later I would learn that while I was playing Mariana on the stage, my future husband, Alfie, and his then girlfriend (who also went to Douglass and lived in the Puerto Rican house) were sitting in the audience. After we were dating, and Alfie realized I had been Mariana, he exclaimed, "Oh my God. That's when I fell in love. With your spirit, with who you were. And then you disappeared! I didn't see you after that."

I did disappear from Douglass around that time, after I received a disturbing phone call from my sister Milagros. My father was very ill—the result of an infection after surgery—and he could not work. He would be okay eventually, but in the meantime my family needed money. So, despite not speaking to my parents, I transferred to Rowan University in South Jersey at the beginning of my junior year so I could be closer to home. I took a small attic apartment in Woodbury, near Rowan, for which I paid sixty dollars a month. I slept on a mattress on the floor and cooked my meals on a hotplate because there was no kitchen in the building.

I once again called on Marta for assistance, telling her I needed a job. She arranged for me to manage the office at Puerto Rican Youth in Action. I helped the migrant kids, processed applications, and did other administrative work, for which I was paid about ninety dollars every two weeks. Marta arranged for me to be paid through grant money from Neighborhood Youth Corps and VISTA. She was a genius at raising grant money through different government programs, so when one account was depleted she would pay me through another. VISTA was paid for by CETA, the Comprehensive Employment Training Act, which paid for young people to have jobs while attending college.

She also made sure I had money to give my father. She secured me a twenty-five-dollar subsidy, to which I added thirty dollars from my pay and sent the money home. This continued for about three years until my father had fully recovered and was able to resume working. However, that whole time I was sending them money, I never saw my father. All communication went through my sister. She kept me posted on his health and the other goings-on in the family.

It was my last year of college—I was graduating early, in January, and needed to plan my next step. My first thought was to go to law school and become an attorney working for the poor, but I hedged my bets and applied to Rutgers School of Social Work and Public Administration Graduate Programs. I was accepted to both but would have chosen law school had I been able to afford it. Back then law students had to attend full time, which made it very difficult for those who had to work. I was already broke even with a job; there was no way I could go full time.

Fate and finances dictated that I chose graduate school. It wasn't that important to me to attend my college graduation, but Marta insisted, saying I needed to be there. I didn't invite anyone except her, not even my parents. By that time my mother and father didn't even know what I was doing with my life. My mother had literally given up on me because she thought I was a rebel. My father and my sisters, on the other hand, were very proud of me, but they were also saddened that I wouldn't see them.

That was a difficult time for me too. There I was, the first Bonilla to graduate from college, and my family would not be there to share it with me. Marta had been the center of my world for so long, and I began to question just a little bit my relationship with her. As my mother had, I found myself wanting to assert my independence from Marta, so when the women from the CETA program offered me a job, I didn't tell her. In reality I was afraid to tell her. I knew she was grooming me for something, perhaps to follow in her footsteps in her work for leftist causes, and my getting a new job wasn't part of her plan for me.

Despite worrying about what Marta might think, that summer I began working at CETA as a job-development counselor. I had no choice; my money situation was desperate, and I was living in a terrible apartment. The guy living below me drank a lot, and he would often knock on my door drunk in the middle of the night. Despite having three locks on my door, I was petrified. The apartment was in the attic of the building; it had one little window and a narrow ledge. I knew this because I'd had to plan my escape just in case. If he broke down my door, I would head out that window. Each night I would sit there shaking as he knocked on the door and called for me to open up. He knew I was there by myself, so I was an easy target. I lived like that for a year and a half, and I wanted out. But in order to do that, I needed a new, better-paying job.

When Marta learned I had moved over to CETA, she was furious. I had never made such a decision without consulting her. But I didn't know what she had planned for me, and I had to make my own way. Marta had become more secretive about her work, almost to the point of being clandestine. In any event she made it clear she had wanted me to stay on at Puerto Rican Youth in Action. At that time she was working for American Friends on an international level. She began traveling to El Salvador for months at a time, and while I never knew exactly what she was doing, I told myself whatever it was, it was in service to God.

Other people who knew Marta started to tell me she was controlling me, and I needed to go my own way. I was shocked by what they said. I loved and respected Marta; I also felt like I owed her for everything she had done for me over the years. So when she called me collect using a codename—Katrina—she had previously given me, I did whatever she asked without question.

I later learned she was working for Bishop Oscar Arnulfo Romero, a politically active Catholic cleric who was murdered in his church in San Salvador in March 1980. Marta was working underground for him, infiltrating part of the movement on behalf of the left. Some believed she was actually there just before Romero was killed. The theory was he had called his disciples to talk about what the El Salvadoran government was doing and that Marta was warned by someone that the military was coming. She was able to get out in time, but Romero and his followers were all killed.

Although the nature of her work was unclear, the fact remained that I was seeing Marta less and less as she was often out of the country. I began to realize how independent I felt when she wasn't around and how controlled I felt when she was. Each time she returned from a trip, things continued as before, with her in control. But as with my mother, I had begun to assert my own beliefs, goals, and dreams for my life. For example, when she criticized my job with the CETA, saying I was working for the establishment, I calmly told her I needed the money. I also declined her offer to stay at her house; instead, I took an apartment I could not afford because I had to gain my independence from her.

I did eventually leave the CETA job, not because of Marta but because I felt I was wasting my time there. I was always looking for meaning in my work, and when I didn't find it I had to move on. When I was offered a position at the Office of Youth Services at North Camden Center, I jumped at the chance. It would mean going to school at night, but it would also enable me to help inner-city youth.

Marta would continue to influence my life on several levels for many years. Even after I met Alfie, and he helped me reunite with my family, Marta remained a priority. Whenever she called and announced she was in town, I dropped everything to pick her up and give her money or a place to stay—anything she needed. Alfie echoed my growing suspicions about her work and mysterious aliases. "Maybe she works for the CIA," he'd say.

Marta and I remained apart from each other for a long time. Our paths did cross once since we split, in—of all places—China. I was part of the US delegation to a 1995 educational conference in Beijing led by Hillary Clinton when, to my surprise, Marta appeared as one of the conference's speakers. Our meeting was cordial but brief, lacking any of the passion or intellectual discourse of our earlier relationship.

Fourth World Conference on Women met in Beijing in September 1995

It wasn't until Alfie's tragic death that I cut ties with Marta for good. She believed that without a husband anchoring me to my life in the academic establishment, I was free to follow her into her world of revolutionary activism. But what she failed to realize was that it was not just Alfie but my work that made my life meaningful. So after nearly thirty years of close friendship and camaraderie, we parted, and rather bitterly at that. I was no longer under her control, and she couldn't handle it.

On the other hand, I am as much to blame for the lack of contact over the years as she is. I have always believed it is important to remain focused on the future, not to dwell on the past. This is both a benefit and a flaw in my personality, especially in personal relationships.

In the course of writing this book, I have searched the Internet for Marta and was pleased to find so much information, including videos about her. She is still advocating change with the same rhetoric but for different causes—for world peace and against global warming. However, I am deeply saddened too, not by the fact that she has grayed and aged and looks more grandmotherly than revolutionary, though she still wears the same diamond-earring studs, but because we have not maintained contact. Watching her online, I am overwhelmed by the feeling that I miss her and still love her.

I know I could not have achieved the academic success I've earned without Marta's help. She was not only my intellectual mentor but my role model for activism and what it can achieve. She inspired me to work for social justice and always to think for myself rather than accept the opinions of others. It was these lessons that led not only to my commitment to helping poor Latinos through education but to my eventual decision to separate from her. Ultimately we could not reconcile our divergent beliefs on how to bring about societal change—Marta working to change the system from outside and me working to change the system from within.

Dr. Santiago and Marta Benavides at the Fourth World Conference on Women, which met in Beijing, China, in September 1995

In the end Marta had cultivated my independent spirit so well that it eventually led me to reclaim my life from her.

CHAPTER 3

Camden: The Early Days and the Road to Academia

I was still in graduate school when I made my first attempt to transform a community through education in Camden, arguably America's poorest and most violent city. Unlike LEAP, however, that experience had a very different tragic and life-changing turn, ending in murder. In fact, it almost ended my work for social justice altogether.

I had moved to Camden from Woodbury to complete my graduate studies in social work at Rutgers Camden, not aware that this was the critical first step in a new phase of my life. But the more I immersed myself into the urban community, I realized that Camden was the place where I could find social purpose and meaning to my work.

Even then, in the early 1980s, Camden was a city gripped by poverty, corruption, and social decline. It ranked among the worst cities in America in nearly every violent-crime statistic and economic measure. Its deteriorating neighborhoods were not safe, its public schools were disastrous, and its streets were ruled for the most part by drug gangs. As businesses and jobs fled Camden, drug trafficking became its principal business. Sadly, not much changed in the ensuing years.

Unfortunately, corruption reigned in city hall as well, crippling the possibility that government could turn things around. Angelo Errichetti, the city's mayor when I moved to Camden, had just been snared in a huge FBI sting, which became known as Abscam, along with numerous US congressmen and public officials, including one of New Jersey's senators, Harrison A. Williams. America was treated to hidden-camera videos of corrupt elected officials stuffing cash bribes into their pockets on a luxury yacht in Miami, money from a phony Arab chieftain meant to influence their official activities. Errichetti went to jail followed by several other mayors in Camden who ran afoul of the law and were indicted and convicted of official corruption.

Nevertheless, the more I learned about Camden and the more I became involved with its people, the more I knew this was the place where I could apply the sum of my experiences and education to do the most good.

When I moved to Camden from Woodbury, where I was employed as a trainer in the federal government's Comprehensive Employment Training Act (CETA) program while I attended Rowan University, I needed a job to survive. Over the years I had never had to worry about the cost of my schooling, which had been fully paid for by a succession of scholarships and grants I had earned at every level of my education. This drove me to become a straight A student throughout college, to assure that the scholarships and grants would be renewed. And, in my early college years, my living expenses, meager as they were, had been paid by the succession of jobs and small stipends Marta Benavides had given me.

But Marta had begun disappearing for longer periods of time and was very angry that I had taken the CETA job in Woodbury, which she viewed as tantamount to working for the enemy. So while I was in Camden, Marta would not be a source of any income.

As part of my graduate studies in social work at Rutgers Camden, I signed on as an unpaid policy intern in the city's Office of Youth Services at North Camden Center, serving a predominantly Latino community in the worst part of the city. It eventually led to a full-time paid position, but before then, to earn money for food and rent, I became a paid tutor in an adult language program for Latino residents in Camden.

It was through the language tutoring program that I met Vilma Ruiz and her sister, Lisette, who lived in the North Camden barrio and, beyond the tutoring, really made me feel welcome. Between my schoolwork and job, I hadn't had time to make many friends. In fact, throughout my school years I had no girlfriends or boyfriends and no social life to speak of. Vilma, who was instrumental in helping me found LEAP, and Lisette both have remained good friends and supporters over the years.

Vilma and I became very close because I knew she had firsthand knowledge of the poverty and violence facing Camden's citizens, particularly the youths who it became my mission to serve. I instinctively knew it was important to immerse myself in the urban community. I knew plenty about life in migrant camps and small towns, but I had never lived in a city. Vilma and I often discussed our plans for the future and what we wanted our work to be about. In fact it was Vilma who first suggested I do my social work in her hometown.

"You have ideas," Vilma told me, "and you're really smart. I don't know anyone your age who speaks like you about what has to be done."

My initial interest in Vilma's suggestion soon turned into a passionate commitment, and when she told me I could stay with her family, it seemed everything was falling into place. The Ruiz family home had a basement that Vilma's parents were willing to rent to me for an affordable seventy-five dollars a month. There were no windows in the basement, and the bathroom was upstairs, yet for me it was perfect because I intended only to sleep there.

The Ruizes were a fixture in North Camden, or, as most people called it, North Vietnam. Nearly everyone in Camden is poor, but conditions in North Camden, where most Hispanics lived, were the worst of the worst. It was infested with drugs and violence. And this was precisely why I felt I needed to be there. I believed I could really make a change. I was full of passion and a new wealth of knowledge. However, as I would later find out in the most devastating way, I was full of naïveté as well.

Vilma's father was a Spanish teacher in the Camden public schools, and her mother worked in a school cafeteria. They were stable and substantial as far as Camden Latinos were concerned. Although they had not been impacted greatly by the culture of drugs and violence in Camden, they were as vulnerable to the same poor conditions and fears as everyone else.

Staying with the Ruizes was the best of both worlds for me. I had the comfort of knowing there were others around as well as the freedom to come and go as I pleased. Vilma's parents weren't too happy about that, though. In the traditional Latino way, they wanted me to stay around the house, have dinner with them every night, and essentially be a member of the family. Perhaps they were just looking out for my safety, but I felt I already had a family, albeit an estranged one, and I was not looking for another. I simply needed a base of operations from which to begin my work in Camden. To be polite I would spend some time with them on Saturdays, but then I would disappear to do my own thing.

Besides our friendship, Vilma and I also shared many political and social beliefs, which I continued to explore despite my already overloaded schedules at school and the North Camden Center. One of our shared political experiences came about because we were both Puerto Rican and trying to find a viable political path to follow.

Under Marta's tutelage I had been discouraged from joining certain political organizations, particularly the Puerto Rican Socialist Party. For reasons I never entirely understood, Marta, who was a progressive and a leftist, had never participated in political groups with a leftist orientation. I had always listened to her, but now that Marta was travelling so much I had a new sense of freedom. Besides, this was the 1970s and '80s, a time when college students were very politically motivated, and it was inevitable that I would be recruited by one group or another.

When it came down to it, I did not care to join a Socialist organization either. But Marta had introduced me to some people involved with *El Comité (el co-mit-tay)*, a New York-based organization focused on whether Puerto Rico should become a US state or be independent altogether. I had always been very passionate about the subject, but like Marta I did not view it from the perspective of the far left. Instead I believed in Puerto Rican independence. Today my opinion on this subject has changed drastically. But in those days, it seemed clear to me that the best thing for Puerto Rico was independence, and at the time El Comité seemed like the perfect group for me. It was very progressive but not Socialist and advocated for an independent Puerto Rico.

Perhaps Marta wanted to ensure my continuing education while she was away, for El Comité had what they called study groups, which I eagerly joined. These groups weren't only about Puerto Rico but involved a host of issues about which I was passionate. For much of my time in Camden, I spent almost every Saturday with my El Comité study group, reading about Darwin, Lenin, Mao Tse Tung, and other political and social theorists. We would read their books and talk about them in group, often relating them to the status of Puerto Rico.

Since I was a student in political science, I enjoyed the work despite the grueling schedule. I also had the notion that if I stayed involved with El Comité, it would somehow lead me to something important, or at least connect me with more people who shared the same desire to transform poor urban communities. I thought it a bit strange that El Comité asked its members to contribute money, but when I told them I couldn't afford it, they let me stay anyway.

My doubts about El Comité continued to grow, particularly after I invited Vilma to come with me to one of the discussions. I explained we studied philosophy and politics, but the group's ultimate goal was an independent Puerto Rico. Intrigued, Vilma joined, but before long she was saying she did not care for the people or the issues they discussed. She said she felt they lacked a real direction or agenda and was suspicious that they asked for money.

Despite her misgivings Vilma came with me to an event in New York. We were expecting a large gathering of people similar to us—in other words, those who knew the realities of what it was like to grow up poor and Latino in the United States. But when we got there, it was just a small group of people. They were Latinos. But that was where the similarities ended. They were essentially a bunch of New York intellectuals. It wasn't the first time I'd heard bourgeoisies spouting flowery language about injustice and positive change, and it wouldn't be the last.

The El Comité members hadn't always been bourgeoisie, though. When I started attending the meetings and study groups, I found that a lot of them had originally been part of the Young Lords, which was a very controversial organization. The Young Lords had begun in Chicago in the 1960s and had spread to other big cities, including New York, with large Puerto Rican communities. They were a Puerto Rican nationalist organization committed to fighting police abuse and other human-rights violations.

El Comité, which eventually evolved and in 1975 was renamed *Movimiento para la Independencia Nacional Puertorriqueña* (MINP)—the Movement for Puerto Rican Independence—was also known for its ability to attract thousands of people to its events. And it was easy to see why because while these events were political in nature, they were also huge parties with musicians, food, and a celebratory air. I was impressed, but after a while I began to see what Vilma was talking about.

There was something about El Comité that made me uncomfortable, and eventually I decided I wanted to stop studying with them. When I told them, they were very upset and sent some women to talk me out of leaving. They asked me why I didn't want to continue. When I told them I had to focus on my work, they didn't accept it. Instead they argued that El Comité's aims should be part of my work.

I disagreed, but it took awhile to free myself of them. Their representatives even followed me to North Camden to observe my work with the kids and try to convince me it was connected with their organizational vision. That was when I realized El Comité was more cult-like and single-issue oriented than socially progressive in the way it operated. I also never knew who was really in charge of the organization. This was always kept secret from the general membership.

One Saturday I got a visit from someone who informed me there had been a growing rift in the leadership of El Comité, and the organization was splitting. True or not, I viewed it as another ploy to get me to stay, and I reminded him that we had never known who the leadership was anyway. He wouldn't reveal any more information to me, so I never did find out who was running the show or its real agenda. This was the final straw, and I left El Comité for good. My political education was progressing as I learned to think politically for myself.

I suppose I could have been angry that I had spent three years of Saturdays studying with them, but I wasn't. During that time I had been constantly reading. It had given me an enormous capacity to absorb knowledge as well as the discipline to focus on my career. The study groups also gave me a greater understanding of Puerto Rican politics, which

Gloria Bonilla-Santiago as an undergraduate student, 1976

complemented what I was learning in graduate school. The books I read at that time—mostly political science, which was the subject of my undergraduate degree—heavily influenced my thinking and my work. They gave me different perspectives on both historical events and what was happening in the present, and ultimately they got me thinking about what tools I would need to effect social change for the future.

While my friendship and association with Vilma endured, I was soon making enough money from tutoring and my job at the North Camden Center to move out of the Ruizes' basement and get a place in the new Ferry Street Station Apartments in South Camden, along the high-speed commuter line that ran from Philadelphia through Camden to the South Jersey suburbs. South Camden, only a block from suburban Collingswood, was still the nicest section of the city. My apartment was only a studio, but I didn't mind. It was the first place I could afford on my own, so it might as well have been a palace.

Marta Benavides visits Dr. Santiago's home, 1987

It was also the place Marta stayed whenever she was in town. I rarely saw her during this time. Nevertheless, she was an important influence on me, although now it seemed to be more about what I could do for her. She would call using the code name Katrina to tell me when she was arriving and when I should pick her up at the airport. She always stayed with me, never in a hotel. I knew she often attended meetings at the American Friends Committee, but I also believed she was carrying on other secretive work as well.

She always took an interest in my work, and while she wasn't there for my college graduation, she was there when I received my master's and doctoral degrees.

I loved my work at the Office of Youth Services and quickly came to view my job there as the start of a new era in my life. Part of my work as a graduate student was to go out in the field and apply what I was learning; however, I would be armed with much more than what I had heard in lectures or read about in books. I had my own life experiences as a child growing up in the migrant camps. I knew what it was like to live in poverty as well as how it felt to be marginalized by society. I was still living in poverty, and I still felt marginalized. Added to that were years of lessons from Marta, who had taught me about working for social justice and facilitated my trips to Cuba and other countries so I could learn about other political systems. During my years at graduate school, Marta was often out of the country, so I had plenty of time to begin implementing all I had learned without her constant oversight.

My work was essentially to provide counseling to Camden's youth and attend my graduate courses at Rutgers. I have always been driven to apply what I learn not to build a successful career for myself but to find the social purpose and meaning in my work. So it was not long before I wanted to take my counseling job a step further.

My experience in the theater, playing Mariana Bracetti, the Puerto Rican independence heroine, had been extremely positive and empowering for me, and I decided to form a street-theater group in Camden to perform at night. I already knew I was good at acting, but now I took a class on how to teach the craft to others. Getting local kids involved in a creative activity would teach them discipline and self-control as well as provide a healthy alternative to the life of drugs, crime, and violence they were bombarded with on a daily basis.

The theater group was called *Alma Latina*, or Latin Soul, and it was wonderful from the start. The kids were twelve, thirteen, and fourteen years old and were considered children in risky environments. They were youngsters in trouble with the law and habitual truants who were referred to me for counseling and support by the juvenile court system, and their attendance was mandatory. Nevertheless, I quickly became very close to them, for they somehow knew I was not there just to teach them how to act. I was providing them with a way to change their lives and showing them there were ways out of the poverty into which they had been born.

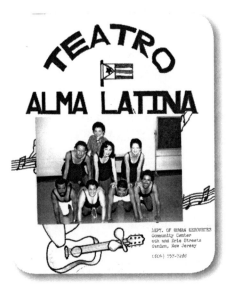

Alma Latina Theatre Group 1979

I wanted them to experience what I had experienced on my trip to Arizona, when I had realized for the first time that there was another world outside the migrant camps. Through their acting I wanted them to realize there was a better life beyond the dark and bleak streets of Camden. The kids knew this, and they loved me for it.

The work was very challenging and drew on all my organizational skills. Since I had been a young child at my father's side, I had been learning how to organize people, and like my father I found I had a natural talent for it. I had honed those skills while working with Marta and the American Friends Committee, and the theater group was no different. I knew in order for the group to have maximum impact, I would have to involve not only the kids but their friends and families as well.

A local woman named Vilma Perez introduced me to people in the neighborhood, and we held block parties to raise money for the theater group. Through these efforts I made many long-lasting alliances such as the one with Yvonne Vargas, one of the referred juveniles; currently she works as a teacher's assistant with pre-K children at LEAP and has two sons who have graduated from LEAP and Rutgers University. Vilma's sister, Lisette, also works at LEAP, and her children are LEAP students. Vilma was on the board of LEAP for a while, and at the time of this writing her son has graduated from LEAP and is on his way to college.

When the theater kids were ready, we began performing in the streets, first locally then traveling to other areas. Every piece we staged had meaning beyond the theatrical, usually combining music with themes of social justice and political ideas but also depicting the gritty and abject poverty of their everyday lives on the streets of Camden. It was very important to me that it was an educational activity as well as a recreational one.

Despite our grassroots fund-raising efforts, I knew I would need a grant to keep the theater going. So it seemed like fate when I met a woman who would become instrumental, albeit indirectly, in its continued success. Not wanting to lose touch with Puerto Rican politics after leaving El Comité, I had become involved with a policy organization called the Puerto Rican Congress of New Jersey. At one of their events I was introduced to Esther Novak, who, despite her Anglo name, was Argentinean. Esther worked for the New Jersey Council on the Arts and knew people at Rutgers, and when I told her about the theater and its financial worries, she told me to send her a grant proposal.

I knew about applying for grants. After all, that was how Marta funded much of her work, and by extension much of my learning experiences. But I had never applied for my own grant before, so I was shocked when Esther announced that based on my application, I would be given $15,000. It was a small amount in the scheme of things, but it would be enough to get the kids uniforms and costumes and keep the theater going for a while. I was even more shocked when Esther called and said she wanted to come see the group perform.

I invited her to our next fund-raiser. It was summer, and we were planning an outdoor festival. Esther quietly watched the street kids perform for a few minutes and then turned to me and said, "My God. They are incredible!" The festival was a huge success. The entire community got involved. The parents brought food, and everyone donated money—whatever they could afford. After that the theater became very popular, and I was overcome with pride because it wasn't just about nurturing the kids' abilities as performers; it was about liberating them from a restrictive environment of violence and crime and getting them to read, think, and learn about positive roles for themselves in society.

Like many of the students I would later meet when starting LEAP, these kids came to the theater group as the products of their environment, meaning they had grown up below the poverty level and had been exposed to drugs, gang violence, and other criminal activities. Through our work at the theater, they were starting to see that despite being from a poor, urban community, they could find a new way of life and achieve great things. They simply needed someone who understood how to motivate them.

Recruitment of students for Teatro Alma Latina, 1979

One of these kids was a boy nicknamed Justo in the streets (later I found out his real name was Robert). Justo was a fourteen-year-old who had lived in poverty and on the mean streets his entire life. He had been referred by the courts but was reluctant to join the program until some of his friends whose lives had been transformed by our work together convinced him to come see me. Like most of the others, Justo wasn't a bad kid, but he was definitely a lost one.

And like so many kids in Camden, he supplemented his impoverished lifestyle with money from selling drugs on the street. It was an enterprise too tempting for him to pass up. Justo was making around $300 a week from his drug trafficking on the street, and this was back in the 1970s. His parents could not control him and had all but given up hope. He was definitely on a collision course with trouble.

I became close to all of the kids I came in contact with and in my theater group, but no one more so than Justo. Camden's youth are tough and often not very open about the hardships they have experienced, but for some reason Justo felt comfortable confiding in me about his life, including his drug dealing and how much money he made. In his performances he was almost cocky and boastful about the street life he was leading and the success he thought he was having as a drug dealer. When I warned him about violence or being arrested, he would just say, "Don't worry, Gloria. I'm going to be okay." I thought, what else was he going to say? By that time he had become used to the money and probably didn't see any way he could earn as much through legal pursuits.

Justo was a generous and good-hearted kid. One day he brought me a bottle of Ralph Lauren perfume. While I was touched that he had gotten me a gift, I also noticed it was one of those sample bottles the salesgirls put out on the counters in department stores. But when I asked where he'd gotten it, he insisted he had paid for it. I hated to push him, but I knew I had to.

"Did you steal this?" I asked, but he shook his head, upset.

"Please don't ask me that. I got it for you. I went through a lot to get it for you."

So I sprayed some of the perfume on my wrist and sniffed, liking the scent. I never bought perfume back then. I had never been able to afford it, and it seemed a bit of a frivolity. But, I reasoned, now that I had gotten it as a gift, why not? Justo was pleased and said it smelled like me. I still had my doubts about how he had gotten it, but I was moved nonetheless, and I left work that night happy in the knowledge that I had touched and reached another kid. Justo was a natural actor. He could read well, was very smart, and became very involved in our group. He loved to perform and became a leader in the theater. Most important to me, he knew I cared about him. It would be the last time I saw Justo alive.

When I showed up at work the next day, the police were there, cordoning off the area with yellow crime-scene tape. At first I didn't think that much of it. Given the neighborhood, it wasn't that unusual. Then I saw the expressions of horror on my coworkers' faces. They told me someone had shot Justo gang style in the head and dumped his body in the alley behind the building that housed my office. Frantically I tried to figure out who might have killed him and why he had been shot. I thought probably he had been murdered by one of his street associates or perhaps a rival drug dealer.

I was convinced the drug gangs who ruled the neighborhood were involved because of Justo's very real portrayal of street life in my theater, and his body was dumped in the alley behind my office as a warning to my theater group and me. But whoever had done it, Justo was gone, and I was absolutely destroyed.

I ran out of the center sobbing and got on the commuter Speed line that would take me downtown to the Ferry Station apartment where I lived. I didn't officially resign from my job until the next day, but I knew when I left that horrible murder scene I was never going back.

I kept seeing Justo's dark, handsome face and brilliant smile and thought about the perfume he had given me the night before. I had always associated scents with memories, and I knew that for the rest of my life I would think of Justo whenever I smelled Ralph Lauren perfume. I have memories of Justo's performing with my theater group, and to this day they stir pain and feelings in me as strong as my memories of the perfume he gave me.

Justo had not only become a friend, but he was also an important role model in the theater group both as a talented actor and as someone who could handle any task I gave him. He had been so smart and, like so many street kids, old beyond his years. He could also manipulate people, skillfully bending the most obstinate to his will. He could go before a judge and spin a story as well as a politician. Above all he was a born leader, someone who could have achieved great things under different circumstances. And now, at only fourteen, life was all over for him. I had lost him, and the guilt was unbearable. I had never before felt such responsibility for another person; I had always thought mostly about the injustices in society at large rather than the circumstances of a single individual.

It eventually struck me that Justo had probably been killed because he had told whoever he was selling drugs for that he wanted to stop, probably as an indirect result of being involved in something positive like the theater group. In that respect I was in awe of his bravery, but even I knew one doesn't tell a drug dealer one wants out. They had murdered him and dumped his body like he was nothing—simply a disposable person. It was symbolic of how people viewed Camden itself: as a place that, like the migrant camps I had grown up in, was outside American society.

The truth was that at the time of Justo's death, I had already begun to question my work in Camden. I knew I was helping the community in some way, but it was like treating a fatal wound with a small bandage. I wanted to be part of systemic change like I had seen Dolores Huerta and Cesar Chavez achieve for the farm workers, but how? I had never worked in a place like Camden before, a city not only impoverished and overrun by crime but rife with political corruption. Justo's brutal murder only confirmed that I was not making the impact I had intended.

I had often teased Marta that she reminded me of Don Quixote because she was at heart a philosopher and always saw the good in life that nobody else seemed to see. Now I felt the same way—like I had tried to make the impossible dream come true, but while tilting against the windmills of injustice I had failed. Distraught and heartbroken, I considered giving up community work and finding something else to do with my life. After all, if a kid like Justo could be cut down so tragically, what was the use?

It was at this darkest moment that I experienced one of the biggest turning points in my life and career. As I fled Camden on the Speed line, a stranger on the train saw me crying and asked if I was all right. I guess I really needed someone to talk to, and, despite my characteristically independent and self-sufficient manner, I began telling him my story. And that was how I met Sidney Katz.

Sidney and I could not have been more different, at least outwardly. He was a white, Jewish guy from Cherry Hill, an affluent New Jersey town. He was also a chemist, a biologist, and the dean of the College of Arts and Science at Rutgers University in Camden. After hearing about the work I had been doing with Camden's youth and how it had ended with Justo's death, he suggested there was a different way I could bring about the kind of sweeping social change I so desperately wanted: a career in academia. He gave me his card and encouraged me to apply for a counseling job in the Rutgers Camden administration, offering to help me get my foot in the door with an interview.

Although I was still reeling from the shock of Justo's murder, I was intrigued by what Sidney was proposing. After all, I had grown up in the migrant-worker camps, first watching my father's work as an organizer and then Marta's work in social justice organizations. I had thought that was where I was headed as well, in some sort of grassroots organization that made changes from the bottom up.

But the more I thought about what Dean Katz had said, the more I began to see the value of a career in higher education and academia. My work with Camden's youth, while important, I realized, was on too small a scale to make a real difference. I wanted to do something bigger, which would affect not just a neighborhood but the larger cycle of poverty that held generations of Camden residents in its grips. I believed if I set my goal to become a professor, it would give me several advantages in this regard. It would not only allow me to educate college students, most of whom came from privileged backgrounds and had no idea what was happening in places like Camden; it would also give me the opportunity to meet like-minded people—professors, politicians, college administrators, and community activists—who were also interested in transforming communities. A university, especially one as large as Rutgers, could be my base of operations from which to carry on my real work.

There was also my personal reality to consider. I was a graduate student with very little money and, as of recently, out of a job. I was not concerned so much with my own welfare, but I had to be pragmatic. How could I hope to help others if I could not even support myself? It did not take me long to follow up on Sidney's advice. The position he had told me about was as an assistant director of the Academic Foundations Department in the Rutgers Camden administration—not a high-level job. Nevertheless, I bought an expensive business suit that I could ill afford to make a

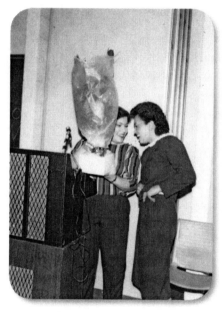

Wanda Garcia, president of the Latin-American Student Organization (LASO) at Rutgers-Camden honors Dr. Santiago with flowers for her support with Latino students, 1983

good presentation at my interview. It turned out that the interrogation—in Spanish, conducted by Wanda Garcia, a student who was active in the campus Latino organization; she eventually became my first hired staff, my right-hand assistant for thirty years, and the maid of honor at my wedding—was more important to my getting hired than what I was wearing. Wanda had been assigned to ask me the Spanish questions in the interview and told me later that I was the only applicant who had responded in Spanish.

Statewide student leadership conference chaired by Wanda Garcia as a student leader. Dr. Santiago provided leadership development training for students (Cook College, Rutgers New Brunswick, 1983).

It was in this unexpected way that I entered the very white, very male world of academia. I had, of course, been involved in intellectual pursuits for years but always as a student. Coming in as a university administrator on the path to becoming a professor was a completely new role to me, and I soon learned the administration at Rutgers had expectations that had less to do with my abilities and more to do with my ethnic background.

When I had accepted Sidney's offer to interview at Rutgers Camden, I had known it would be a long road to acceptance. I would have to pursue my own education, which would now include a PhD, while working full time and teaching classes. However, I had not realized how much time and effort I would need to claw my way out of the box in which my colleagues were so determined to keep me.

CHAPTER 4

· ·

Surviving in Academe as a Latina Scholar

My entire career at Rutgers Camden has been about being an engaged scholar within both the community of the university and the community outside the walls of academia. As an applied scholar, I came to understand that the role of a research university needs to be about engagement in creating innovative efforts to reinvigorate its civic mission—to call on faculty, students, and administrators to apply their skills, resources, and talents to address important issues affecting communities, the nation, and the world.

Perhaps the most important accomplishment in my more than thirty-year career at Rutgers Camden—more than the gains I personally made as a minority Latina scholar—was convincing the university its best interest was in applying those resources and talents to the development of a truly community-based charter school.

It can be argued that a university such as Rutgers has significant academic and societal influence beyond its campus boundaries. Rutgers certainly has world-class faculty, outstanding students, state-of-the-art research facilities, and considerable financial resources that give it the credibility and stature needed to help drive institutional and field-wide change rapidly and in ways that will ensure deeper and longer-lasting commitment to civic engagement in the community at-large.

In particular, because they set the bar for scholarship across higher education, research universities are well-positioned to promote and advance new forms of scholarship that link the intellectual assets of higher education institutions to solving public problems and issues. That is a premise clearly tested and proven in Rutgers's engagement in the development of LEAP.

My three-decade journey at Rutgers Camden, from an entry-level position in administration to the highest rank of distinguished professorship in the university, has provided me with the opportunity to build a leadership agenda for renewing the civic mission of higher education. That has been accomplished through the Center for Community Leadership, which I created as the principal vehicle for the university's support for LEAP, and the center's impact on Camden's most valuable resources: its children and families.

In building that leadership agenda, I have also created new scholarships that have benefited me immensely in my teaching career as well as the students I have taught over the years.

I have created a new scholarship of discovery in harmony with the educational needs of Camden's children through the LEAP Academy University Charter School, which is a successful model for the transformation of urban schools. I mastered the scholarship of integrating different disciplines of study by applying them to community development, education, and public policy through the creation of new academic programs, grants, and applied research that is relevant to the community and its educational needs.

I learned the most from the scholarship of application by building an educational pipeline from infancy to college along Cooper Street, a broad avenue that once divided Rutgers Camden from the city but now unifies the university and its surrounding community. It's an educational pipeline of more than thirteen hundred students at LEAP today, with a 100 percent high school graduation rate and 100 percent college placement for all its graduates since the initial graduating class in 2005.

And from the scholarship of teaching—today we have more than one hundred Rutgers college students participating in service learning courses through various academic units, all related to engaged scholarship—I learned to incorporate new knowledge from practice back into the classroom. From this experience I have taken away what I believe is the most important lesson of teaching: that service learning leads to student engagement and effective instruction, which helps those students improve academically and develop stronger ties to their schools, communities, and society.

Throughout my career, my commitment to engaged scholarship through service learning and community-based research has helped burnish the image of the Rutgers Camden campus, an image that in recent years has suffered from questions about its role in the community. By speaking publicly about engaged scholarship and encouraging other institutions to implement similar approaches to research, universities not only help promote these models but also send messages to the public that they are responsive to community needs and are committed to contributing more meaningfully and directly to solving societal problems and issues at the local, national, and international levels.

The narrative presented here portrays my own experience as a faculty woman of color who has had wonderful and challenging experiences in academia. That certainly was not the expectation at the beginning of my career. As a Latina scholar, I was a newcomer to Rutgers University in 1981, at a time when the academic world was defined and controlled by discourses that did not address the realities of my Latino community, a world that did not affirm our intellectual contributions and one that did not seriously examine our Latino community culture and identity.

Early on in my career, a top administrator said to me, "Someone who looks like you will have a very difficult time making it at Rutgers." He meant female and Hispanic. I think he said it without animus or bias but simply as a statement of fact about the white–male-dominated culture at the university. I took it as an admonition that I would have to work harder and smarter than anyone else just to survive.

Back then Latinas could not be taken seriously as scholars because of the expectations of failure. We were expected to choose roles that were less defined for us. Part of the problem was there were few Latina tenured-scholar role models in the field. Other women scholars of color will find these experiences very familiar. Like other successful women of color who work in white-male-dominated professions, which was and is the case at most universities, these women have much to say about the way they managed to attain their positions despite the anomaly of their gender or race. They have much to say about how they developed confidence in their competence and authority and what they accomplished by exercising their professional power.

Many of these successful women felt discriminated against based on gender and race inequality that structured their professions. Many times I found myself studying the familiar stories of how they responded to discriminatory treatment in order to understand how other professional women made sense of their realities.

Two of these women at Rutgers were Hilda Hidalgo, a PhD in the School of Social Work, and Miriam Chaplin, an education professor at Rutgers Camden. Hilda overcame discriminatory hurdles as a woman, a Latina, and an avowed lesbian to become an assistant commissioner of education in New Jersey and cofounder of such important organizations as ASPIRA and the Newark Urban League. She inspired a generation of Latina women in academia. Miriam overcame hurdles as an African American woman to chair the English Department at Rutgers Camden and become a nationally recognized expert and author on literacy in America.

When I arrived at Rutgers, colleagues told me that historically, faculty women of color often were invisible, marginalized, and hidden within departments of traditional Latino and African American studies. Others were afraid to identify themselves as Latinas because they thought assimilating was an easier way to be accepted into the mainstream culture of academia. Many other minority scholars had a sense of not belonging in the organization, perceiving themselves as cultural outsiders, and feeling isolated and invisible. Some of my Latina colleagues described barriers to advancement including bias and gender-role expectations and perceived a double standard of discrimination.

An early teaching experience of mine is illustrative of the marginalization and senses of misunderstanding and isolation many minority scholars feel. Most Latino faculty members wind up teaching Latin-American studies or Spanish language and cultural classes. Since I was then teaching in the Graduate School of Social Work, it was assumed I would teach courses that focused on Hispanic social issues in America. I was assigned to teach classes on social welfare policy, or, as I called it, the sociology of the poor. When my supervisors gave me a course titled "Groups at Risk" to teach, I had to ask: "What the hell is that?" They politely explained it was, as the title implied, a class about groups that were at risk in society.

Now it was my turn to educate them. "There is no such thing as 'groups at risk,'" I said. "Rather, it is about groups living in risky environments." The point, I continued, was to change the conditions, remove the risks, and allow people to thrive. I insisted I was not getting my PhD to teach a course about defeatism. I wanted to teach the history of social work, the policy of change, and, most importantly, how things could be different moving forward.

Three years later Provost Gordon promoted me to director of the Office of Hispanic Affairs while I finished my doctoral studies. Once I earned my PhD in sociology in 1986, he appointed me as an assistant professor in the School of Social Work and director of what is now the Center for Community Leadership. Later the provost would relinquish the Camden Social Work Program to the Rutgers administration in New Brunswick.

Dr. Santiago's tenure party with Alfredo Santiago and Walter Gordon, at their home 1991

While my faculty position reported to New Brunswick, I remained physically teaching on the Camden campus and conducting research on children and families until 1991, when I received tenure and founded the Center for Community Urban Leadership under Provost Gordon to house all my projects and innovations, most importantly the research on creating an alternative community-based school in Camden.

Once the transfer of the School of Social Work was complete, I was assigned to a new provost in New Brunswick—Joe Potenza, who was also the university's vice president for academic affairs. I remained at the Camden campus, still reporting to New Brunswick. Under Provost Joe Potenza I got to build capacity for my Community Leadership Center in Camden. He assigned an associate provost, Barbara Lee, to work with me in overseeing my center and other initiatives while I continued to work and grow my programs in Camden. It was a fortuitous assignment because Barbara Lee understood the community agenda I was pursuing and became a key supporter in my efforts to convince the Rutgers administration to become engaged in the Camden community.

First graduation ceremony of Parents as Partners for Educational Change Program, July 27, 1996. Barbara A. Lee, associate provost Rutgers New Brunswick; "Jack" Ewing; Gloria Bonilla-Santiago.

From the beginning I consciously made a decision and promised myself to frame my experience at Rutgers to be different from that of any other minority Latina scholar despite the isolation, marginalization, and discriminatory practices against minorities at that time. I decided my experience had to be different—that I would persevere, overcome the challenges, and create a safe space for others and for me. It was in this capacity that one of my later provosts in Camden, Roger Dennis, described me as a "tenacious force of nature." I became resilient and coped with every challenge I faced.

Most importantly, I had a vision for my work. I designed new microenvironments to survive, balancing my personal life and work, learning to accept being underestimated at times and not taking things personally. I simultaneously held dual duties and identities—trying to be successful in the organization while trying to change its culture. I remember taking on as many nontraditional roles and duties in my department as I could, teaching courses that were new and difficult, designing new programs to build minority capacity, creating space for my research agenda, fund-raising for my own projects, and bringing money—significant amounts of money—to build capacity for my work.

All that time I understood that aligning my research work with university priorities would be one way to stay alive while preparing and training for tenure. I became a social entrepreneur, using social and intellectual capital as assets to support my work by building relationships inside and outside academia. As a result, I became savvy and influential in both arenas. Other scholars who were doing similar work around the country legitimized my work, and my relationships in the outside political world were critically important in moving my agenda forward.

I worked long hours, and staying focused on what was important became a priority. The community became my lab and my platform for applied research. Learning the politics of organizational savvy and training a team of qualified staff became critical for my survival. At the same time, I decided early in my career to apply for Leadership New Jersey and later Leadership America, the Hispanic Women in Leadership program at the national level, and others. These programs taught me the leadership skills I needed to survive in the mainstream world of academia.

Understanding the politics of tenure and the process of promotion at the university also contributed to my success in that I was invited to come up early for tenure. It normally takes at least six years to get tenure, but I was promoted in my fifth year by leveraging the fact that I was being recruited by another institution to become a tenured faculty. At the same time, Governor Florio had appointed me as the only woman to the State Management Audit Commission, whose members included a former governor, several former state cabinet officers, business CEOs, and organized labor leaders. Because the commission had broad executive authority to examine management practices at state institutions, which included oversight of Rutgers, Provost Gordon pushed for my early tenure to protect me from any repercussions at the university and because he felt my work deserved it, and I was ready.

I was determined not to allow any obstacle to get in the way of my academic advancement. I developed an attitude of success early in my career, particularly after I was encouraged to follow an administrative route in academia instead of seeking advanced degrees to teach because it would be less hard for me. I was determined to prove that advice wrong, and I did.

Nevertheless, many times I felt isolated, alone, and marginalized from the rest of the academic world because I stayed true to my passions to build an education pipeline for pre-K to college for poor kids and their families rather than go into a mainstream world of traditional administrative academia or research simply to advance a personal agenda.

I looked for ways to grow and learn from the best, to pass the difficult test of life experiences with high marks, and to stay calm no matter what happened. I asked for advice and did not try to solve things by myself. I built a kitchen cabinet of experts I could rely on for advice. Three of the most important advisors in my cabinet were Bill Kornblum, James Jennings, and Joe Nathan. Dr. Kornblum, a renowned City University of New York (CUNY) sociologist who was also my PhD advisor, is an internationally recognized expert on the people and sociology of New York City and has written numerous books on the subject. Dr. Jennings, a professor of urban planning and environmental policy at Tufts University who has held similar posts at Harvard and the University of Massachusetts, is an expert on Puerto Rican politics and the Puerto Rican experience in America. And Joe Nathan, an education professor at the University of Minnesota who is the acknowledged founder of the charter school movement in America, was one of the most important advisers and supporters of my efforts to build LEAP. To this day I still rely on them for advice.

I also used that time to fund raise and bring as much money as possible to the Rutgers Camden campus to secure support for my work, the LEAP initiative, and other important projects. I knew the only way to build capacity for the community and support for my projects was to raise the money by myself, and I educated myself on the intricacies of public and education finance; I became expert in the procurement of government and foundation grants as well.

Today the total I've brought into LEAP and Rutgers exceeds $85 million, making me one of the university's top moneymakers. Provost Roger Dennis said I was very good at fund-raising because I always had a hook, meaning I knew what issues the important foundations were interested in and were likely to fund—for example, the Robert Wood Johnson Foundation and urban health, the Knight Foundation and literacy, and the Prudential Foundation and charter schools.

At the very beginning of turning my vision into reality, I was able to raise $2 million with the support of the Delaware River Port Authority (DRPA) and the Prudential Foundation to plan for Project LEAP. (I describe this process in detail in chapter eight, in the LEAP case study.) At that time I also had the support of Governors Florio and Whitman and many other leaders in the state who believed in my leadership and ability to get LEAP completed.

Former Camden Provost Roger Dennis toured the LEAP Academy Elementary School construction site in 1999 (Elk Lodge No 293—Camden, NJ, eighty-four-year-old building that marks the very beginning of downtown Camden along historic Cooper Street).

From the outset, however, Rutgers University saw my efforts as purely a research project, as a way to advance my academic standing and career. The administration thought I would write a book about my work. They never thought I would actually build a school for poor kids within the university. The administration didn't understand that, as Roger Dennis put it, my avowed goal was "to change the world through projects that improved the lives of people."

Soon after the charter law was enacted, and I was advocating for Project LEAP, I was informed by Provost Gordon that the Rutgers Board of Governors would not allow me to file a charter application with the Department of Education for LEAP to be a part of Rutgers. The board was mainly concerned with the administrative structure of such a school and the financial obligations Rutgers might have to assume.

Recognizing my problem, Provost Gordon gave me permission to seek advice from the governor and others about my alternatives. That evening I called a group of political stakeholders in Trenton—such as state senators Donald DiFrancesco and Jack Ewing, legislative leaders who were influential with Governor Christie Whitman and had convinced her to sign the charter proposal into law—to inform them of my predicament at Rutgers.

Early the next morning, I was awakened by a phone call from Rutgers President Francis Lawrence, who bluntly said, "Dammit, Gloria! Who told you we weren't going to let you file the charter application? You got a lot of people upset about this." He then invited me to join him at a Board of Governors Executive Committee meeting to discuss the future of Project LEAP and work out the details of Rutgers's involvement.

I went to the meeting with Provost Gordon and was given five minutes to explain why this project was so important it needed to be part of the university. I took three minutes and explained that Project LEAP was my vision for a pre-K to college pipeline for attracting minority students to Rutgers. At that time, I explained, Rutgers, which is the state university of New Jersey, had less than 1 percent undergraduate minority students in a state that has very large African American and Hispanic populations. I told the board the LEAP kids would become the new generation of college students for years to come at Rutgers.

After much discussion, the board of governors gave me approval to pursue the filing of a charter application. But the university's leadership directed me to return in three weeks with a comprehensive plan for financing school buildings and providing an administrative structure that would benefit the university and the community.

*Rutgers former president Francis L. Lawrence and Rutgers
Board of Governors tour LEAP Academy, 1999*

I remember leaving that meeting feeling that in many respects, I had won a battle and lost the war because I had no idea where I was going to get the money for a school building. But I was encouraged by the level of the university's attention to my project, from the president and senior vice president to the board of governors. It told me that my school was not being dismissed as the wild idea of an overzealous professor but was under serious review and consideration.

Vice-President Joe Seneca was assigned to follow up with me. And in a series of exchanged memos, oversight of the LEAP project was reassigned to Rutgers Camden under Provost Gordon, and the conditions for the final board of governors approval of the LEAP project were spelled out.

As a result, I was reassigned to report to Walter Gordon once again in the chancellor's office in Camden. Associate Provost Barbara Lee, who had been the instrumental person supporting my efforts and mentoring me through the administrative process during that time, was asked to transition the project to Camden.

In a memo she laid out the terms of governance for LEAP that the board of governors would accept. Her memo, in part, read:

> Dr. Seneca has determined that the school should be an independent legal entity reporting to a LEAP board of trustees, which in turn is subject to regulation by the commissioner of education. Dr. Santiago has stated that she is willing to live with a governance model in which the school is a separate legal entity if Rutgers provides the services that it would have if the school had been a subunit of Rutgers. (Lee, B.A., 1996)

It was exactly the administrative structure I had wanted for LEAP, and now I had support for it from the university. But there were additional hurdles to get over, since Vice-President Seneca had made it clear this was not going to be an easy process, and all of the conditional items needed to be approved by the board of governors. I was under a lot of pressure to get a lot done quickly, including the charter application, which was due soon after on October 15, 1996. I was able to get the board's support to file the application, but the university's governors remained very concerned about my ability to get the funding for the facilities and operation of the school.

In a memo to me, Joe Seneca delineated the university's concerns and set a number of conditions for final approval of the LEAP project. In part the memo said:

> As the board resolution acknowledges, your energy in getting the project to this point is to be commended. At the same time, the board, President Lawrence, and I continue to have concerns about several unresolved issues regarding the project and I believe that in order for the project to be successful the following factors need to be

addressed as expeditiously as possible: 1) A suitable site for the school and a fully documented financial plan for the purchase or lease of that site. 2) A fully documented estimate of all renovation costs for the site (including asbestos and lead paint removal, if necessary). 3) A fully documented estimate of the costs of the school's furnishings and equipment. 4) A fully documented annual operating budget, which must include repayment of the school's financing as well as complete personnel cost (including benefits) for the extended school day and year; round operation envisioned for the school as well as all other operating expenses such as insurance, maintenance, and security. 5) If the fiscal participation of any governmental agency (such as DRPA) is envisioned as part of the charter school plan, a formal letter of intent from that agency detailing its commitment. (Seneca, J.J., 1996)

I was given a very short time to come up with a plan to address the concerns raised by Vice-President Seneca. In reality I am convinced he and the board never believed I could meet their conditions in time to open the school in the fall of 1997. Indeed, very few people at Rutgers believed I could get it done. But I had a plan.

As part of my research strategy, I already had a working group, and Rick Wright, who had been chief of staff under former Governor Florio, had made himself available to support my efforts. Rick had been involved since I'd begun to formulate my ideas for LEAP. He helped me put together the contingency plan for financing the school buildings and operations. Since he had been with me throughout the process of designing and building the school, and he knew state government inside and out, his advice was invaluable. He also had friends and contacts at the Delaware River Port Authority (DRPA), which became a key source of funding the project. Together we were able to construct a comprehensive finance and organizational plan for Vice-President Seneca in a matter of weeks.

At that point in time, Walter Gordon retired. When I first had come to Rutgers, he had been skeptical of my ideas and ability to survive at the university but later became one of my staunchest advocates, so I had moments of trepidation about who might succeed him. My concerns were eased, however, when Roger Dennis, the dean of Rutgers Camden Law School, was named to replace Walter and became my new provost.

Without reservation I can say Roger Dennis was the best provost and chancellor I've ever known. I do know that without his vision and commitment to the growth of anchor institutions such as Rutgers in a poor city like Camden, LEAP may not have become the school it is today. Certainly it would have been a much more difficult and longer task to make LEAP a reality without his support.

Roger Dennis's ideology was very different from any other provost's or chancellor's under whom I had worked. His underlying philosophy was that Rutgers Camden could not be an island in the community, and he believed in an urban agenda for the university. His agenda was to expand university growth onto Cooper Street, in effect opening that side of the Rutgers campus to the city, and he saw my school as part of an opportunity for community development. Consequently Joe Seneca assigned Roger to mentor me in finalizing the project.

Roger used to say I was actually his boss, and he would poke fun at me, saying he could not mentor me because he was the one who was learning from this great experience of community entrepreneurship. He also often used a football analogy to describe our working relationship. He would say I was the quarterback, and he and the Rutgers Camden staff were merely the linemen and running backs in the LEAP project.

He embraced my work by making it part of his own agenda for the campus. He aligned the university's vision with my vision for Cooper Street and empowered me to get the funding necessary to build LEAP. He provided guidance and support and leveraged university resources so I could do this great work. As a result he became the first urban provost of Rutgers Camden, with a new vision for the campus, making it an urban campus within the university.

His support was also invaluable in getting things done with the central Rutgers administration in New Brunswick. He knew the university inside and out, and when facing delays or difficulties in dealing with the administration or getting expeditious responses on issues, he would say, "Rutgers may have been founded in 1766, but it is still studying ideas that came up in 1768."

He always acknowledged my efforts as part of his plan to rejuvenate the forgotten city and as part of a living laboratory for incubating new ideas and entrepreneurial capital projects for LEAP and the Rutgers Camden campus. He always saw LEAP as a leading project in the university's expansion onto Cooper Street and into the community. Consequently there was jealousy from other faculty and administrators who did not understand the work, and who suggested I was his favorite and often tried to sabotage or silence my efforts. They failed, however, because Roger and I were determined never to allow those things to get in the way of our agenda of community expansion.

Roger was the kind of person who did not have time for small talk and did not brook petty jealousies. He was too busy transforming the campus and the city, and I was focused on saving the children and building the LEAP schools on Cooper Street.

In one brief moment in 2005, at the first graduation of LEAP high school students, Provost Dennis showed he understood the importance of my work and our shared vision for Camden. That night his remarks urged the graduates to use the social capital they had acquired at LEAP to be self-confident and proud of Camden as their city.

LEAP Academy founding class of 2005 graduation day

"I want to talk to you about an experience I guarantee you will have at college," he told the graduates. "You will be sitting around talking with your fellow students, and one of them will say, 'Wow! You are from Camden. That's amazing!' Whatever is meant by the statement, I want you to embrace the comment. Define yourself as the kid from Camden. Camden is an amazing place. Tell your friends, 'Everyone at my high school went to college! My hometown has two world-class hospitals. My hometown has a great state university. My family and my community really, really want me to succeed.' Tell them you think Camden made you who you are: a committed, concerned, effective young adult. Tell them you are Camden!"

Class of 2005 graduation ceremony with Provost Roger Dennis

Those sentiments, in one way or another, have been expressed at every succeeding LEAP high school graduation.

Dr. Santiago with Julio
Atenco, class of 2005

Roger also played an important part in restoring my spirit and desire to work after the most tragic event in my personal life. On November 27, 1996, my life changed forever when my beloved Alfie was in a terrible car accident, struck down by a drunken truck driver near our home in Voorhees, New Jersey. He lingered in a coma in a Philadelphia hospital for more than thirty days before he passed away on December 30, 1996. Alfie's death came at a critical point in the development of LEAP and redefined my career.

In his new role as provost, Roger was in the process of negotiating my tenured faculty line from the School of Social Work in New Brunswick to the Department of Public Policy and Administration on the Camden campus when Alfie's accident occurred. I remember going for an interview with the top faculty in the Public Policy Department as my husband was in a coma in the hospital. The interview, in my mind, did not go well since all that mattered to me at that time was Alfie. I remember most of the department's faculty was white males from the Political Science Department; there was no diversity and no one from my academic areas of social work or sociology. And I really could not focus on what they were asking because I was so worried about my husband's condition.

I told them about his accident and how I could not focus on the interview. They said they understood my concerns and acknowledged they were impressed by my accomplishments. But I left the interview without much hope or expectations. A couple weeks later, however, I was pleased to learn I was invited to be part of the faculty of the Public Policy Department. Somehow the department faculty accepted my transfer with full support, perhaps acknowledging my growing stature at the university, and this became my new academic home.

A week later Alfie died, and soon after that I went to see Roger Dennis on my first return to campus after my husband's funeral. As I waited outside Roger's office, many Rutgers faculty and staff stopped to pay their respects and offer condolences. But I was still in shock and probably in denial of what had happened, and as I waited to see Roger, I kept asking myself, *What am I going to do now?*

Before Alfie's death I had been preparing to interview for the presidency of a women's college, a position Alfie and I had felt might be a real career choice for me. But once he died, everything changed. My spirit was broken; my dreams were gone, and all I felt was pain and agony. I was in a mode of shock, anger, rejection, and acceptance (SARA), a condition that would affect me for nearly a year. I soon realized all I wanted to do was to build my school for the kids, and I decided to focus on Camden's children and families. In a sense Alfie's death liberated me to find my true passion and love for what I really wanted to do: save kids' lives through education. I knew all I needed was time to grieve and get better.

Roger came out of his office that day and asked me to walk with him. He wanted to know how I was doing. I knew he was concerned for me and thought he might want me to take a leave to resolve my grief and plans for my future. I told him I did need time to get through this, but I had decided the best way to deal with my loss was to come back to work right away.

He told me to follow my heart and do what I thought was best for me. And, erasing one of my concerns about the future, he assured me he and the university would always be there for me. I told him I just wanted to build the school. He simply asked, "When do you want to begin?"

I went right back to work and began where I had left off. I followed up with the Rutgers team assigned to work on LEAP, and everyone was surprised by my early return and was supportive of my efforts. I began by writing an execution plan for LEAP. We set up the governance structure according to the charter we had received from the state. Rutgers got three seats on the LEAP Board of Trustees to represent the university's interests in the new school.

Rutgers derived benefits from the arrangement mostly from professional-development opportunities for research, teaching, and learning with the creation of LEAP. The benefits included establishment of the Centers of Excellence at Rutgers, a dual-degree program for LEAP high school students, and the newly established Alfredo Santiago endowed scholarship for LEAP students to attend Rutgers University as their first-choice school.

LEAP was incorporated as an independent nonprofit entity with the Rutgers Centers of Excellence supporting operation of the school. The component Center for Community Leadership became the administrative arm to provide oversight and management of the growth and expansion of LEAP. This structure allowed for decentralized governance and entrepreneurial research projects to emerge out of LEAP working in collaboration with the university.

I was assigned to teach two courses a year—a two-course reduction in my teaching responsibilities—as I was entrusted to oversee implementation of the LEAP school model for the university.

LEAP opened its doors on schedule in September 1997. Its first classrooms were in trailers, acquired with a Prudential Foundation grant, on a vacant lot near the Rutgers Camden campus while I waited to lease or build a new building on Cooper Street. We began with pre-K to third-grade classes with three hundred students selected through a lottery to allow for equity and diversity. We had an additional five hundred parents on a waiting list hoping for opportunities for their children to attend LEAP.

LEAP operated for two years in the trailers, which gave me the time to fund raise with the DRPA for the lease and purchase and renovation of a historic 1920 building at the intersection of Seventh Avenue on Cooper Street, adjacent to the Rutgers campus. We moved the school, with pre-K to eighth grade, to this new site in 2000. Fifteen years later, LEAP is at thirteen hundred student capacity with infants and pre-K to twelfth grade in five buildings on Cooper Street, including a STEM elementary and high school. We have the authority to grow in three years to serve eighteen hundred students—more than 15 percent of Camden's public-school-aged population. As noted by Dr. Michael Palis, previous dean of the College of Arts and Sciences at Rutgers University Camden, "LEAP has been a model for community building, leadership and engagement ... It actually is a national model of how the public school system can serve urban students and how these students can make success stories out of themselves." In chapter 8, in the LEAP case study, I document the success of LEAP and the implications for its growth.

LEAP began as a startup organization as I was learning to become an entrepreneurial faculty member with dual roles in academia as a research scholar and as an applied scholar. This experience taught me great lessons. First, it taught me the importance of recognizing the role I played as a minority faculty member in shaping the education, research, and service functions of my institution. As a result, I experienced rejection, joy, pain, loss, and, most important, reinventing myself as I transformed Cooper Street into an education miracle. The many faces of happy children and families as part of the transformation of a community of learners have exhilarated me and provided the energy for my life and work.

As a Latina scholar, I learned to multitask and focus on my work, combining practice and scholarship as guides to influence my research and teaching. I also learned that to be of great service to society, one must first learn to be both humble and savvy at the same time. It was not enough to be as good as anyone else; I had to exceed those expectations to achieve excellence and be noticed.

I learned that being underestimated was okay if I could use it to move my work forward. I always say I made it to being a distinguished professor at Rutgers because they were not paying attention. Rather, I surprised folks as I was bringing the resources and working on my ideas.

The academic journey has been incredibly rewarding, painful, and transformational. I created new teaching and learning, developed new knowledge, and influenced university governance on the importance of community and university partnerships for the good of all. I recognized that as a professor and leader in a university that is not racially and ethnically diverse, I needed to tap into a new kind of intellectual power and innovation to achieve excellence.

I was breaking new ground and barriers as a minority faculty person with a new role and a new voice with power and influence that came from outside, not inside the organization. I built space and discourse for others to follow. I created space and voice for a minority community that had been left behind within the echelons of academia.

It was during this time that then Rutgers President Francis Lawrence broke ground with a diversity plan to transform and educate the university about the importance of racial and ethnic diversity to the mission of higher education, the importance of faculty diversity (or the lack thereof), and the importance of diversity as a harbinger of Rutgers's continuing educational, academic, and societal legitimacy.

Second, I learned that working in academia and staying the course for thirty-plus years was a lifetime journey worth taking. On this journey I learned to clarify my life mission and vision. Many prestigious job offers came my way, but I resisted the temptation of what I considered instant gratification and remembered that the worthiest goals take time and energy to achieve. Consequently, I became part of building a culture of excellence and developing an education pipeline for infants to college.

Many times I made fear my friend so that I could open my mind to discover many possibilities that were not obvious at the time. As a result I zeroed in on the goal that had the most depth of meaning for me: to save kids' lives through education and send them to college. That part of the journey has been the most gratifying.

In the end I have understood that changing the culture of a university begins with defining one's role in it. I took extraordinary steps in creating a new experience with meaning, which produced extraordinary results for me. At the same time, I shared the experiences and alienation of many minority women who had gone before me. They saw themselves as outsiders within the academic setting.

Because of the marginalization that exists in academia, I believe women, both minority and nonminority, are more able to see the bias and exclusion that may operate in academic centers as well as other problematic dimensions of that culture. As cultural outsiders, women in general may be better able to advance change to improve academic culture.

The next step, I believe, is to leverage the awareness of academic women to develop a broader vision of what the university culture can and should be like.

In this chapter I have related my struggles and successes within academia and with the Rutgers University administration to bring my vision for the LEAP Academy University Charter School to reality—a vision to transform a poor, minority, urban community through education.

In the next chapter, I will recount the story of my political education outside academia and the struggles and successes I achieved in the political world and with government to make LEAP a reality. In terms of chronological order, many of the political efforts parallel my work within the university setting to build my school on Cooper Street. In that respect, the political story of LEAP will take a step back to the beginning.

CHAPTER 5

The Politics of Transforming Communities through Education

If you want to work for change and social justice and don't want to run for public office, own the policy because knowledge is power!

—*Former New Jersey Governor Jim Florio*

G overnor Florio offered this advice when I first met him and sought career direction, and it is probably the best political guidance I've ever received. It certainly was critical advice given where I was in my life in the late 1980s and the nonpolitical direction I had chosen for my academic and professional career.

I was well schooled in political theory and philosophy, having earned my undergraduate degree in political science, studying the political systems not only in America but in the many foreign countries I visited.

But I had very little practical experience in politics. In fact, I had long shunned participating in organized party politics first at the behest of my intellectual mentor Marta Benavides, who believed change could be achieved only by working outside the system, and then because of a growing personal aversion to politics as a practical way to solve serious problems.

The more I formulated my ideas to create an urban community school, however, the more I realized the road to education reform in cities such as Camden was not through city hall or the local board of education but in the state capitol of Trenton, where education policy for New Jersey was legislated and administered. That was where Governor Florio's advice to "own the policy" benefited me immensely in navigating a treacherous world of politics. He also offered me opportunities to learn the political ropes in Trenton and then provided the seed money to finance a landmark study on alternative public schools that led to charter school legislation and the creation of LEAP.

In the late 1980s, I was in my early thirties and was an assistant professor at the Rutgers University School of Social Work in Camden, building an academic career in social policy and research with a concentration on Hispanic issues. I had founded and directed the first Office of Hispanic Affairs at Rutgers Camden, a two-desk, one-room office where the phone was audaciously answered, "Office of Hispanic Affairs," proving a lesson I had learned early in life: present yourself with authority, dignity, and respect, and you will be seen with authority, dignity, and respect. I had earned a master's in social work from Rutgers and a master's in philosophy and a PhD in sociology from the City University of New York in 1986. I wrote my dissertation on the plight of Puerto Ricans and migrant workers in New Jersey and was cited as supportive evidence for legislative reform in the treatment of those migrant workers.

I was married to my soul mate Alfredo (Alfie) Santiago, who was quickly rising in the administrative ranks at Rutgers; he became my moral compass as well as a sounding board for all my ideas and was the most ardent supporter of my professional activities. I did not know of "power couples" back then, but in the university community and among Hispanic activists, I'm sure we qualified as one. All in all, I was on a tenure track to academic success. Personally this place was further from my roots in Puerto Rico and the migrant worker camps than I had ever imagined.

The social policy I taught, studied, and researched at first to advance my academic career became increasingly centered on education issues and finding ways to help poor urban Latinos break the cycle of poverty and violence that had them in its grip nearly everywhere, but with particular ferocity in the city of Camden, where I had chosen to stay and work. From the sanctuary of the Rutgers Camden campus, a fenced compound of tree-lined walkways and university buildings that was forbidden territory for most of the city's poor, I could see the devastating effects of poverty, violence, and official neglect.

A short walk onto Cooper Street, which bordered the campus, provided striking evidence of the distress. Once a thriving commercial thoroughfare anchored by the townhouse mansions of the Campbell Soup family and an imposing federal court building, the street had deteriorated into block upon block of shuttered and abandoned buildings and closed stores and offices. The federal court building still stood but as a foreboding symbol of authority rather than justice.

A visit to the heavily Hispanic North Camden Section of Camden, just blocks from the Rutgers campus, where I had lived in a barrio basement room when I first had come to Camden, was equally despairing. Block after block of deteriorating row houses and empty lots strewn with debris and garbage were evidence of the abject poverty and official neglect.

In the late 1980s, the city of Camden was predominantly African American with a fast-growing Latino population. Whites and the middle class had long abandoned the city. Camden ranked at the bottom of nearly every measurement of social capital—employment, housing, income, education—and at the top of nearly every negative statistic of crime and violence. At the time 40 percent of the population lived below the poverty level, and two-thirds of Camden's adults depended on public assistance as their main source of income. Crime and violence were rampant, and drugs and drug gangs ruled the city. Nowhere in Camden was it safe after dark. City hall was riddled with corruption. Several mayors in succession ended up in prison. Social services were nonexistent or at best ineffective. The public schools were leaderless and failing. For nearly everyone in Camden, life was a struggle to survive.

Over time, with Camden as the stark, debilitating backdrop, the academic policies and ideas I pursued at Rutgers evolved into a vision not just to build a school but to develop a comprehensive program of education and services centered in a community school that could actually change people's lives. It was a program I believed would lead to the transformation of an entire community.

That vision was shaped not only by what I saw firsthand in Camden and studied at the university but also by the many life lessons I had learned, first while growing up and working in the vast fields of New Jersey and Florida agribusinesses at the side of my father, "Don" Pedro Bonilla, as he organized and managed crews of migrant workers with fairness and justice. As a child, I would sit on his shoulders at union meetings, where he taught the disenfranchised workers the way to build consensus and give them voice and power. Next, under the tutelage of Marta Benavides, the mysterious Central American revolutionary and social activist, who vigorously pushed me to pursue formal education and activism as the best ways to bring about reform and change. And then as a community organizer on the streets of Camden, following the principles of sociologist Saul Alinsky.

My first attempt at community organizing turned out to be a failed effort to overcome governmental obstacles. That part of my career ended with the murder of Justo, one of my teenaged street-theater performers, who defied the drug gangs he worked for as he tried to find a better life for himself. But it was an effort that gained me valuable street smarts and an understanding of the distressed urban conditions for poor people. And it landed me in academia at Rutgers.

The conclusion of my academic studies and experience was clear: the poor people of Camden needed help in every facet of their lives—jobs and job training, health care, legal services, and education. Any solution had to be comprehensive to address those needs. It had to be community based and driven. And, since Camden was a city of children, with nearly half its residents under the age of twenty-one in the 1980s, I believed the best place to start to fix the broken community was education—good schools and good teachers for the youngest in the community. Save the kids first, I thought. Involve the parents, and the families would follow. And in the process the community would be transformed.

In my mind I had gained the knowledge that Governor Florio said was essential to bring about change and social justice. Now I had to find a way to turn the power of that knowledge into reality, fully realizing that the road to education reform and change was not through academia, where I had established myself, but through state government in Trenton, where education policy and practices were set and regulated and where the major currency was and is politics.

The door to the state capital opened for me when Jim Florio was elected governor of New Jersey in 1989. It was his third attempt for the state's highest office, having lost in the Democratic gubernatorial primary in 1977 and again as the Democratic nominee in 1981 to Republican Thomas Kean, then by less than eighteen hundred votes in the closest statewide election in history. Given where I was in my life and thinking, Jim Florio's election in 1989 was an important and fortunate development. Coincidental as it may have been, his election created opportunities in government and politics at the state level that were beyond my expectations and, in retrospect, eventually led to the enactment of measures that enabled the creation of the LEAP Academy schools.

Gloria Bonilla-Santiago sponsors fund-raising event in Camden, NJ, for James Joseph Florio during his first successful election for governor, 1989

I had known Jim Florio since the early 1970s, when he first had been elected to the state assembly and then in quick succession to Congress in a district that included Camden. He developed a reputation as a thoughtful, policy-oriented officeholder whose politics were streetwise and urban tough, and independent of the corruption of local government. I was drawn to him as a forward-thinking politician of ideas. He was involved with many of the same community organizations I was, and we shared a common urban orientation. Through the years we talked often about urban issues, particularly as they impacted the city of Camden, and I often sought his advice and counsel.

As Florio recalled:

> I think it might be an overstatement to call me her philosophical or political mentor, but yes, perhaps we could say I am a little responsible for her ability to navigate politics and Camden entanglements. We've

always had an affinity for each other because in many respects we shared the same background. I came out of the Office of Economic Opportunity's (OEO) War on Poverty, community action groups, and working with the local people in Camden. Gloria was always involved in neighborhood actions and activities. We got along very well because I was—more than I suspect most Camden city politicians were—a little more interested in substance. And she was clearly a substance person. We interacted quite a bit, and she would ask for advice, and I would tell her who to steer clear of and who to interact with. I always tried to emphasize that good policy is good politics. (Florio, J.J., 2011)

It was important for my future too that Jim Florio not only knew about Camden but came from South Jersey. Historically in state politics, there are two New Jerseys: North Jersey and South Jersey, and they are usually in conflict with each other even to this day. It isn't delineated on any map, but feelings ran so strong that as late as 1981, there were nonbinding referenda on the ballot in several of the eleven southernmost counties testing voter sentiment for secession from the north.

North Jersey, facing New York City to the east, had most of the state's population, business, and industry. And South Jersey, facing Philadelphia to the west, had significant open spaces in the Pine Barrens, extensive farms and agribusinesses, and fewer people. As a result most of the money, power, and major government programs flowed to the north from Trenton, and invariably the south got the smaller piece of the pie. With Florio in the governor's office, there was a better chance for the south to be heard and the imbalance to be corrected.

To my advantage also were the people Florio brought with him from South Jersey to state government—aides and confidants who became friends and supporters and were subsequently instrumental in making

LEAP a reality. Three of them were particularly important in advancing my work. There were his chief policy advisers: Brenda Bacon, who later, as a Camden County freeholder and original LEAP Academy board member, provided invaluable advice and political direction; Rick Wright, who directed funding to the LEAP project study and provided critical counsel on operating a charter school; and Peter Burke, an always positive and cheerful CPA who was a prodigious fund-raiser for Florio and US Senator Bill Bradley, and an important facilitator for LEAP while serving as the vice chairman of the DRPA. In the process, Peter became LEAP's financial guru and the first and only treasurer of the board of trustees that built and manages LEAP.

Many of the new governor's advisers had been with him since his earliest days in politics in the 1970s, when he had defeated the local political machine in Camden to win a state assembly seat. Florio said:

> Even before I went to Congress, I had this working group
> of people who shared the same value systems. They
> were smart people, interested in policy, but all came to
> understand, as I did over the years, that politics is part
> of the process. You've got to become minimally involved
> in politics in order to make policy. It is a lesson I think
> Gloria learned very well. (Florio, J. J., 2011)

My first taste of Trenton politics came as a member of the governor's transition team, traditionally a place where not much serious work is done but prospective government appointees are auditioned and screened. Instead, I saw the appointment as an opportunity to begin explaining my ideas—my vision of transforming communities through education. I made a point of selling my ideas to the connections, the people in Trenton who could collaborate on making my vision a reality. "Vision to connections to collaboration" became the political mantra I diligently professed in Trenton.

Florio said he chose me for his transition because of my credentials as an urban community organizer. He said:

> We were looking for a cross-section of people from New Jersey, and not only was Gloria a community activist, she is one of those people who has that wonderful combination of being a policy person, someone who truly understands policy, and is a great administrator. And she is ferocious when she becomes involved in the things she believes in. (Florio, J.J., 2011)

Jim Florio was not the first or last to label me *ferocious* or *tenacious* or *relentless* in advocating for causes. These are traits I actually believe I had in common with him. I also admired his skill as a political infighter, and in fact he was a champion boxer during a stint in the navy and bears the scar of a sunken left cheekbone, broken in the ring. I've described him as an accomplished political boxer. In turn he has called me a "verbal pugilist."

Adhering to Florio's career advice, I've stuck to policy and resisted all offers to run for public office or take government jobs, even when a cabinet-level position as commissioner of the State Department of Community Affairs was offered in a later administration. I tell everyone who wants me to run for public office that I have a job in academia at Rutgers that affords me more freedom and independence and resources to pursue my goals than any government or political position ever would. I chose a career that allows me the freedom to express my opinion and to do things from an academic perspective. And, I'm convinced, that kind of freedom has shielded me in the political world.

As it is, the most political activity I've participated in was serving on the Platform and Credentials Committees at the Democratic National Convention that nominated Bill Clinton for president in 1992. That activity introduced me to a lot of people who went on to hold important positions in the Clinton administration. That same year I was elected to the Electoral College, to cast New Jersey's electoral votes for Clinton. It was essentially an honorary position but meaningful to many of the politicians I had to deal with later.

Even though politics has been an integral part of everything I've accomplished, I grew to dislike it, particularly the practice of what I call *traditional politics*—the things politicians have to say and do to stay in office and get things done, almost always to benefit their political party or themselves. The people, their constituents, especially poor constituents, often place third in their considerations. Compounding this problem for Hispanics in New Jersey is that historically they have been underrepresented in the state legislature and therefore overlooked when it comes to serious social reform. Even today, in 2012, Latinos, who are the largest minority group in New Jersey at 17 percent of the population, hold only six of 120 seats in the state legislature, a very poor and politically weak representation of 5 percent.

Dr. Santiago represents New Jersey as electorate at the 1992 National Convention of the US Democratic Party

Despite my dislike of politics, I did understand the very important distinction between the practice of traditional politics and inherent political savvy, or street smarts, as some may call it. My background and life experiences in the migrant worker camps, on the streets of Camden, and in academia, where politics can be as intense as in any institution, have given me an abundance of political savvy as well as the smarts to know when and how to use it to best advantage.

Being politically savvy is an art. The art is knowing who the players are, where they stand, where the power base is, where the controls are, and how you can use all that to your advantage. Coupled with my relentlessness in pursuit of an agenda, I came to believe that anything is possible. And despite my distaste for the practice of politics, I developed the greatest respect and admiration for many of the legislators and officeholders, whether Democrat or Republican, I came to know and work with in bringing the vision of LEAP to fruition.

The Florio transition led to a number of other government activities and appointments in Trenton, and for the next six or seven years I made the forty-mile drive between the state capitol and Camden on Interstate 295 two or three times a week to testify and fulfill committee responsibilities, making many connections that would help me immensely years later.

Following the transition team, my next assignment in Trenton was an appointment to the State Commission on Sex Discrimination in the Statutes. The commission had been created during the administration of Governor Brendan T. Byrne in 1978 to research and restore equality and fairness among the sexes in New Jersey statutes, I suspect partly in response to failure of equal rights amendments and proposals in the 1970s. In 1990, when I joined the commission, its chair and "heart and soul" was state senator Wynona Lipman, a Democrat from Newark who was the first African American woman ever elected to the state senate in New Jersey in 1971, and one of the most remarkable women I've ever met. She was rail-thin and soft-spoken but morally tough and constant. And more than anyone, she taught me the power of ideas and knowledge in getting things done in a political environment.

Senator Lipman became my mentor on public policy, particularly on how to maneuver issues successfully through the legislative process. Nothing I learned about advancing a policy agenda came from books. I learned it from watching Wynona and how she handled people and legislators with so much class and elegance. She taught me it was just as important to research the legislator as it was to research the legislation at issue. Study the values of the legislators, she said. Find out what they care about. And then get them to do the right thing.

I recall an incident in the state senate when Wynona cornered a recalcitrant senator over the issue of welfare reform, leaning into him and, with a steely gaze and self-assurance, said, "I know what you believe. It's time now, and you have to do the right thing, Senator. I just expect that. That's all!" Five minutes later, when the issue came to a vote, he did the right thing. A valuable lesson learned.

Dr. Santiago alongside Nancy Starrett at a press conference discussing her study Hispanic Women in New Jersey: A Survey of Women Raising Families Alone, New Brunswick, NJ: Rutgers University, 1988

Senator Lipman's staff aide on the commission was a young attorney, Alma Saravia, who became my close friend and adviser and later counseled LEAP through several legal crises. Importantly to me also, the commission's work gave me insight and understanding into how unfairly women and minorities had been treated in many New Jersey statutes. It all served to further my political education.

At the same time, I was appointed by state senate president John Russo, a Democrat who years later would cosponsor charter school legislation, to a legislative advisory committee on women's issues. On the committee I helped research and advocate for legislation that was sponsored by Senator Lipman to create Hispanic women's resource centers in New Jersey. When it passed the legislature, it was signed into law by Governor Florio and created two centers, in Newark and Camden, to offer courses in basic language skills and English as a second language, job counseling and referrals, self-help programs, and information and referral services for Hispanic women in crisis. Significantly it was one of the first state initiatives designed to assist Latinos, a fast-growing segment of New Jersey's population. And it added to my credentials as an adviser to the governor, an urban specialist, and a Hispanic researcher.

About a year into his term, Governor Florio created a seven-member governor's management-review commission to look at management practices and budget policies in all state departments, agencies, and institutions, and propose cost-saving measures. The governor appointed me as a member and later as chair of the commission, explaining he chose me because of my administrative abilities and the fact I was an "outsider" who wouldn't be unduly swayed by "insider" politicians. As Florio put it, "I knew Gloria to be very articulate. She stood out clearly. She was not anyone's person. And she certainly was not shy" (Florio, J.J. 2011).

I greatly appreciated the governor's confidence in me, but my resume as an assistant professor at Rutgers paled by comparison to the six other members he appointed, all men who had reached the top of their professions.

Besides me, the commission included former governor William Cahill; Stanley Van Ness, one of the state's most prominent African American attorneys, who had served as New Jersey's first public advocate; John Petillo, PhD, a former Catholic monsignor and chancellor of Seton Hall University, who headed the state's largest health insurance company; E. James Ferland, chairman and CEO of Public Service Electric & Gas Co.; Howard Williams, head of the United Food & Commercial Workers, one of the state's largest unions; and Martin Brody, CEO of Restaurant Associates Industries, one of the nation's largest restaurant operators.

James Joseph Florio, former governor of New Jersey; Gloria Bonilla-Santiago; Stanley C. Van Ness, former New Jersey state public advocate (Management Review Audit Commission, 1993)

I still recall the first session of the commission, when I greeted Governor Cahill at the door of the State House conference room where we were meeting and asked if there was anything I could get for him. He said yes and requested a cup of coffee, which I poured and placed in front of him at the conference table. After the very long organizational session, Governor Cahill apologized for having mistaken me for a commission staffer. Cahill, a Republican, was a feisty, straight-talking Irishman who had been an FBI agent before his election to Congress and then as governor of New Jersey. And, overlooking my youth and inexperience, I think it was my feistiness he came to admire and respect.

When I told my chancellor at Rutgers Camden, Walter K. Gordon, about the gubernatorial appointment and scope of the management-review commission's work, which included a review of Rutgers's financial status as the state university, he expressed concern for me as an untenured professor who might have to make high-level decisions impacting Rutgers.

To protect me, Chancellor Gordon said he would recommend bringing me up early for tenure. Even though it was early in my academic track, he said, my research, publications, and work at Rutgers supported early tenure for me at that time. Walter also arranged for me to meet with Rutgers President Francis Lawrence to coordinate efforts on the commission, and Lawrence invited me to receive a crash course in university finances and policies to assist me in any review the management commission might undertake of the university's practices and budget.

Chancellor Gordon was a traditionalist and old-school academician and hadn't always been a staunch supporter of my ideas or extracurricular activities. In fact, he had doubted my ability to gain the traction necessary to be successful at Rutgers. It hadn't taken long for his opinion to change, however, and after ten years of working closely together, he was solidly behind my work and career path. True to his word, Walter successfully shepherded my early tenure recommendation through the university's stringent and restrictive review process.

The experience on the governor's management-review commission was very rewarding for me personally. It gave me keen insight into the workings of the legislative and executive branches of government and the management of large and complex organizations, which served me well in creating and developing the LEAP Academy. It also broadened my connections to include some of the state's most influential and important government and corporate leaders, who would later prove valuable in bringing LEAP to fruition. And it instilled in me the confidence that I could hold my own in a high-level, highly political setting.

During that time Governor Florio and I periodically resumed our discussions of urban issues. Mostly Florio and I, with his top policy adviser Brenda Bacon as my advocate, talked about our experiences in Camden and shared ideas on what might be done to deal with the city's enormous problems. Our focus invariably turned to education and the city's failing public schools. We didn't specifically discuss charter schools, an idea that was just emerging elsewhere in the nation, but, rather, generally discussed education policies that might have worked to bring about change in public education.

The governor hoped to create a model school with innovative teaching and practices that could be adapted for struggling public schools, which was not incompatible with my idea to develop community schools in Camden that could educate children and provide a wide range of services to help their families and begin the process of transforming the community.

In 1993, in the fourth year of his term, the governor asked me to put my ideas on paper and take a proposal to one of his top aides, Rick Wright, who had been assigned to oversee the state's efforts to help the city of Camden. In many respects the state was actually running the city, which had huge management and budget problems. As it turned out, meeting Rick proved to have important unforeseen, long-term benefits for me in developing LEAP and the concept of a community-based school.

Rick Wright was tall and lanky with a friendly, outgoing nature that belied a deep intellect and an understanding of finance. He was Princetonian through and through. He lived in Princeton and was a graduate of Princeton University, where he had been a roommate and teammate of Bill Bradley, the future Knicks pro basketball star and US senator, who had led Princeton's basketball team to national prominence in the 1960s. Rick had held a number of top positions in the Florio administration, first as chief of staff, then as policy advisor, and was associate state treasurer when assigned to go to Camden to watchdog the city government and find public and private entrepreneurs who could get something done in the distressed city. Rick recalls:

> I had never been to Camden in my life when Governor Florio called me into his office and said he wanted me to go down and take a look at Camden. On my first visit, he instructed me to take a specific route, coming off the Walt Whitman Bridge then driving through the center of the city and ending at the small building along the

waterfront where the governor had his office. I realized later he wanted me to see how bad it was. In those days there literally was barbed wire around the buildings where you worked. It was really kind of dangerous. But he wanted me to see it firsthand. (Wright, R., 2011)

The meeting with Rick Wright on my proposal took place in a dilapidated office building on Cooper Street. He gave me fifteen minutes to make my pitch, which was why I did not bring any university aides or any of the parents I had begun to organize to push for school reform, a tactic of packing meetings that helped me many times in dealing with public officials. I realized I had to make the case one on one with Rick as strongly and succinctly as possible, so I briefly sketched out a proposal for an innovative alternative community school with parental engagement, teacher development, and merit pay and a wide range of family services, including a health center and job and legal counseling. What I did not realize was that Rick was not evaluating my proposal on its merits but on my ability to implement the proposal effectively and overcome the serious obstacles to getting things done in a city such as Camden.

Rick says:

> Gloria walks in and sits down and starts talking, and my honest impression is that I was not even listening to what she was saying. I was watching her body language, and she was so forceful and enthusiastic and knowledgeable about schools and Camden and Rutgers, I began thinking this is something I would probably want to bet on. That's what I reported back to the governor. I always had the impression this was one of the projects Governor Florio wanted to get done and was simply looking for validation that Gloria was the person who could do it. (Wright, R., 2011)

When Rick told me the governor had approved my project, he asked how much seed money I would need to get started. I had no idea how much funding was available or would be needed to undertake and complete the strategic planning for the community-based school I envisioned, so I boldly calculated it would cost $1.5 million. There was no pushback, leading me to figure later I probably could have asked for more. No matter; I was ecstatic that my project was under way, and I had the adequate funding to research and develop a strategic plan that would meet my academically trained standards.

Former Chancellor New York City School, Joseph A. Fernandez, New Jersey Education Commissioner, Leo F. Klagholz, Gloria Bonilla-Santiago, Rutgers New Brunswick Joseph Potenza, Rutgers Camden Provost, Walter K. Gordon, meeting on the Charter School Law, 1993

The source of the funding was to be the DRPA, the bistate agency regulating port activities on the Delaware River in Philadelphia and Camden and operating bridges and transportation facilities servicing South Jersey and southeastern Pennsylvania. The agency's reserves and resources served very much like a piggy bank for the governments in both states, and the intense politicking that went on at the agency was aimed primarily at assuring each state got its fair share of the funding.

That's one reason Governor Florio had dispatched Peter Burke, who lived in Williamstown near Camden and was a CPA familiar with public financing, to the port authority, naming him DRPA vice chairman, the senior position held by a New Jerseyan, to represent the state's interests. Another Florio administration official who ended up at the DRPA with Peter was Paul Drayton Jr., who, as CEO over the course of nearly fifteen years, assured the DRPA became LEAP Academy's largest financial benefactor. Peter Burke worked with Rick Wright in securing my initial DRPA grant.

Rick recalls:

> We leveraged a lot of DRPA money for Florio projects, and Peter was instrumental in everything because so much of the money came through the DRPA. Peter was the guy I used to talk to. We were on him all the time. Every dime that came through DRPA, we had it going here. We had it going there. We were leveraging everything. Peter loved it. (Wright, R., 2011)

It shouldn't surprise anyone that Peter Burke ended up as my financial adviser at LEAP, though *wizard* is probably a more apt description. He has been the only treasurer LEAP has had since its founding.

But with planning hardly under way and the $1.5 million DRPA seed grant still outstanding, disaster struck—certainly disaster in my mind, anyway—when Jim Florio failed to win reelection as governor in November 1993. He lost to Christine Todd Whitman after a bitter campaign over Florio administration tax hikes and policies. Christie Whitman was a wealthy Republican and the daughter of one of New Jersey's truly iconic GOP figures, Webster B. Todd, whose political resume dated from the Eisenhower presidency. Whitman lived on an estate in Somerset County, near horse stables where she regularly rode. She had defeated Florio on an antitax, antispend platform, and I was convinced someone with her background would have little or no interest in solving urban problems—certainly not the problems of Camden or, for that matter, South Jersey. She had made it clear during the campaign too that much of what the Florio administration supported would likely not be a part of her agenda.

The Florio headquarters on election night was upbeat and celebratory because late tracking polls had shown that the governor had closed a big gap with his Republican challenger and may have pulled ahead by as many as 10 percentage points. The balloon- and banner-festooned hotel ballroom was jam packed with Democratic loyalists and campaign workers as well as officeholders and Florio administration staffers looking forward to another four years in Trenton.

The mood changed dramatically as the results from across the state were reported, and the tally turned against Florio. The cheers turned to tears. The band stopped playing, and I left the headquarters that night fearing my DRPA grant was dead and my dream of a community school was delayed if not permanently then for a long, long time. I was not the only one with that view.

Rick Wright notes:

> When Florio lost, we had ten or twelve major urban projects, not just Gloria's, underway in the state, each one at a point where they really needed Jim Florio to win to take them to the next stage. We were not optimistic the incoming Republican administration would continue to support those projects. (Wright R., 2011)

That night I shared Rick's fear that the campaign had been so bitter, the incoming governor would retaliate against anything the Florio administration had initiated. As it turned out, those fears were unfounded.

CHAPTER 6

. . . .

The Power of Community Advocacy

Creating schools in which all the nation's children receive
high quality education will not be easy. But behind every
significant achievement are dreamers and visionaries ... We
must have a vision, but we must also have the will to act.
Forging that will is perhaps our greatest challenge.

—*Cherry A. McGee Banks, professor,*
University of Washington, School of Education

S oon after Governor Jim Florio's November reelection loss, two
of his appointees to the DRPA—Peter Burke, the agency's vice
chairman, and Paul Drayton Jr., its chief executive officer—paid a surprise
visit to my office on the Rutgers Camden campus to present me with a
$1.5 million check from the bistate agency to finance a three-year strategic
planning process for Project LEAP Academy.

It was a grant I had thought was lost because of Florio's defeat at the polls, setting back my dream of creating an alternative community school in Camden for a long time. Under normal circumstances a government action of that financial magnitude would not be completed during the lame-duck period of a governor's term, the period between the election and swearing-in of a new governor, but would await a decision by the incoming governor.

I was told Governor Florio interceded to move the grant. However it was accomplished, what mattered to me most was that my vision to transform a poor and distressed community in Camden through education was back on track. And I had the resources to complete a thorough and comprehensive strategic plan for my community school.

To this day Peter Burke is fond of telling anyone who will listen that the only reason I keep him involved as treasurer of the LEAP Board of Trustees and for years as a valued financial adviser is I expect him to walk into my office again someday with a million-dollar check. In reality, there is no price that can be placed on the services he has rendered to LEAP through the years. And in fact Peter returns his annual consulting fee as a contribution to LEAP's scholarship fund. It is this kind of dedication and support from many people like Peter outside the field of education that has enabled LEAP to survive and excel.

Rick Wright, Governor Florio's top aide assigned to oversee state business in Camden, had worked with Peter on the DRPA grant and said they had been directed by Florio to "get Gloria's project done"—in other words to deliver the financing before his term ended. As it was, my Camden project was one of only a few of the Florio urban initiatives under way that survived the change in administrations.

Rick Wright, Florio administration associate treasurer, director of economic development, chief of staff, speaks to the attendees of the first LEAP Academy ribbon-cutting ceremony, 1997

Nevertheless, Rick is convinced I could have saved the initiative on my own:

> Gloria is a survivor. Part of her brilliance is that she is thinking a step or two ahead of everyone else, and it would surprise me if she hadn't made the connections in Trenton with the people who could help her in the new administration. (Wright, R., 2011)

That may have been true, but because of Governor Florio, Rick Wright, and Peter Burke it was unnecessary to involve those connections to obtain the DRPA grant.

With the money in hand, the real work to create a strategic plan for the Project LEAP community school began. The grant was under the auspices of the Center for Strategic Urban Community Leadership (CSUCL), which I had created at Rutgers Camden several years earlier as a vehicle to promote community initiatives, to train community leaders, and to teach community development. I believed it was important for the university to maintain control of the Project LEAP planning process through CSUCL, and it allowed me to manage dispersal of the DRPA funds.

Project LEAP participated in a Puerto Rican parade, 1995

One of the first things I did was hire former New York City schools chancellor Dr. Joseph A. Fernandez, EdD, a controversial figure in the field of education with a national reputation for innovation in urban schools. Fernandez, a high school dropout and former gang leader, had earned the highest academic honors in his career in education and achieved remarkable results in reforming urban schools in New York City and elsewhere. And he was Hispanic.

I contracted with Dr. Fernandez and his Florida-based education-consulting firm, School Improvement Services Inc., to lead the Project LEAP study. Fernandez had developed a program known as School-Based Management (SBM), which was attractive to me because it gave teachers, principals, and parents strong voices in the decision-making process at the school level. Community influence in a community school, notably through parental involvement, was an essential component of my vision. The SBM program had been adopted by nearly 250 schools in

New York City before Dr. Fernandez was fired by the city's school board in February 1993, ironically because of parental anger over his "rainbow curriculum," which advocated teaching about sexual identity issues as well as allowing distribution of condoms to high-school students.

Along with his academic credentials, however, I knew Dr. Fernandez would have an even more important role in the strategic planning for LEAP. As the leader of the planning process, he would be the lightning rod for dissension among study stakeholders and opposition from external sources such as politicians, academicians, or educators. He had the independence, credibility, and standing to deal quickly with any controversial issues.

For myself I chose the role of principal investigator, a term applied to academicians conducting research. It allowed me to participate across the board in each of the ten Project LEAP working groups we established. "You be a part of the working groups," Fernandez told me. "I'll lead the process. Let me take the heat."

Former chancellor New York City Schools, Joseph A. Fernandez;
associated director of Community Leadership Center, Wanda I. Garcia,
MSW; and Gloria Bonilla-Santiago, working group meeting,1993

The objective of the collaborative planning process for Project LEAP, as stated in its final report, was "to create a compelling vision and critical interest for an innovative alternative approach to serve the educational needs of the children of Camden." In every facet of the endeavor, I always placed children first. The aim was to design a model pre-K to eighth-grade science, math, and technology magnet school that would provide educational, human, health, legal, and business services for five hundred students and their families in the Camden community. It was an ambitious objective indeed. The process was fueled from the beginning by a simple question: If we dream, what should this school look like?

At the outset there was none of the heat Dr. Fernandez had predicted. We had the enthusiastic cooperation of the sixty members of the project working group. We had a unified purpose to achieve an innovative educational approach. And, significantly, we had the resources to conduct the most comprehensive and thorough strategic plan we could envision.

We adopted the step-by-step planning principles laid out by one of the foremost authorities on strategic planning, W. J. Cook Jr., in *Strategic Planning for America's Schools*, published in 1990 by the American Association of School Administrators in Arlington. Virginia. In one year's time, we produced a landmark 159-page report, "Camden Counts: A Strategic Plan for the Project LEAP Academy," which served as the road map for creating my comprehensive model school, including family services. And we initiated a feasibility study that served as the basis of a financial plan for LEAP. Even before a charter school law was enacted, my community school was on its way. And in the process, we compiled volumes of research and empirical evidence that supported the later adoption of New Jersey's charter school law.

The first step in our planning agenda was identification of stakeholders and creation of a partnership that would have the widest possible representation and participation of community interests. We drew active participation from Camden residents as well as other traditional institutional stakeholders including Rutgers University administrators, faculty, and students; Camden public schools' superintendent, board members, central administrators, principals, teachers, parents, and students; the Camden mayor's office and social service agencies; public and private community organizations; members of the Camden clergy; the Camden business community; and the Delaware River Port Authority. There were even nurses to help us design a health clinic and architects to help us design a facility. We wanted everyone to own a piece of the policy.

The high level of project participation was impressive. In that regard Camden public schools' superintendent, Dr. Roy Dawson, served on the working group and, in the early phases of the project, made significant contributions regarding school administration, as did Camden's mayor, Dr. Arnold Webster, who had served as the city's school superintendent before his election as mayor. Unfortunately, later in his term as mayor, Dr. Webster was indicted and convicted of accepting bribes in city hall and was in jail when Project LEAP was completed.

Rutgers former president Francis L. Lawrence, Chancellor of Higher Education Edward D. Goldberg, Rutgers Camden Provost Walter K. Gordon, former Rutgers New Brunswick Provost Joseph Potenza, Rutgers School of Social Work Dean Mary Edna Davidson, and former mayor of Camden Arnold Webster, 1993

The participation of Rutgers Camden gave the project instant credibility. It assured that the study would be conducted in accordance with the highest academic standards of research. And it assured the final report would be free of any political influence or pressure. The initiative also reflected a desire and commitment by Rutgers Camden to increase its involvement with the greater Camden community after years of neglect and ill feelings between the school and city residents, and to channel more university resources to the people of Camden.

Rutgers Camden faculty members from eight fields of interest—health, human services, law, civic service, business public policy, parental involvement, and leadership development—were drawn to the project. Those faculty members and the students they brought with them to the project represented the Rutgers Camden School of Law, School of Business, the Social Work Department, several departments in the College of Arts and Sciences, the Center for Strategic Urban Community Leadership, and the Nursing Department.

When I presented the Project LEAP proposal to the top Rutgers administrators in New Brunswick and received $1.5 million to underwrite the project, I think they believed I was going to do a research project and then maybe write a book about it. That would become a problem later on.

That was never the belief on the Rutgers Camden campus, however. Chancellor Walter Gordon and most of my faculty colleagues in Camden knew I was doing something significant beyond research. They understood that there was a movement to reform public schools. They knew how bad the Camden schools really were. They knew they were part of a movement to introduce legislation and that there was going to be a law enacted. I had funding to pay for the research that would assure the project was done the right way. And, I believe, they knew how relentless I would be in pursuing a cause in which I believed.

One of the Rutgers Camden faculty members who became very involved with Project LEAP was Dr. Miriam Chaplin, an African American tenured professor in the School of Education. Thinking far ahead, I hired Professor Chaplin to conduct interviews and evaluations of public-school teachers in Camden, with the specific intention of creating a file of prospective teachers to hire for LEAP Academy.

Dr. Miriam Chaplin (in black suit), LEAP Academy planning group, 1993

Of course I was fully committed to the prospect that this project was not simply an academic exercise. The prevailing view in academia is that academic professionals are supposed to be detached, conducting research and examining both sides of an issue—not, as in this case, actually building and running an off-campus school in the community. But, contradicting that tenet, I fervently stood for doing something real. And that fervor, I believe, is what made my vision for a community school so interesting to legislators and people outside academia. As it was, I had brought other experiences with me into academia from a life shaped by work in community organizing and social justice. In my heart I was doing things not just to advance my academic career but for the greater good of society.

That was why the stakeholders who were of particular importance to me and my reform agenda were the parents of children who would attend my school. I believed a key component—perhaps the most essential component—in organizing a successful community school was parental engagement. To that end I had begun to organize local parents to support the creation of an alternative community school even before Project LEAP got started.

When I received the DRPA funding, I hired two Camden parents—Norma Rosa Agrón, a Latina, and Shantay Clark, an African American—to go door to door in the poorest Camden neighborhoods to solicit involvement from parents with school-age children. They organized their search on the basis of neighborhood demographics, Norma in the Latino barrios and Shantay in the African American neighborhoods, because it was often a dangerous task in both communities. The threat of violence and a distrust of authority figures were palpable in those neighborhoods. But Norma and Shantay's persistence and persuasiveness, not to mention their strong commitment to the idea of a community school in which parents had a say, paid off. By the time the LEAP Academy charter school opened its doors nearly three years later, more than five hundred parents, who were my foot soldiers in the school reform battle, had been organized and trained. I can say without equivocation that there would not have been a LEAP Academy without the parents. When LEAP opened its doors, Norma, a single mother of three who had come to Camden from Puerto Rico in 1986, became the school's coordinator of parental engagement, a position she held for more than ten years, and Shantay Clark became a trainer in the LEAP parents' academy.

The parents we recruited were mostly women. Many of them were unemployed and receiving public assistance. Only a few had formal education or had graduated from high school. But their message was a powerful one, simpler and more poignant than any of the other project stakeholders. These parents were not asking for anything for themselves. They simply wanted a better school and better educations for their children. They wanted only an opportunity for their children to escape the poverty and violence that gripped their lives in Camden.

As the Camden Counts project and feasibility study for a community school was unfolding, I obtained a $75,000 grant from the Prudential Foundation in Newark to develop a LEAP parental training program, which would educate parents on their responsibilities and involvement in the school. At the time the Prudential Foundation was headed by Gabriella Morris, who became a good friend of LEAP and a supporter of the charter school movement. And the initial grant from Prudential turned out to be a down payment on significantly greater funding for LEAP over the years.

Besides training parents on what it takes to make a community school run properly, we offered them lessons in civics and the tactics of civil protest. We taught them what to say, how to lobby lawmakers, how to protest, when to make noise, and when to be quiet. We even taught them how to dress for success and how to speak in public. It brought back vivid memories of my childhood, when Marta and my parents had taught me what to do on the picket line or in protests and how they would tell me when to hold a sign up and when to lower it.

The sixty stakeholder members of Project LEAP were assigned to ten working groups to research and design instruction programs for students, leadership training and professional development programs for administrators and teachers, and a comprehensive school-linked health and human services program that included a hospital-operated health clinic. The working groups also planned a school-linked law clinic, a job-counseling clinic, and a community-outreach program that included public information and parental involvement components. There was even a physical design working group with architects among its members charged with identifying a location for the Project LEAP Academy and developing a design for space utilization in the school.

Focus group with Camden city parents, 1993

Looking at LEAP today, all of those programs have been fully implemented. The LEAP Family Health Clinic, located in LEAP's pre-K to eighth-grade elementary school, is operated by Camden's Cooper University Medical Center, which has become one of the region's most outstanding hospitals. The clinic provides a full range of health care and services, including prenatal care, for LEAP families, most of whom have no health insurance.

The project's working group as a whole, under the direction of Dr. Fernandez and his staff, met nearly weekly in full-day sessions between January and October 1994. The group meetings served as vehicles to discuss and analyze issues from all the stakeholders and led to the production of a unified strategic plan. Joe Fernandez had managed a school system in New York City with hundreds of schools and millions of stakeholders. His ability to lead a large group of stakeholders would lead us to success. One of the most informative and valuable undertakings by Project LEAP was the focus groups. Dr. Fernandez led a total of fourteen group sessions with five distinct groups of stakeholders in Camden. The sessions followed a fixed professional format with the same broad topics covered in each one. The sessions were designed to assess problems and issues in the community and in Camden schools as well as barriers and challenges to reform. Focus groups were conducted with teachers, administrators, school support personnel, parents of public-school children, and students. The sessions were held in local schools and on the Rutgers Camden campus. They were videotaped and transcribed, and the information they produced proved absolutely critical to the development of a viable strategic plan.

The number one issue raised over and over again during the focus group sessions was security and safety in schools. The issue came up most frequently in the focus groups conducted with parents and schoolchildren. They said most of all they wanted to feel safe in school. But sadly they didn't know what safety was or how to describe a secure environment. They didn't know what a good school—a safe school—looked like. They couldn't even dream of or speculate about it because they had never experienced it. And that was why we incorporated safety into every facet of our plan for a community school. I wanted to create that vision for them.

We also planned for clean schools because the kids and their parents talked about how dirty their schools were, how the classrooms and hallways and particularly the bathrooms smelled bad. We also found that the problems of safety and cleanliness were worse in the poorest-performing schools. As a result I developed a bathroom test for schools. Whenever I visit a school in the United States or on an overseas consulting tour, I make sure to check the condition of the bathrooms. If they are relatively clean and appear safe, I believe there's a chance the school is being run properly.

Dr. Fernandez also conducted site visits to model schools in the region—schools with high levels of achievement and performance. And in coming to grips with the thorniest issue on our agenda, school governance options, I led a team on visits to a half dozen states across the nation where alternative schools, notably charter schools, were already in operation. From our research we learned three states—Michigan, Minnesota, and California—had the most mature charter school programs in place. In Minnesota I met with Joe Nathan, recognized as the nation's foremost authority on charter schools and one of the founding fathers of the charter movement. I was most impressed with the progressive nature of the charter schools in Minnesota, the first state to pass a charter school law, although the facilities in Michigan were better. In my mind I was already combining features of both states to bring home to New Jersey.

Joe Nathan, leader of the Minnesota charter school movement provides professional development training for LEAP Academy teachers, 1997

Working group of teachers in the planning process of LEAP Academy, 1993

Since the early stages of the Project LEAP planning process, a major focus had been on the development of a governance structure, particularly to define a formal relationship between Rutgers Camden and the Camden public schools, which had legal and fiscal responsibility for public education in the city. As a result of our research, site visits, interviews, working-group meetings, and focus groups, three models for governance of the Project LEAP Academy emerged—a shared governance school, an independent school, and a charter school.

Under the shared governance approach, Rutgers Camden and the Camden Board of Education would share responsibility for the operation of LEAP Academy. In essence, LEAP would become a new magnet school within the Camden public school system, and the annual operating costs would derive from the per-pupil funding formula used for other Camden schools. Like the other Camden schools, LEAP Academy would be required to adhere to the policies and rules of the Camden Board of Education regarding both students and employees, including collective bargaining agreements. A major advantage of the shared governance model was that it built on existing working relationships between Rutgers Camden and the Camden board and provided an established legal framework and a source of financial support for the operation of LEAP Academy.

The independent school model positioned LEAP Academy as a separate entity from the Camden public schools in a manner similar to private and parochial schools. The independent model required that separate legal and fiscal support structures be developed by Rutgers Camden or an independent agency designated to operate the school. As with other nonpublic schools, the independent model required a separate funding mechanism, through grant solicitations or other sources, to underwrite operating costs for the school and staff.

The charter school governance model, which would give LEAP Academy both autonomy and fiscal support, was already established as a popular approach for educational reform in some states across the nation. And at the same time the Project LEAP research was being compiled, New Jersey had begun exploring the adoption of charter school legislation. We quickly saw that the major advantage of the charter-school governance model would be access to state public education funds while limiting state and local bureaucratic obstacles that usually accompany such financial support, so schools such as the proposed LEAP Academy could remain autonomous. Another advantage would be that the charter school reported to the State Department of Education and not the local school board.

The heat Dr. Fernandez had predicted came when it was time for the Camden Counts project to select a preferred governance option.

The parents we had recruited and organized to support Project LEAP Academy were adamantly opposed to the shared governance option, threatening to withdraw from the initiative if "their" new school was given back to the failed Camden school system they were desperately trying to get away from. In a sense, I was pleased and proud to hear it. I was pleased because I also had reservations about having to deal with and adhere to all the policies and rules of the Camden Board of Education. There would have been very little new about my school. And I was proud because those parents, most uneducated and barely speaking or reading English, had understood perfectly well what the consequences of the various governance options would be. I also knew that without parental involvement, my dream of creating a community school would not be possible.

First graduation ceremony of Parents As Partners for Educational Change Program, July 27, 1996

Much of the research compiled by Project LEAP showed the independent school model was the least likely of the three governance options, primarily because of the issue of finances. The Project LEAP feasibility study had revealed there were numerous foundations, institutions, and corporations willing to provide significant program funding, even some financing for facilities. But without support from the per-pupil public-school funding formula, the need to fund operating costs year in and year out loomed as an insurmountable obstacle under the independent governance model. Tuition of any kind was certainly out of the question. There was no way our parents could afford to pay for this option. There was also strong opposition to this option from the Catholic clergy, who did not want any new competition since they were already struggling with recruitment of students to parochial schools.

It was obvious from our research that the charter school model was the only viable option for Project LEAP Academy. It would offer funding to operate a school and provide the autonomy necessary to institute educational reforms.

But when we announced the decision to pursue a charter school option, all the Camden Board of Education and Camden City officials withdrew from participation in Project LEAP. That was followed by the state's largest teacher's union, the New Jersey Education Association (NJEA), coming out in opposition to any charter school project.

And, of course, the decision to pursue a charter school also meant we had to go back to Trenton for enabling legislation. The dynamics in Trenton had changed significantly since Florio's defeat in November 1993. For one, both houses of the legislature were controlled by Republicans, whose track record on supporting urban education initiatives was not as strong as the Democrats. And, as far as education policy in the new Republican administration was concerned, Governor Christie Whitman was an avowed proponent of school vouchers. In her campaign for governor, she had won important support from Bret Schundler, the Republican mayor of Jersey City, who was one of the state's most vocal advocates of vouchers. So early in her administration, Governor Whitman fulfilled her campaign promise by convening a blue-ribbon commission to examine the issue of vouchers. She appointed a former Republican governor, Thomas H. Kean—who, during his term in office, had earned the honorific title Education Governor primarily for his higher-education initiatives—to lead the commission, and she named Schundler a member. It meant that school vouchers would be the all-consuming education issue in play in Trenton.

The outlook for charters, however, was not as foreboding as it may have seemed. First, legislators in both parties were already exploring the charter school issue and considering legislation. Second, I had broadened my contacts and connections during the Florio administration to include some of the most influential Republicans in the legislature. Early on my policy mentor in the legislature, Senator Wynona Lipman, a Democrat, had introduced me to Republican legislators she said I would have to get to know if I was serious about pursuing my ideas for an urban community school. Two of the most important Republicans she pointed out were Senators Donald DiFrancesco and John H. Ewing.

I had served with Senator DiFrancesco on the State Commission on Sex Discrimination in the Statutes, which he had cochaired with Senator Lipman, and when Republicans took control of the legislature in 1994 he was elected senate president, a powerful position that at that time put him next in the line of succession for governor. More important to me, no legislation could be posted in the senate for a vote without his approval.

As for Senator Ewing, he was the leading Republican authority on education issues in the legislature in 1994 and had assumed the chairmanship of the Senate Education Committee when the GOP took control. He emerged as my champion in Trenton, and I am convinced that without him charter school legislation would not have been enacted when it was, and LEAP Academy would not have opened its doors as soon as it did or been as successful as it has been.

In that regard Jack Ewing was perhaps the most unlikely advocate for urban schools and schoolchildren in the legislature. He was a wealthy suburban Republican who had retired in 1967 as board chairman of Abercrombie & Fitch before entering state politics. That same year he had been elected to the state assembly and ten years later had moved up to the senate. When I met him, he had twenty-five years of experience in the legislature. Senator Ewing lived on an estate in a huge, rambling Colonial-era home in Somerset County, just a mile or two from Governor Whitman in a part of New Jersey known as "horse country." His personality was unassuming, and he was dignified, self-assured, and soft-spoken. I seemed to have an affinity for soft-spoken politicians, lawmakers who did not have to shout and scream to get their way but instinctively knew which political buttons to push to get things done. And Jack Ewing certainly knew how to make good policy look like good politics.

Soon after I explained my concept of a community school to Senator Ewing, I invited him to come to Camden to see firsthand the condition of public schools. We were allowed access to only a handful of schools, and I'm convinced if I had asked to inspect the sites on my own, permission would not have been granted. The senator was visibly saddened by the deteriorated conditions of the classrooms and buildings, the demoralized teachers and students, and the lack of books and basic resources, and was appalled at the thought that these schools might be the best in the city. Needless to say the schools had not passed my bathroom test. From that point on, Jack Ewing became my biggest booster in Trenton.

Senator Ewing's right hand on education issues in Trenton was Melanie Schulz, the executive director of the bipartisan Joint Committee on Public Schools, which was cochaired by the senator. The committee had been formed by both houses of the legislature in the 1970s, when the controversial Abbott school funding decision was made by the state Supreme Court. It had been created to provide ongoing study of public schools and their financing, administration, and operation as well as to make recommendations for legislative action. A major function of the committee was to merge and find compromise between legislative proposals introduced in the senate and assembly.

I had learned early on that there are actually two governments in Trenton and probably in every state capitol. There is the government that changes every four years or so according to the election cycle, and there is the government of bureaucrats and committee staffers not dependent on elections who really run things. Melanie, who for years had been a committee staffer in the senate before moving to the Joint Committee, was among the latter. Slender and petite with a sharp intellect and no-nonsense attitude, she knew as much about the legislative process and the legislators themselves as anyone I met in Trenton. In that capacity she played an important role in the enactment of charter school legislation.

As Melanie recalls, after returning from a Washington, DC, conference of educators on the cutting edge of charter schools in January 1995, Senator Ewing asked her to draft a charter school proposal. And within a month, in a remarkably quick turnaround for major legislation in Trenton, Senator Ewing introduced a bill in the senate. At the same time, two assemblymen, Democrat Joseph Doria and Republican John Rocco, had written their own charter school bill and introduced it in the lower house. It was not a companion bill identical to Senator Ewing's, however, and it would take months of work and negotiations to hammer out a final draft—a task that fell to the joint committee to coordinate.

Joe Doria and John Rocco both had backgrounds in education. Doria, who eventually became assembly speaker, a state senator, the state commissioner of community affairs, mayor of Bayonne, and a college professor, compiled a remarkable record in his more than two decades as a legislator. During his legislative career, more than 240 bills he sponsored were signed into law, probably a record for any legislator, and he earned his doctorate in education from Columbia University, writing his dissertation on the charter school movement.

Assemblyman Rocco, mayor of Cherry Hill and a former school principal who had earned a doctorate in education from Rutgers, was chairman of the Assembly Education Committee when the debate over school vouchers and charter schools arose.

By the time a final version of charter legislation was drafted, Senator John Russo, a Democrat and the immediate past senate president who had appointed me to the legislative commission of women's issues, had signed on as the senate cosponsor of charter school legislation with Jack Ewing. If someone had created a wish list of sponsorship for the charter school proposal, they couldn't have come up with four more influential sponsors.

But even with such powerful sponsors, it took nearly a year of negotiations and bargaining—with education policy people in the governor's office, with school administrators, with interested parties, with other legislators, and with opponents such as the NJEA—to get a final version of the charter legislation written and passed in the legislature.

Work on the charter legislation continued through the summer of 1995 even though the summer months traditionally were a break period for the part-time New Jersey Legislature. It was a good time in the legislature to work on a charter bill, Melanie Schultz recalls, because most of the focus and attention on education policy in Trenton was on the fight between proponents and opponents of school vouchers.

Melanie notes:

> During our charter law journey that year, we would convene nearly on a daily basis, sometimes just a small group of people. Most times legislators would be involved. Sometimes there were people who were thinking about doing a charter school. Sometimes there were interest groups. Or attorneys like Chris Christie [the future governor of New Jersey] who represented Edison Schools, a for-profit education company that was interested in what our legislation was going to look like. With everyone we would sit around the table, and we would talk about different ideas and things that would be in the legislation and how it would be implemented. And we would have hearings—not only committee hearings in Trenton but public hearings all over the state.

> Gloria was a part of all of that. I can't count the number of times we went to Camden or asked Gloria to come to Trenton to give us her take on different provisions being drafted for the legislation. She knew all the experts on charter schools in the country and had access to them. And she had an incredible amount of research and evidence on a new kind of school she was compiling as a part of the Rutgers study [Project LEAP] she was leading.

> She actually was planning to build a charter school before there was a charter school law. The volumes of information in her study answered so many of the

questions we had about this reform, and much of it served as the basis for the legislative proposal we wrote. So we went to Camden often.

After all these years, I still have lots of notes in the files on different provisions, some of which made it into the bill and others that didn't, written on Gloria's office typewriter or even on napkins—things Gloria wrote. She was definitely a person who was always at our table. She was there, or she always had someone there. Jack Ewing and I got very close to Gloria and her people. We became more than colleagues. We really became friends. And that has lasted all through the years. (Schulz, M., 2011)

As the journey toward a charter schools bill Melanie Schulz describes progressed, I was called on numerous times to testify in support of charter school legislation. I also brought in charter school experts to testify, such as Dr. Fernandez and Joe Nathan. I believe, however, that my secret weapon in the campaign to win legislation that would allow me to build a community school was the cadre of parents I had recruited from the barrios and poor neighborhoods of Camden.

Melanie recalls:

When Senator Ewing and I first met Gloria, her hook was that she knew in order to turn around anything in education, she had to take on the parents first and make them aware of what they needed to do to help their children get a better school. She recruited all these parents, and she would bring them to meetings and hearings. Not all of them every time. But a handful, five or ten, up to thirty or fifty depending on how loud or large a presence she felt was necessary.

What was fascinating to us was the way the parents evolved. Over time they evolved like butterflies. Gloria gave them an understanding of the nuance of meetings, the importance of how they should present themselves in a professional manner, the way they should look, and the way they should express their opinions. She gave them the experience of participating, made them proud of who they were, and gave them confidence. All of it changed the dynamics of shaping charter legislation, made a huge impression on legislators, and made the parents valuable participants in the process. That's what she gave to them. (Schulz, M., 2011)

I would bus my Camden parents to all the important meetings and hearings in Trenton and elsewhere. We would pack lunches for them and prep them with testimony or the points they should make when lobbying lawmakers. For many it was like a Sunday excursion. Some were welfare mothers who said the trips to Trenton were much more meaningful than sitting and watching TV all day. They would pack the hearing rooms and fill the galleries in the legislative chambers. They would walk the hallways to promote their cause. They were enthusiastic and inquisitive and had all the time in the world. And their presence alone proved effective in moving the legislation to enactment.

The parents were helpful and persuasive in other ways too. During deliberations on the charter bill, Senator Ewing asked me to meet with a legislator who was not convinced charters were the way to go and was important to getting the bill passed. But Senator Ewing warned me the legislator was not one who stayed focused or paid a lot of attention to details. So I decided to bring six or seven of my Camden parents to the meeting, which had been set at a Trenton restaurant called Something Special near the State House. All of them were welfare mothers who had been through the Project LEAP training for parents and were dressed in their best Sunday-go-to-church finery—floppy hats, flowery dresses, and heels.

When we arrived at the restaurant, the legislator was already there, seated at a small table for two in a corner of the dining room. I apologized for not giving him advance notice of my Camden parents' accompanying me. No matter, he said, and quickly arranged to have us all seated at a larger table. After enduring several hours of stories about Camden, the legislator graciously picked up the tab for lunch. And he became one of the charter legislation's staunchest proponents. As for my parents, it was probably the best meal they ate that week.

I did not get everything I wanted in the final version of the charter school legislation, but as it is in crafting any major reform, neither did anyone else. I was pleased that authorization and approval of charter schools were established at the state level with the State Commissioner of Education rather than in the local districts, which most likely would have crippled or severely delayed the program. I was just as pleased that the legislation permitted and encouraged establishment of charter schools in urban districts and in partnerships with institutions of higher learning, but this was a provision that would become a problem for me at Rutgers even before the legislation was enacted.

We were also able to include an important provision on teachers' unions. They would be allowed to organize teachers, but charter schools would not be subject to existing contracts in a local school district. While upholding the right to organize, the provision recognized that charter schools operated differently, and teacher responsibilities extended beyond the classroom to include, among other things, longer school days and years and before- and after-school activities.

I was disappointed the final version of the legislation did not include financing for the construction or acquisition of buildings for charter schools. Facilities funding was something assemblyman John Rocco had strongly advocated, but there was no will in the legislature or Whitman administration to tackle an issue that could have run into hundreds of millions of dollars and most likely would have killed the possibility of passage.

Also, because charter schools would be autonomous in local school districts, they could not benefit from or use the local districts' bonding or public referendum authority. To this day the lack of a facilities-financing program in the New Jersey charter schools statute has cost the state millions and millions of matching federal education dollars. It is a shortcoming in the New Jersey law that remains to be fixed.

There was, however, another important financial clause included in the final charter school legislation—a provision that permitted charters to acquire property by "lease with an option to purchase." Several years later it would allow the LEAP Academy charter school to acquire its first elementary school building.

Opposition to the legislation was not as strong as many of its proponents had anticipated. Some local school boards were pensive at first but eventually were satisfied that per-pupil funding would remain in the districts and that charters would not impact the districts' bonding capacity. The public school administrators were concerned that in the proposed legislation, heads of charter schools could call themselves whatever they wanted and might not have the appropriate credentials for the job. The proposal was amended to require that the individual who leads a school must hold a principal's or supervisor's certification from the state.

The major pushback on the legislation came from the NJEA, but again it was not as strenuous as anticipated. The union lost on a number of issues, such as authorization of charters and the charter exemption from local-district teacher contracts, but won compromise on others, including retaining the right to organize. The NJEA's major concern was over a provision that allowed for unlimited propagation of charter schools and encouraged the state commissioner of education to promote the establishment of charters as official policy. The union feared thousands of charter schools might be created and had drawn a line it would not back down from on the issue. It wanted language in the proposal limiting the number of charter schools in New Jersey.

The compromise written into the legislation was to limit establishment of charter schools in the state to 135 in the first forty-eight months of the program, after which the limit would be lifted. As it turned out, only a few dozen charter schools were opened in the first four years of the new law. And to date, after more than fifteen years of a charter-school program in New Jersey, the number of charters in operation has not reached 135. In the end the NJEA, preoccupied with its fight to prevent school vouchers, signed off on the charter proposal as the alternative of lesser evil.

It was the political argument on the viability of charters over vouchers that charter-school proponents such as Senator Ewing used to convince Governor Whitman to embrace the concept as a part of her educational-reform agenda. In several meetings with the governor, arranged by Senator Ewing, I had come away with the fear that she was too wedded to school vouchers ever to endorse charter schools as an option. I felt she didn't fully realize how bad conditions were in urban school systems. But she did express a deep concern for the children trapped in those schools.

In the end, I believe, Senator Ewing convinced Governor Whitman that if she wanted to have an educational reform achievement in her first term in office, the votes were there for a charter school program but not for school vouchers. To date, school vouchers have not been enacted in New Jersey and remain a very controversial and contentious issue.

With the concurrence of the governor and nearly all interested parties, a final version of the Charter School Program Act was in position for a vote in both houses of the legislature by October 1995. The governor even expressed to me her hope that I would be the first applicant for a charter and possibly the first to open a charter school in the state. I assured her I was already preparing the information needed to apply.

Before a vote occurred, however, a serious problem arose with the top Rutgers University administration in New Brunswick, no doubt exacerbated by a provision in the charter legislation that read: "A charter school may also be established by an institution of higher learning ... located within the State in conjunction with teaching staff members and parents of children attending the schools in the district."

I had helped write that into the legislation, and apparently the realization that Project LEAP, which I was leading as a Rutgers professor, was not simply academic research but a plan to build and operate a school had raised concern within the New Brunswick administration. Rutgers Camden Chancellor Walter Gordon had also confirmed to the Rutgers Board of Governors that I intended to file an application for a charter school as soon as the law was enacted.

On his way back from that board meeting, Walter called me from his car and said, "Gloria, I don't think they are going to let you file for a charter school. They thought you were just doing a research project."

But Chancellor Gordon, who fully supported my project, also noted he was soon retiring. An acting Rutgers Camden provost, Roger Dennis, had already been designated, and he told me, "Gloria, you've got my permission to do whatever you need to do."

In my mind that meant I had permission to go outside the university system—a step that would be viewed as near sacrilege in the world of academia. So I made several calls to Trenton: one to senate President Donald DiFrancesco, who was fully onboard with the charter legislation and aware of my intention to file an application for a charter school, and another to my friend and supporter Senator Jack Ewing. I asked them to alert the governor's office to the problem I had encountered with the Rutgers administration over filing a charter-school application.

The word already circulating on the Rutgers New Brunswick campus on the subject had nearly panicked my husband, Alfie, who worked in New Brunswick and was the highest-ranking Latino in the university administration. Alfie told me there had been a closed-door meeting of Rutgers administration officials on my project, and some of his colleagues had advised him he should do something to "control" me because the university was not going to let me file. Alfie was convinced we might be punished or sanctioned, perhaps even dismissed, over the issue.

In a reversal of our roles throughout the years, I became the consoler, trying to assure him we wouldn't be fired, but even if we were, we would be able to find jobs somewhere else in academia. The argument was little consolation for Alfie. When he came home from New Brunswick on the day Chancellor Gordon called, he cautioned me to be careful. I told him it was too late; I had already placed calls to my friends in Trenton on the issue.

Later on the president set up a meeting for me to attend a board of governors meeting to present the project. I stalled, figuring I had overplayed my hand and anticipating a difficult and contentious meeting in New Brunswick. I sought the advice of my friend Alma Saravia, the attorney who was Senator Wynona Lipman's aide and confidant and counsel to the State Commission on Sex Discrimination in the Statutes, on which I had served. She was already helping me prepare a charter-school application. Alma said by all means I should have legal representation at the meeting, and she arranged to have a Philadelphia attorney who was a law partner of hers and specialized in education issues accompany me to New Brunswick. When we—the lawyer; my top assistant, Wanda Garcia; and I—arrived at the meeting, I realized how seriously the New Brunswick administration was taking the issue. Chairing the session was Joseph Seneca, a nationally renowned economics professor who also served as Rutgers vice president of academic affairs. He was the university's chief academic officer, who conducted the school's disciplinary hearings.

Chancellor Gordon, who met us before the meeting, asked me who the third person was I had brought with me. I explained he was an outside counsel from Philadelphia, and if they wouldn't let him participate I would not meet. Walter went back into the conference room and, after ten minutes, emerged with Joe Seneca. Clearly annoyed, Seneca told me I did not need outside legal representation, that the lawyers on the Rutgers side of the table represented both the university and me. Thinking as quickly as I could, I said the Philadelphia attorney did not represent me but the interests of the five hundred parents who were participating in Project LEAP with the full expectation and commitment that they would have a new school for their children.

Whether it satisfied the Rutgers officials or not, the attorney was allowed to stay, and the meeting continued. A deal was worked out that a nonprofit organization would be established to run any school that was created, alleviating Rutgers of that responsibility. And Chancellor Gordon agreed to reduce my teaching responsibilities by 50 percent so I could fund-raise and develop an operating plan for the proposed school.

But Seneca also ruled that before permission would be granted to file an application, a financial plan on how the school would be paid for and how operating costs would be met would have to be submitted. He gave us one week to produce the plan. That deadline might have seemed impossible, but it was one I knew I could easily meet because of the extensive financial information and operational plan we had developed for Project LEAP and the Project LEAP feasibility study we were conducting under Camden Counts.

I was elated. The charter legislation was about to be enacted, and my differences with Rutgers had been resolved. However, the worst personal tragedy I have ever experienced then occurred when my beloved husband was crushed in an auto accident with a drunken truck driver who ran a red light. The days at his bedside were the most excruciatingly painful and emotionally draining time of my life. I lost interest in my career, in my dreams for LEAP, and in life itself.

After Alfie was buried, I wallowed in grief and tearful depression at home, cared for in shifts by a succession of family and friends, most often by my cousin, Sonia Gonzalez, and my mother. I did not think at all about my work or Project Leap or the charter-school legislation that had just cleared the state legislature.

Just days after Alfie's funeral, the phone at my home rang, and my mother, who was overseeing my convalescence, answered it. She listened and then, covering the receiver, told me in Spanish it was the governor's office.

"The governor is going to sign the charter school bill into law in her office tomorrow, and she is inviting you to be at her side when she does it," she said.

Former Governor Christine "Christie" Todd Whitman, Assemblyman John A. Rocco (Republican, Camden), former New Jersey state senator John "Jack" Ewing presenting the charter school law certificate to Dr. Santiago, 1997

With a heavy sigh, I told her to say I regretted I couldn't be there, that I was still recovering from the loss of my husband.

"But it's the governor," my mother insisted.

I declined again, saying I was not up to going out in public yet.

My mother, who had strongly opposed my independence and pursuit of education as I grew up—because of it we didn't speak for years, and I came to believe she never fully understood what my work was about—raised the phone and firmly, in perfect English, said, "She'll be there!"

CHAPTER 7

. . . .

Alfie: True Love and Unspeakable Tragedy

T his chapter about my late husband, Alfredo (Alfie) Santiago, is the most difficult for me to write not only because of how much he meant to me and my work in education and because of the emotion his memory evokes but also because of the deeply conflicted feelings I have over what my life with Alfie might have been and what my life has become as a result of his death.

I do suspect LEAP may not have become what it is today if Alfie had lived, our perfect marriage had continued, and we had pursued our professional careers more diligently than fulfilling my dream of building a school to transform a poor urban community through education.

I miss him every day. He was my confidant and comrade, conciliator, friend, and lover, and my soul mate in everything I thought and did during the all-too-brief thirteen years we were married. I tell people we had a century of love and marriage in those thirteen years, but my tears swell and my heart aches for just a few more hours or minutes with him.

Our life together couldn't have been more perfect.

Summer 1985, Gloria and Alfredo Santiago

Alfie was the highest-ranking Latino in the Rutgers University administration when he died. From my early years at Rutgers Camden, when I was adjusting to academia and earning my advanced degrees, through the difficult times trying to convince the Rutgers administration to recognize its obligation to the community outside its ivy-covered walls and support my vision of transforming a poor minority community through education by allowing me to open a charter school, he was my eyes and ears and adviser at the university.

More important than anything else, Alfie reunited me with my family, effecting reconciliation with my father and mother after a nearly ten-year separation during which we hadn't spoken with each other, and I had rejected their religion and culture to pursue my education. As much as I missed them, I may never have reconnected with my parents if

First Christmas tree given to Dr. Santiago by Alfie, 1981

I hadn't met Alfie. He was at heart much more the Latino traditionalist than I was and refused to marry me until I reconciled with my family.

But all that—the love and life we had, the plans and dreams we made together—ended in one tragic moment in 1996.

It was on the eve of the passage of the charter school law that would enable me to build LEAP—a historic legislative victory for New Jersey's children—that tragedy struck, nearly derailing my work and my life forever. On one awful morning, fate, in the form of a drunk driver, stole Alfredo Santiago from me in a tragic accident.

I had met Alfie in 1981. He was a quickly rising star in the central Rutgers University administration in New Brunswick and headed an organization of college faculty and staff—the Hispanic Association of Higher Learning. I was a young social activist and recently hired administrator on the Rutgers campus in Camden. I had not yet earned my PhD and was just becoming acclimated to life in academia.

One day the phone rang in my office in Camden—the Office of Hispanic Affairs, which I had just created. When I answered, the caller introduced himself as Alfredo Santiago. "I have heard so much about you," he said, which I thought was rather interesting because I was so new to Rutgers. "There's a group of Latinos at Rutgers, and we know who you are from what you've been doing in Camden and in the Puerto Rican community in the state," he said, "and we would like you to get involved in our organization."

It sounded interesting, but I already had enough on my plate at Rutgers Camden, trying to get the Hispanic Affairs office established and trying to solidify my career in academia. "I don't need to be involved with anything else," I told him and thought my matter-of-fact tone would settle the matter.

But Alfie was persistent, and, as I was to learn, like me he didn't shy from a challenge—an attribute that would benefit us tremendously in the years to come. He called repeatedly, saying, "Just come for lunch ... I would like to introduce you to the association members."

Finally I agreed, curious to find out what the association was all about, and penciled him into my schedule. But as I drove to New Brunswick to meet him one day, I had nothing but my own work in Camden on my mind. When I turned in to Cook College on the Rutgers campus, he was waiting at the curb to greet me. When he saw me, he waved and flashed a wide, welcoming smile, but there was something else I noticed about him that sparked a long-lost memory.

I took one look at his distinctive, long-lashed green eyes and said, "Oh my God, I remember you!" I had seen him ten years earlier, when I was starring as Mariana Bracetti in a play about the Puerto Rican independence leader at Rutgers's Douglass College, where I had been a student. He had been with a group of students who had come to congratulate me. We hadn't spoken, but I could never forget those eyes.

Years earlier, as a young girl in the migrant worker camps, my mother had taken me to a Latino spiritualist in Vineland in an attempt to cure a chronic stomach ailment. I think the medical care my father got me had more to do with my recovery, but I never forgot the prediction the spiritualist made about my future, saying there would be three men in my life, and one of them would have green eyes.

Alfie was a tall and strikingly handsome man, always impeccably dressed, impressively articulate and with an air of confidence and reserve that was not common to the Latino men I had known while growing up in the migrant camps.

Over lunch Alfie told me about the association and its efforts on behalf of Latino students at Rutgers and then took me to a meeting to introduce me to the association members. That was how our relationship began—with a common commitment to Latino students. He later told me I made a very strong impression on the group.

"It's not just who you are," he told me, "It's how you walk into a room. You make an instant impression, and when you left they were ready to elect you as the association's new president."

Alfie was chairing the group at the time but told me he did not want to continue in the role. I came to learn he was excellent at managing and providing support but did not want to be the face of any organization. He thought I would be better suited to that and tried repeatedly to convince me to take a leadership role in the group.

But I told him I was tired of being in charge, and I meant it. I had been in one leadership role or another since Marta Benavides had come into my life—as a teenager at the camp for young student leaders in Arizona, on the trips to Cuba, as the head of the Puerto Rican Youth Association, and on several migrant worker reform committees. And since joining Rutgers, I had been heading the state's Hispanic Women's Task Force. Now I had just started a new job, my first real job in academia, and wanted to focus on that for a while.

I did agree to participate in Alfie's association, however, and attended regular meetings around the state, perhaps subconsciously more interested in seeing him again than in the association's business. I did find the networking opportunities very helpful; I met many Latino academics who were important later on in my career, including Carlos Hernandez, who became president of the New Jersey City University, and Hilda Delgado, the first tenured Hispanic faculty member at Rutgers, who became my role model of a Latina in higher education. But I soon tired of the meetings. I was willing to participate in an organization that discussed serious issues of social justice but not one where I felt everyone attended either to find new jobs or to socialize.

It was soon after I told Alfie that I would no longer attend association meetings that our relationship became personal and romantic. A few days later, a beautiful bouquet of white roses arrived at my office. There was no card, but a few minutes later my phone rang, and it was Alfie asking how I liked the roses.

"Why white?" I asked, and his answer surprised me a bit.

"Because you're so pure and the real thing, and I want to take you out to dinner," he said. When I didn't say anything, he added, "I'm not trying to … I just want to get to know you. I know you don't date anybody, and

I know you're reserved, but you are just somebody I want to get to know, and I think you might want to get to know me."

I agreed, and I remember our date as if it were yesterday. I had never had a boyfriend in high school or college, always more interested in furthering my education and pursuing academic and social justice goals than dating or socializing. So the memory of my first date with Alfie remains clear and present.

It was summertime, and Alfie took me to a small Italian bistro in a South Philly neighborhood that was becoming gentrified. I wore a white dress, conservatively cut as all my clothes were, because I knew that color would please Alfie. He looked so handsome dressed in a light linen suit with a crisp white shirt and bright-yellow tie. He was always stylishly dressed; he never wore jeans, even on casual occasions.

We had instant rapport that quickly turned to affection. We found we complemented each other perfectly both personally and professionally. In a lot of ways, Alfie and I were very different from one another, although those differences served only to strengthen our bond. Alfie was also of Puerto Rican descent, but his background was quite different from mine. His parents were working class and a lot better off than my parents. After leaving Puerto Rico, his parents had settled in the Bronx, New York, and that was where Alfie had been born. He was the third child of five and the only boy, so he had learned from a very young age to respect and revere women.

When Alfie was still a kid, his parents had bought a home in Jersey City. There he had attended Catholic schools from kindergarten all the way to Saint Peter's College, a Jesuit school where he had majored in political science before getting his master's in public administration.

He was very well educated and could even speak and write in Latin. He was also involved with Esperanto, which is both a universal language and an apolitical movement for linguistic equality. This commitment continued even after he joined Rutgers. I was not an Esperanto but was supportive of his efforts with the movement.

One of Alfie's great loves was writing, and he was excellent at it. It was one of the things I admired most about him. He and I collaborated on several memos for Rutgers. We would brainstorm ideas, and then he would put them into words. He was a tremendous help to me in turning my ideas for a community school like LEAP into writing. Far from being the nonintellectual I had first believed him to be, he was brilliant and forward thinking.

As progressive as he was in his profession and ideas, he was also in many ways a Latino traditionalist, especially when it came to family. In that respect he was similar to my father. So when I told him of my estrangement from my family, he understood my reason for it, yet at the same time it was contrary to everything he believed in.

By that time I had not spoken to my parents for nearly ten years, ever since I had decided to move in with Marta Benavides and continue with my education rather than migrate with my family to Florida. Although I dearly loved my family, including my mother, I felt restricted by them and, in many ways, by the traditional Latino culture to which they adhered. In short, I knew I would never achieve the things I had dreamed of as a child unless I struck out on my own. I may have left with Marta, but she was simply the catalyst. Long before she had come into the picture, I had known that my mother would never accept who I wanted to be. Since it was my mother's deepest desire that I would get married and raise a family, it seemed fitting that Alfie, my future husband, would reunite us.

While Alfie never judged me or the situation, I knew it was inevitable that he would try to mend the rift with my parents, especially after we got engaged. "You know," he said, "I come from a big family, and we're religious." I understood that. After all, it was how I had grown up as well—family and religion were everything. But when faced with my mother's lack of understanding or support, and her expectation that I would marry another migrant worker, work beside him at home and in the fields, and have children, I felt I had no choice but to leave.

"You know what?" he said. "I'm going to bring you back home."

I raised an eyebrow at him because he had never met my mother.

"Let me call," he said.

"It's going to be bad," I warned, but I knew that wasn't going to stop him.

So Alfie called my mother and explained who he was. I heard him on the phone with her and smiled because he was working her. He was using all his skills to win her over.

My mother was friendly enough to him, but she wanted to know why I didn't get on the phone. "Well, why is she not calling? Why is she not talking to me?"

"She will," Alfie said, knowing I was terrified to speak with her after all the time we had been separated. I knew that while my mother was already warming to charming, elegant Alfie, nothing had been resolved with me.

When we first walked into my parents' home, I was nervous and nearly numb with foreboding, understanding what this day meant for all of us. My mother greeted us warmly, and I could tell she was genuinely happy to see me. But I also sensed she was still very angry for all the years of silence between us. I dreaded being alone in a room with her, for she would surely make her feelings known, and I wasn't ready for that. After all, if it hadn't been for Alfie, I wouldn't have been there at all. Throughout our visit that day, she had eyes only for him, but I knew there would come a day when years of emotion would come to a boiling point.

My reunion with my father—who had always been more supportive of my pursuit of education and independent ways—was much easier. When we first arrived at the house, he was in the basement, afraid he'd get too emotional when he saw me. Finally he came out and embraced me wholeheartedly as we both cried tears of joy after having been separated for so many years.

In keeping with Puerto Rican tradition, my mother cooked a great meal for us, knowing I would love that after such a long absence but also to please Alfie, the one she really wanted to know more about. Sharing a good meal is an important way Puerto Ricans communicate with each other and convey their feelings and values. As she prepared the meal, and my father went out to get dessert, my mother asked Alfie to join her in the kitchen, which was strictly her domain, to talk.

I was not invited; I was left alone in the living room to contemplate the walls and tables full of pictures and icons of Jesus Christ and Catholic saints as well as pictures of my sisters and brother and the Kennedys, especially Jack and Robert, who my mother reveres to this day. My spirits were lifted by the many pictures on the walls of me when I was growing up. I had left years ago, but it made me feel good and reassured me that my mother still considered me a part of her family.

Dinner was pleasant since all my mother did was talk and talk about our family and our life: the entire story of how we came to the United States, about our farm back in Puerto Rico, and how she hated the wintertime in this country. She also asked Alfie many questions. She kept looking at me as if she wanted to hug and kiss me, and I thought, *Tell me how much you missed me.* But her pride would not let that happen, and I did not want for a second to engage in any conversation, fearing it would turn into a confrontation. So I made up an excuse that Alfie and I needed to leave early but said we would be back for a visit the following week.

On our next visit, my mother once again lavished all of her attention on Alfie. As she handed him a cool drink, my mother glanced at me and then back at Alfie and said, "I have to tell you her story." I guess she thought he'd be shocked to find out I had abandoned my family at such a young age.

"I already know everything about her," Alfie replied. "You know, she had nothing here to look forward to for a while." And he let her know how hard I had worked and studied all those years to get where I was.

By our third visit, I was used to my mother's cordial but cool treatment of me and her doting on Alfie. She would serve him food, stand over him, and ask a million questions, trying to find out more about him. But on that day, she took him to another room. She said she wanted to speak with him privately, but I could still hear what they were saying.

"Look me in the eyes," she demanded of Alfie. "I want you to know she's my daughter, and if you're going to marry her, you'd better be good to her. She is a very special type, you understand?"

That was when I knew that despite everything, my mother not only still loved me but she was very proud of me as well.

"I'm going to be the best *Yerno* [son-in-law] you ever had," Alfie said, smiling.

Then she kissed him, officially accepting him into the family. She had also gone a long way toward forgiving me, but we still faced one more hurdle to total reconciliation. It was the summer before Alfie and I got married, and we had gone to visit my mother. She was upset with my father because she felt he had gotten too involved in the church and had been neglecting her and the family.

And then she finally said it: "You of all people should understand me because you left us, and you haven't been here." As my mother proceeded to tell me loudly how angry she had been with me and still was, I began to sob. It was as if a dam had broken after all the years of holding in the loneliness without my family. Once the tears started, I couldn't stop.

Alfie had been outside, but he must have heard me because he rushed into the house. "I think that we have to go," he said firmly to my mother, but, ever respectful, he added, "Dona Lila."

When we left, and after I finally found my tongue, I told Alfie, "I'm never going back there again. She said horrible things to me."

Two days later my mother, who was even more stubborn and unforgiving than I imagined I was, did something I had never expected. She called Alfie and said, "I need to talk to her. I need to apologize. I was upset. She needs to understand that she put me through so much."

We had put each other through so much, I thought, but I did not want to open old wounds, just heal them and move on. I told my mother I would come home that weekend to see her, but I didn't want to talk about it anymore. She had said her piece, and there was no point in rehashing the past.

After that conversation things between us changed drastically. My mother had always equated obedience with respect, and when I left my family she took it as the ultimate insult. Now, however, she began to think of me not as the defiant young girl who discarded her family and the Latino culture but as a strong woman who had endured great sacrifice in order to pursue her dreams. I became someone she respected and often turned to for guidance. She would become one of my staunchest supporters and my support in the dark days ahead.

But those dark days were still many years in the future. For the time being, Alfie and I were incredibly happy. He valued me not only as a life partner but as an individual committed to making the world a better place. We connected on many levels, including intellectually. As a feminist and a passionate supporter of women's issues, he had found most women he knew too traditional for him. Alfie was a very spiritual person, and he told me he wanted a different kind of woman—one who would

Wedding, August 13, 1983

be a leader in her own right. At our wedding he first committed himself to being married to me, and then he also vowed to be my partner in social justice because he knew that was what I stood for.

Alfie fulfilled that promise every single day of our marriage. He was my champion and soul mate. When I was preparing to defend my dissertation, he would hold my hand and say, "Repeat it to me; repeat it to me." I can't count the number of times he rode with me on the train to New York—to CUNY, where I earned my PhD in sociology—calmly prepping me for classes and my defense.

In the years that followed, I began winning awards for my work. Alfie was never surprised that I was being recognized; rather, he expected it, and he was always the first to arrive at the presentations. As the plans for LEAP began to form, he became my most trusted adviser, advocate, and moral compass. He loved the idea of establishing scholarships for needy students so more of Camden's children could have opportunities for a better education.

PhD graduation, City University of New York, Graduate Center, New York, 1986

But Alfie didn't just support me professionally, and he had not only given me back my family. He had also brought me back to God and the church, both of which I had rebelled against ever since my teenage years. I wouldn't say education had become my religion, but it had become my life. My family had practiced a mix of Catholicism and Spiritualism, so I had these things ingrained in me. To this day my father is very religious and is a church leader. It is a way of life for him and for my mother.

As a child I had always believed in God, but as I witnessed life in the migrant camps I realized religion would not lead me or anyone else out of poverty. It began to seem that religion was more of an obligation than a useful tool to building a better future, and, as with so many of the other beliefs I had grown up with, I turned away from it. I wanted to learn about the larger world, about logic and science, and religion did not seem to have a place in any of that.

Meeting Alfie changed everything. He was very religious but in a very different way than the people I had been around as a child. He went to church not because he thought he should but because he felt a deep spiritual pull to do so, and he reminded me of my own beliefs that had been buried for decades.

Perhaps it was because our relationship was so perfect that I always had a fear I would lose him. I didn't worry about other women; rather I was afraid something bad was going to happen to him, that something would happen to take him away from me because our life together seemed too good to be true.

We had built our dream house in Voorhees, just a short fifteen-minute commute for me to Rutgers in Camden, with a large yard and a garden that reminded me of my childhood on the farm in Puerto Rico. Alfie drove over an hour each way to his office in New Brunswick, where he was the senior vice president of the university's fund-raising arm, the Rutgers Foundation. It was a long commute he willingly undertook because he said my work should always be our priority.

Alfredo Santiago; Mr. and Mrs. Joseph H. Rodriguez, federal judge District Court for the District of New Jersey; Gloria Bonilla-Santiago; Efrain Blassini, chair of Hispanic Affairs at Rutgers, at Rutgers Foundation Reception

It was November 26, 1996, the day before Thanksgiving, when my worst fears were realized. Alfie and I were going to spend the holiday with my parents, and we had taken a rare day off from work to prepare. We were going to get haircuts and then go to the bakery to pick up the sweets my father loved. Over the years Alfie and my parents had formed a very special bond, and he looked forward to our visits and holidays with them. We had spent the night before relaxing in front of the television; Alfie munched on popcorn, and I was so tired I fell asleep in his lap.

I was still sleeping the next morning when Alfie jumped up and began dressing. It was early, around six thirty. "Don't open your eyes," I heard him say. "I'm going to the office, but I'll be back soon."

"Hmm-mmm," I said, opening my eyes anyway. The first thing I noticed was he didn't have a tie on, which struck me as a bit odd because he always wore a tie to the office. He was also leaving his briefcase behind. The only thing he had in his hand was his mobile phone. This was strange too, but I figured it was because he didn't have any meetings that day. I went back to sleep, and he jumped into his new car and headed off to New Brunswick.

He'd had the car, a Mazda sedan, for only a few weeks. In the beginning of November, I had gone out of town for a National Council La Raza board meeting. I traveled frequently, and whenever I returned Alfie would be waiting with sushi or wine or a card or some flowers—something to welcome me back. This time, however, when he came to get me at the airport he announced he had a surprise.

"Don't be mad that I didn't consult you," he said, "but I know you'll be happy with it."

Then he led me out to the lot where he had parked his shiny new black Mazda. I was taken aback because Alfie usually never did anything important without discussing it with me. He certainly didn't make financial decisions or large purchases like this, I believed, without consulting me. It really bothered me, but he was so happy I didn't have the heart to spoil it for him.

"Well, that's really nice," I said, but I couldn't resist asking why he hadn't called me. He explained he hadn't expected to buy the car, but the dealer had given him such a great price he couldn't refuse. He apologized for not calling because he thought I would be as pleased as he was with the new car. With a sigh I got in to find that Alfie had the flowers and sushi waiting for me as always. I tried to be happy about it, but I felt uneasy and not just because he had bought the car without me. There was just something about that car I didn't like.

I was awakened that fateful morning by the ringing doorbell. I sat up and looked at the clock. It read seven thirty. Alfie had been gone about an hour. When I answered the door, it was the police telling me I had to come with them. Alfie had been in a car accident.

Alfie had deviated from his regular commute; he had taken a different route to his office. I initially speculated that because it was such a long drive from our home to New Brunswick, he perhaps thought this new way was faster and would allow him to get back sooner so we could start our day. I will never know for sure why he chose that route. I do know, however, that had he gone the usual way, he would not have been at that intersection at that horrible moment. Instead, he was traveling on a long, wide road, with a clear, unobstructed view. As I later learned, Alfie had had a green light and was driving through the intersection when a large truck, driven by a drunken driver in need of sleep, seemed to come out of nowhere. According to the police, the truck was going so fast Alfie had no time to react.

The truck struck the passenger side of the Mazda with such force that it slammed the car into a tree on the other side of the road. When the police arrived, they found the truck on top of Alfie's car. The vehicles were so mangled that they had to cut into the car to get him out. By that time a half hour had passed, and he had already slipped into a coma when they loaded him onto the helicopter.

When I got to the scene, frantic and still wearing my pajamas, all I could think about was getting to Alfie. But there, in the middle of everything, the police told me I had to fill out all this paperwork. I learned that the truck driver had not even been hurt. He had been well enough to be arrested and taken away in handcuffs. He would eventually be charged with vehicular homicide. His company, knowing I would file suit, declared bankruptcy to avoid paying for his tragic error, and I would have to hire a lawyer to seek redress. But on that morning, and for several weeks afterward, none of that mattered to me. The only thing on my mind was helping Alfie heal.

When I finally got to the hospital and spoke to the doctors, I could barely process what they were telling me. Alfie had suffered what's known as a *diffuse axonal brain injury*. All the damage was on the inside. To look at him, one would never know he had been hurt. He had no cuts or bruises. He appeared to be sleeping, but the part of his brain that allows a person to wake up and move around was horribly damaged. Even if he lived, they told me, he would require round-the-clock care as he learned to walk and talk all over again.

For the next six weeks, Alfie lingered in a coma. I did not leave his bedside. I didn't eat or sleep, and I certainly did not think about my work. My entire reason for living was in that hospital room, and my future all hinged upon whether my husband opened his eyes. As time went on with no improvement in his brain activity, it started to become clear that he would never recover.

The chances became slimmer with each passing day, and eventually the doctors approached me with what they called my "options." They explained that while Alfie's brain was essentially dead, his body, for the moment, was still very much alive and would be as long as we kept him hooked up to machines. Since we were such a young couple, they told me they could extract his sperm and impregnate me. After much contemplation about it, I told them no. As badly as I wanted to have Alfie's child, I could not imagine raising it without him. It just didn't feel like the right thing to do. Since my options did not include living the life Alfie and I had dreamed about, the only thing I could do was let him go, and on December 30 he died.

I buried my beloved Alfie on January 6, 1997, the Three Kings Day celebrated as Christmas in Puerto Rico. We had to have a two-day funeral because so many people wanted to pay their respects. Still in deep shock, I numbly watched the endless line of family and friends, Rutgers faculty and staff, legislators and politicians, all representing every community and walk of life—black, Hispanic, Jewish, academics, many involved in social justice work and many parents who were helping me get my dream of LEAP off the ground in Camden. It was incredible to see how many lives Alfie had touched, and my only regret today is that no one recorded all the wonderful things mourners said about him. He was dearly and truly loved.

Alfie's father had helped me arrange his funeral. We prepared a program with many pictures of Alfie and me during our marriage and backed it with salsa music, just like Alfie would have wanted it. When it came time to choose a burial site, I remembered Alfie had told me exactly the place where he wanted to be buried. It was a beautiful green place with flowers on Route 70 near Camden that, from a distance, looked more like a park than a cemetery. We had driven past it once, and Alfie told me that when he died it was the kind of place where he could rest in peace.

As time went on, I would learn much more about the amazing things Alfie had done for others. About a month after he died, I received an envelope with a letter and a check inside. It was from a colleague of Alfie's from the National Fundraising Research Society. They had often traveled around the country to attend conferences, and on one such trip, when they arrived at the airport, Alfie's colleague discovered her ticket had been canceled and her credit card was not working. She was stranded. Without a second thought, Alfie reached into his wallet, pulled out his credit card, and bought her a ticket. After hearing of Alfie's death, the woman wrote to repay the debt and tell me how devastated she was. He had rescued her and never said a word to me about it.

He also never told me he had been supporting his father's with his Jersey City home. I didn't find out until after the funeral, when his father told me. "You know, he wanted to do that. I thought he told you." But

Alfie never liked to broadcast the wonderful things he did for people—not even to me.

While I had sat at Alfie's bedside all those weeks, the world and my work were moving on without me. The bill to create charter schools, for which I had been fighting for three years, finally passed through the legislature and was about to be signed into law by Governor Whitman. In early January, only a few days after I had buried Alfie, I received that call from the governor's office saying Whitman was going to sign the charter bill into law in her office the following day, and she wanted me to be there. So, on my mother's insistence, I was.

A few weeks later, I attended the state of the state address in Trenton, and again I would not have gone had it not been at the urging of my mother, my staff, and the parents who had helped me advocate for the charter bill. That day, as Governor Whitman gave her address, she asked me to stand. All eyes turned to me as she said, "Here's a woman who's been a wonderful advocate for New Jersey's children, and even after tragically losing her husband in a car accident, she is still here for them today." The room erupted in applause as everyone rose to give me a standing ovation. Many of the people in the legislature knew me already, for I had been a thorn in their sides for the past three years. With many, however, I had formed friendships based on mutual respect and a common commitment, and now, in the face of my greatest loss and my greatest victory, they were there to show their support. As I stood there before them, tears streaming down my face, my sense of accomplishment was shadowed by unimaginable pain.

On my birthday, January 17, the phone at home rang. The man calling introduced himself as the owner of a local jewelry store. "I thought your husband would have come in already, but since it's your birthday, I figured I would call to see if he's ready to pick it up."

I didn't know what to say. I had no idea what he was talking about, but I braced myself for more devastating news. It had been hard enough when they took Alfie to the hospital and found his Christmas card to me in his jacket pocket.

"He bought it for Christmas, but I couldn't get it done in time, so he planned to surprise you on your birthday," the jeweler said. "Just come."

When I got to the jewelry store, I found that Alfie had bought me a diamond ring—a significant "upgrade" from the small one he had given me when we'd married. Somehow he had managed to put aside the money to buy this new one. I could not suppress the suspicion that this jewelry store, not his office, was where Alfie had been headed on that fateful morning. I will never know. But as I placed the ring on my finger, I felt as if he had died all over again.

After I lost Alfie, I was broken. I went to a dark place I had never been before. I was lost, and I lost confidence in myself. I had always been able to see my way through a difficult situation, whether it was a migrant camp or the challenges of getting legislation passed, but I couldn't see how I would ever get past Alfie's death. This was not something I could logically think my way out of. I knew I would have to look someplace else for answers.

This was a turning point for me, spiritually speaking. I had always had a belief that something bigger and unexplainable was driving me forward. For want of an adequate reason, I used to call it the "universe." Now I realized it was God to whom I could turn for strength to get me through this agony.

I also could not have done it without my mother. She became my rock, providing her particular brand of tough love to get me out of my depression. At that time everyone was doing everything they could to help me through my sadness, but it was useless. I refused to eat, and I didn't care about anything. All I wanted to do was sleep. It was like I was locked into some sort of purgatory from which there was no escape.

One day my mother walked into the room and stood over my bed. She knew the usual comforting words weren't going to work with me, so she said, "You know, you are going to be okay. I don't know where you get it from, but you are going to be okay because you have that strength of being cold and distant. Otherwise how could you spend ten years without me or your family? You're going to be okay."

"Mom, why are you doing this? Why are you saying these things?" I said, jumping up from the bed.

"Because I want you to get better," she insisted. "I want you to come back from wherever you are and be the strong woman I know you can be."

Well, that got my attention. I realized then what I had been doing to myself and that my mother was trying to snap me out of my depression.

"You are strong," she said. "You've got what it takes. I know you loved him, but you know how you can be so cold? Use that now!"

Cold was the wrong word, but I knew what she meant. She was telling me that the same tenacity and determination that had propelled me to success would help me recover from the loss of Alfie. And despite my pain, I knew somewhere inside me that she was right. I got up and took a shower—a ritual cleansing much like the showers my family used to take each year on January 6 to celebrate Three Kings Day—then went downstairs for the first time in days. My mother was waiting for me at the stove, stirring a big pot of something that smelled delicious.

"I think you're ready for some soup now," she said.

All my friends and family told me I should leave after Alfie died, sell the house and start over in a place that didn't have so many memories of him. My mother even suggested I move back in with her and my father. When I refused, my cousin, Sonia, offered to come and stay with me. Still I was unsure what to do.

"Don't do anything yet," my father advised. "Give it some time, and when you're ready you'll know what to do."

He was right. Having a place where I could be comfortable and safe and feel like myself had always been very meaningful to me. When I was a child, that place had been Cowtown or under my bed in the migrant barracks room I had shared with my brother and two sisters. When I grew up, it was the home I shared with Alfie, and while I didn't want to leave that home now that he was gone, I also knew I needed a fresh start. I had some money set aside, so I hired a decorating company and moved into the basement while they renovated the house from top to bottom.

They started with the bedroom. They took everything out, including his clothes and our bed, which I gave to my sister. They repainted the room, changing the colors from dark to very light. I went upstairs only when the head decorator needed my approval on something. We got rid of all the furniture in the house. I even redid the kitchen counters.

In the end Sonia did move in. She had stayed with Alfie and me before, when she first came to the States from Puerto Rico. We'd had an apartment in Cherry Hill, and she had been attending Rutgers as an art student. When they had seen her work, they had immediately accepted her even though she hardly knew English, and I got her a scholarship to pay for her education. In that way I was like her Marta. The following year she moved to the Rutgers Camden campus because I wanted her to experience dorm life.

Now that I was alone, I was grateful when Sonia returned. She settled into the spare room and stayed for ten years. She bought her own place a few years ago, but we remain very close. She is like the daughter I never had.

Marta also reappeared at that time. She, of course, offered her condolences for Alfie, who she had gotten to know well over the years. But, in typical Marta fashion, she also returned with an agenda: rescuing me from what she called my "bourgeoisie" life and bringing me back into the fold of social activism and revolutionary change. Specifically she was planning to relocate to the mountains of El Salvador and wanted me to join her in the "great work" she was now doing to save the environment.

I immediately said no. I couldn't go anywhere, I told her. I was still in mourning, plus my family, my work, and my life were in New Jersey. At the time I was still working out the details of Alfie's estate, including a battle I was having with my mother-in-law over one of his insurance policies. When I confided in Marta about this, she made it clear she had no patience for what she considered petty concerns. She insisted, "You need to give all this up. Just give it to your mother-in-law."

She thought with Alfie gone, she could control me again, but this time I was not having it.

"You tell me I'm a bourgeoisie," I exploded. "But who's wearing the Lacoste shirt? How do you pay for all this stuff anyway? You're always asking me to contribute to your causes. I am always giving a hundred dollars, two hundred dollars to you, but I don't know where it goes. Look at the clothes you're wearing." I knew she was angry, but I just kept going. "And who's this Katrina?" I said, finally questioning her about the codename she insisted on using whenever she called our house. "Alfie always wanted to know about that."

Marta was furious with me. "You know what? I'm not talking about this anymore. Obviously, Gloria, you made your life. You've made your choice."

I had cooked rice and beans for her, and she ate the meal in silence. Finally, as she was leaving, she said, "You know, this might be the last time we talk. But I want you to think about the things you said. And I'm sure you'll come to your senses, and we'll be in touch again."

That was the last I heard from her. While Marta had genuine sympathy for me over the loss of Alfie, she also believed his death should liberate me from what she considered a bourgeoisie existence. Instead, it had finally liberated me from her. I was free to continue my work in Camden to transform communities through education.

And continue I would, but with Alfie never far from my thoughts. To this day his memory serves as an inspiration and a guide to me. As a tribute to his life and his passion to provide quality education to all children—and in keeping with LEAP's mission to send all its students to college—I established the Alfred Santiago Endowment Fund in 1999.

The scholarships provide financial assistance to LEAP graduates who enroll full time at one of Rutgers University's three campuses. Each year it is awarded to LEAP graduates based on academic merit and financial need. There is a preference for Latino and African American students entering what are considered nontraditional areas of study, including business, science, engineering, and premed. Students who remain in good standing in school can renew their scholarships each year in four- and five-year programs.

Alfie and I had hoped to have children of our own one day. After his death, however, I began to think of all the LEAP students as our children, and I know there is no better way to honor his life, his passion, and his commitment than to help those children continue their educations and break the cycle of poverty.

Conclusion

The death of my husband Alfie forced me to make some life-changing decisions. While in a sense liberating me, Alfie's death left me with difficult questions and challenges with regard to my own professional career and the future of the community school I was planning to open in Camden.

His death came at a critical point in terms of education reform in New Jersey and my career in higher education. The charter school enabling legislation had just been signed into law by Governor Christine Todd Whitman, and she had just recognized me to a standing ovation in her 1997 State of the State Address for my education reform efforts and work on the legislation. I had also convinced the Rutgers University administration, after a long and contentious struggle, to allow me to open a school in Camden under the newly enacted charter law, giving me only months to actually get the school in operation.

My first emotional response to Alfie's death was to give up my life as I knew it and to reflect on my career interests and search deeply for what really mattered in my life. All my life, I was preparing myself to lead and excel in an institution of higher learning. And, all of a sudden, that was no longer my primary interest. My passion became clear. The dream of transforming a poor, minority inner city community through education became my priority. The longer I grieved, the more I came to realize that I had been liberated from family and domestic obligations to pursue my education vision and the development of LEAP. In a sense, I came to believe Alfie was telling me to pursue my dream, to focus on making my vision a reality, and to build LEAP. And that's the decision I chose to make. Our family, Alfie's and mine, would be LEAP, and all the children of LEAP would be ours.

Following is an annotated and referenced case study of the LEAP experience and experiment presented as a Comprehensive Model with Lessons from an Inner City Success and Implications for Growth & Replicating the LEAP Model.

CHAPTER 8

The Leap Case Study—
A Comprehensive Model

I. Introduction of the LEAP Case Study

L EAP is a student-centered learning educational enterprise that supports underserved students in one of the poorest cities in the United States—Camden, New Jersey. With over sixteen years of planning, implementation, refinement, and expansion, the LEAP Academy University Charter School has produced 100 percent high school graduation and college placement rates since its first graduating class in 2005. This has been accomplished without any screening or "creaming" of students, but instead working with all students—and their parents and community—through a comprehensive support system and a pedagogy driven by student-centered learning. The experience of the LEAP Academy and its attainment of positive outcomes for low-income African American and Latino students provide a number of practices that are at the core of how to best develop educational structures and contexts that lead to high performance and college readiness for underserved minority students.

The LEAP (Leadership, Education and Partnership) Academy University Charter School is a comprehensive public charter school serving fourteen hundred students in grades Pre-K through twelve. The school provides a college preparatory education with an emphasis on the content areas of science, technology, education, and mathematics (STEM), as well as specialized career academies in business, liberal studies, and social sciences at the high school level. Developed in partnership with Rutgers University, the school also responds to the imperative for institutions of higher education to be more accountable for and engaged with community development and school reform in ways that foster reciprocity and shared responsibility. The founding philosophy was one reflective of three interrelated components: student-centered and student-nurtured learning; parental empowerment; and community engagement.

LEAP Academy has developed a number of research-based approaches that have proven successful in increasing the preparation of minority students for postsecondary education and their attainment of positive educational outcomes, including: a virtual "pipeline" of learning from birth through college; college access for all; strong parental engagement that centers on inclusion, preparation and support; comprehensive, school-based health and wellness services; entrepreneurial governance focused on accountability and resources development; and support for educators anchored in collaboration and focused on strengthening teaching and learning. LEAP internal and external structures are all focused on preparing students to enter and succeed in college. College Access Centers provide direct services to students and teachers to ensure that every student keeps up with the academic rigor of a college preparatory curriculum, while also leveraging exposure and providing guidance, so that students can build the motivation, self-assurance, and familiarity with college culture. Basically, LEAP works on building hard and soft skills that will make the transition to college meaningful and successful.

LEAP Academy was one of the first thirteen charter schools that opened in New Jersey in 1997 and the first in the city of Camden. Rutgers University played a leading role in developing and sustaining the school from its planning phase and has remained the school's main partner. A cluster of Centers of Excellence to support the school's work channel Rutgers's resources and facilitate the opportunity for LEAP students to participate in dual high school/early college enrollment. The Rutgers Community Leadership Center, a research- and practice-based academic center, leads the partnership and sponsors a full service Early Learning Research Academy for infants, toddlers, and preschoolers.

From inception, LEAP Academy had a dual focus on closing the achievement gap and ensuring college preparation and completion between African American and Latino students who are poor and mostly first-generation college students. All stakeholders at LEAP have embraced the importance of placing college and career readiness at the center of its normative structure—one that promotes high expectations for every child, family engagement; high academic rigor, exposure, and cultivation; consistent attention and intervention from birth through college; and collective accountability for results.

Several elements have contributed to that success, including:

1. a focus on building an educational pipeline that sustains children—and involves parents—from infancy through college to ensure that academic and socioemotional needs of children are addressed as early as possible and that children exit this pipeline ready for college and career;

2. a rigorous academic program that emphasizes the STEM disciplines and is grounded on rich experiences that focus on building mastery, fostering a love of learning, and transitioning to college;

3. a systemic strategy for building capacity from within for a school that is grounded on performance-based evaluation and the ongoing provision of professional development options aimed at guiding teachers to work differently in improving student learning and academic growth;

4. extended time to allow for expanded opportunities to engage in a variety of learning modalities that lead to better outcomes for children and increased engagement with families and community;

5. a college-going culture throughout all grade levels that integrates families, teachers, and students and is sustained through college access centers at each school building and across grade levels;

6. a process for support and engagement of alumni as the educational pipeline extends to college and the school taps on the social capital that the alumni can generate to sustain the LEAP model and its impact;

7. establishment of strong and sustainable partnerships with local universities and organizations that provide resources to sustain and enrich the LEAP experience; and

8. development of structures to strengthen parents' capacity and self-sufficiency by keeping a two-generation focus that binds families and children together and transforms the school into a hub for services and support.

Over the last sixteen years, the integration of these strategies into a comprehensive model has proven to be successful in working with minority children and families. We believe that our experiences in building the LEAP model can be measured and become replicable and scaled up in other communities.

Since 1997 LEAP Academy has made important gains and established a strong educational foundation within the community of Camden.

Despite numerous social, economic, and cultural barriers, the LEAP school has not only provided hundreds of children with a comprehensive education and access to tertiary educational opportunities, but it has also empowered them and their families as individuals. This holistic, comprehensive approach has resulted in advances within individuals, families, and the community demonstrating evidence that new perspectives and strategies are needed, particularly in communities such as Camden.

Former LEAP Principal Dr. Juan Rosario, Assemblyman John A. Rocco (Republican, Camden), Former NJ state senator John "Jack" Ewing, and Gloria Bonilla-Santiago at ribbon-cutting ceremony of LEAP, September 15, 1997

The challenges are formidable, and the degree of commitment required is significant in relation to improving educational systems. But LEAP has proven that when community resources are limited and the environment is antagonistic to student learning, these obstacles can be overcome by implementing practices that are student-centered, engage families, have a collective sense of accountability, focus on development, and build social capital.

The best indicator of academic success for LEAP Academy students is its graduation and college placement rate. *LEAP graduates and places in college 100 percent of its students.* This places the LEAP Academy within the top performing schools in the state. Since LEAP is a K-12 system, the New Jersey Department of Education (DOE), beginning in the third grade, assesses students. Over the last few years, the school has seen a steady growth pattern in performance in the New Jersey Assessment of Skills and Knowledge (NJASK) and the High School Proficiency Assessment (HSPA), with the school meeting growth targets for every grade span. Another important observation shows that overall the longer a student stays enrolled at LEAP, the better the student performs. Another important factor is the college retention and graduation rates of LEAP alumni. Data provided by the DOE reports that 80 percent of LEAP graduates remain in college sixteen months after high school graduation. The data is from the National Student Clearinghouse, which reports that it collects student-level enrollment data from 95 percent of institutions of higher education nationwide. LEAP works closely with its alumni base and also collects information on a regular basis.

The LEAP Academy case study defines college access programs to be precollege interventions that explicitly identify increasing college readiness and/or college enrollment as a primary goal of the school. It further examines seven additional best practices under four factors that have supported our successful college efforts: (1) student, (2) teacher development, (3) organizational, and (4) stakeholder alliances that have been essential for the model effectiveness.

Figure I. LEAP theory of Action

ASSUMPTIONS	ELEMENT OF CHANGE	OUTCOMES

1. Goals for student achievement are realistic and achievable

2. Content standard and grade level expectations for college and career readiness are well defined

Instructional Leadership Teams define student learning objectives which are aligned to a challenging curriculum and promote student growth. Teachers use curriculum materials that allow instruction aligned with grade level content for all students including Student Learning objectives and growth.

Increased access to quality Professional Development to enhance school leadership, improve teaching and Increase student learning.

Educators improve their instruction to become highly effective

Barriers to student success are eliminated

3. High quality assessment systems are designed to align to academic expectations and measure student growth.

4. Goals for all School Leaders, including Directors and Principals, are aligned to student achievement and growth.

Support from the Board of Trustees (or District) provides Teachers, School Principals, and Directors appropriate resources to improve their practice.

Research based interventions are incorporated into each school to address specific needs

All students achieve higher academic outcomes.

All students graduate from high school ready for college and careers

II. Background and History of Camden

By the end of the twentieth century, Camden, New Jersey, was a ghost of its former self. In the 1930s, Camden represented 47 percent of the county's population and 55 percent of its tax base. But by 1990, these figures had fallen to 17 percent and 5 percent, respectively.[1] A variety of social, economic, political, and environmental changes occurred within the second half of the century, culminating in a vicious cycle leading to Camden's decline. As demographic changes occurred and socioeconomic conditions failed, Camden's educational system deteriorated progressively as well. To gain a better appreciation of how these factors interacted to result in the city's unfortunate condition, some understanding of Camden's background and history is important.

Camden's External Climate

Many contributing factors resulted in the decline of Camden's educational system over several decades. However, the most significant was the growth of the suburban sprawl after World War II, which occurred throughout the United States. Perhaps more than any other phenomenon, this accounted for Camden's precipitous decline. Between 1945 and 1965, the Federal Housing Administration created attractive financing packages for race-restricted families in suburban areas to purchase homes. This prompted a migration of many middle class families away from urban regions such as Camden. The development of more comprehensive highway systems, which facilitated suburban travel to and from cities further, facilitated this social migration.[2] Of course, as the middle class vacated urban centers such as Camden, small businesses found they had few customers remaining. As a result, small businesses soon followed, and seemingly overnight, many urban regions felt the void left by what

---

[1] Casey, Path Forward.

[2] Ibid.

was referred to as the "white flight."[3]. Over a few decades, a dramatic change in urban demographics occurred, and cities such as Camden were particularly affected. By 1990, approximately 86 percent of Camden's residents were racial minorities, and the tax base for the city had dropped elevenfold from prewar periods.[4]

In addition to the suburban migration, Camden suffered other major commercial setbacks. RCA, which employed around eighteen thousand workers at one time, was sold in the 1960s and eventually downsized in dramatic fashion. In 1967, the New York Ship Building Company closed, which employed more than thirty-five thousand local residents. And in 1980, substantial downsizing of the Campbell Soup manufacturing plant resulted in additional loss of jobs.[5] In 2000, Camden's unemployment rate was nearly three times the national average at 15.9 percent.[6] Between the loss of middle class citizens, small businesses, and major manufacturing companies, Camden experienced a sudden and significant shift, resulting in tremendous environmental pressures on the city's stability and ability to successfully function.

A snapshot of Camden's housing situation in the late 1990s provides a sobering perspective of the city. In 1999, 86 percent of homes were valued at $50,000 or less while no homes were valued in excess of $100,000. Camden's entire property wealth was estimated at only $250 million, and a marked increase in abandoned housing units occurred. More than 78 percent of these abandoned structures were located within one block of known illicit drug markets.[7] In addition, more than a third of Camden's municipal lands were vacant manufacturing sites, of which half were contaminated and categorized as brownfields. Estimates to clean up such environmentally hazardous sites averaged between $200,000 and

---

[3] Ibid.

[4] Ibid.

[5] Ibid.

[6] Ibid.

[7] Ibid.

$300,000 per acre.[8] These developments notably resulted in negative effects on Camden's tax base. With fewer residents and declining property values, tax rates were forced to increase. This resulted in Camden's property taxes exceeding national averages by far. Yet despite higher rates, city staff and services were progressively cut in an attempt to stay within municipal budgets.

The loss of employers and the increasing cost of living in Camden soon led to social and economic declines subsequently. In 2000, over a third of Camden residents lived in poverty, and 27 percent depended upon public assistance. This latter figure compares to 14 percent in nearby Philadelphia. Likewise, more than two-thirds of households were single parent households with more than half the population being under the age of eighteen years.[9] Regarding public health, only one in six had some form of health insurance, and only a third of infants received routine prenatal care.[10] Crime, which had been a long-term problem for the city, also worsened with over five thousand youth arrests annually in 2000. Homicide continued to be the number one cause of death for ages fifteen to twenty-four years. Illicit drug trade was estimated to employ over two thousand Camden residents during this time, with many workers being children. Higher wages within this illegal industry, which more than doubled traditional employment, was a powerful incentive for many.[11]

Finally, the political environment over the past decades was relatively unfavorable to Camden. Local politics played a significant role in the city's failure to overcome its challenges as county interests often overpowered municipal policies. For example, despite a tax collection rate of only 78 percent for Camden, the county by law received its full portion from the collections. This effectively reduced Camden's collection rate to

---

[8] Ibid.

[9] Ibid.

[10] Ibid.

[11] Ibid.

only 65 percent.[12] State politics were also disadvantageous. New Jersey encouraged municipalities to operate independently without any incentive for collaboration. For many self-sufficient cities, this was effective; but for cities such as Camden needing support, further isolation occurred. Likewise many state policies in the 1980s and 1990s were selectively more favorable to suburban regions (for example, policies concerning low-income housing) or financially unfair to debt-stricken municipalities.[13] These policies perpetuated Camden's rising debt and interest payments while further depleting the city's resources and ability to rebuild. As a result of these interconnected events during the latter half of the last century, Camden was crushed under a tsunami of negative factors, culminating in its current state of deterioration.

Camden's Educational System

The effect of Camden's external environment on its public educational school system has been profound, to say the least. Being a publicly sponsored institution, the economic impacts affecting the city of Camden naturally resulted in marked educational declines. Similarly, social and community effects resulting from a variety of pressures reduced the resources available to assist with educational needs and participation. Even the preponderance of youth demographically created a burden of volume not easily managed without additional resources and support. Camden's educational environment at the end of the twentieth century was not surprisingly poor given the challenges the city faced.

Economic figures regarding student education was a telling sign in relation to the city's educational collapse. Among Camden's youth population, 85 percent qualified for free lunch programs. Unfortunately schools were unable to meet such demands in Camden, and many students were reported to leave midday to find lunch elsewhere, often

---

[12] Ibid.

[13] Ibid.

failing to return to school.[14] In 2000, the average amount of money spent on additional education support for classrooms in Camden was $82 per student, with the average extracurricular expenditures being $74 per student. Comparable figures for schools in the county were $127 and $238 per student, respectively.[15] In many instances, classrooms lacked basic infrastructure such as desks, books, and computers to facilitate learning of educational standards demanded by the state and by federal agencies. Likewise, laboratories often had little to no laboratory equipment necessary to perform laboratory experiments.[16] The significant economic declines of the city thus translated into marked shortcomings within Camden's educational environment.

Economics naturally spilled over into performance deficits within these educational settings. As of 2000, only half of all Camden residents age twenty-five and older had a high school education, and only 7 percent had a college degree or higher. Unfortunately these rates had changed very little between 1980 and 2000. As one might expect from these statistics, Camden's dropout rate was extremely high being reported at 50 percent during the 1990s.[17] Underlying this tendency to drop out of school was a sentiment among children and families that their capabilities were naturally substandard. Repeated failures, lack of encouragement and support, and a lack of future opportunities strengthened these negative sentiments and fostered a culture condoning educational discontinuance.[18] The combination of these growing social and cultural effects in addition to poor infrastructure and school supplies posed serious challenges for attempts to improve education.

Among Camden students in 2000, only 49 percent were able to pass

---

[14] Jonathan Kozol, Savage inequalities: Children in America's Schools (Random House Digital, 2012).

[15] Casey, 2001.

[16] Kozol, 2012.

[17] Casey, 2001.

[18] Kozol, 2012.

state reading standards during annual assessments. This compared to 85 percent of students throughout New Jersey during the same time period. In addition, the literacy rate among Camden residents was reported at 51 percent compared to 79 percent in the state.[19] This demonstrates an ongoing problem, which was perpetuated generationally throughout the community. Not only did parents lack positive experiences of education and life opportunities in the city to help guide their children, but an environment of mistrust between residents, law enforcement, and public officials existed, which hindered participation of the community in the educational setting. Approximately half of residents stated they would not report crimes to law enforcement due to fear and mistrust, and very few Camden residents served in municipal governance.[20] Given these baseline findings, significant barriers existed in achieving community and parental involvement in the development of educational system solutions.

As one may imagine, a city handcuffed financially by falling tax revenues and heavy debt had little to offer educators in terms of financial incentives. A typical school in Camden in the 1990s often utilized teachers who were yet to be certified and who had not developed proficiency. On a regular basis, once these teachers gained proficiency and certification, they soon left Camden for the suburbs being attracted to such areas by higher incomes.[21] Others frequently chose to relocate to safer environments after having their homes vandalized. For some, the realization that the difference they were making in terms of children's lives was minimal at best failed to support a desire to stay. Consistently good teachers relocated away from Camden, creating a continual turnover of educators and an educational culture with little interest and commitment in improving.[22]

Camden in the latter half of the twentieth century went from boom to bust. A combination of circumstances resulted in a mass exodus of

---

[19] Casey, 2001.

[20] Ibid.

[21] Kozol, 2012.

[22] Ibid.

middle-class citizens and businesses from Camden, once a thriving urban center of commerce and manufacturing, almost overnight. The subsequent economic, social, and political events perpetuated this cycle of despair, and by the late 1990s, Camden represented one of the worst environments to live within in the state, if not the nation. The effect this had on the educational system and students of Camden was tremendous as reflected in the statistics shared. Options were limited, funding was scarce, and levels of discouragement were high. The city of Camden in 1997 needed a revolutionary approach to its educational problem, and exploring the literature hoped to find such an approach. In the subsequent section, an overview of the literature evident at the time will be described.

The LEAP Academy story originates as a result of a major debate about how to best address inequality in education and improve low-performing schools in Camden City. It is within this context that LEAP emerges as an option to curve low attainment and substandard education for children and their parents in Camden.

The city has a long history of challenges on all fronts—absence of a local economy that produces jobs and a tax base to sustain city government; a dysfunctional city government that is overly dependent on state aid to provide the most basic services to its residents; a staggering rate of violence mostly related to drug trafficking and gang activity; a chronic underperforming school system with students failing in almost every educational indicator and dropping out of school; a physical environment characterized by decaying housing, abandoned neighborhoods, and a lack of safe public spaces; and a history of political corruption and dysfunction. (Gillette, 2009; Nowak, 2009; Casey Foundation, 2001) Today, Camden is known for its designation as America's second-poorest city, with 45 percent of its families living below the poverty line and with children carrying the biggest burdens. Most Camden families (72 percent) are headed by a single parent and often this parent is young, uneducated, and has been raised in poverty.

Single-headed households are also more likely to be in government assistance and to not own a home, and they tend to be very mobile. What is alarming is that these families are the product of multigenerational poverty that traps them in poverty cycles. The fact that Camden is so young, with 35 percent of its population under nineteen years, creates an opportunity and a challenge as to how best to educate the next generation. Camden has historically failed in this battle and today has some of the worst public schools in the state of New Jersey. As of 2010, only 6.8 percent of the city population graduated from college and, in contrast, 73.3 percent remain in the category of not having any college preparation. This results in young people that are unprepared for the demands of the changing labor market, therefore reducing their capacity for being able to accomplish critical steps to a better quality of life that can take them out of poverty—meaningful employment, capacity to own a home, capacity to have credit, and a lower dependency on government assistance. In 2011–12, high school graduation rates plummeted by 7 percentage points to 49.3 percent, down from 56.9 percent the year before. The graduation rate statewide is 86 percent, according to the New Jersey Department of Education. Three of Camden's schools are the lowest performing in the state, and 90 percent are in the bottom 5 percent. Less than 20 percent of fourth-graders are proficient in language arts literacy, and just 28 percent of eleventh-graders are proficient in math. In 2013, the 13,700-student Camden school district became the fourth school system to come under New Jersey state control.

III. Theoretical Foundation and Literature Review

In developing an understanding of knowledge present at the time the LEAP case study was being formulated, a collection of research literature relevant to urban education and educational perspectives from the 1990s is provided. Many of the core concepts considered in the development of the LEAP model were innovative considerations, which were subsequently embraced and expanded. Also notable was the heightened public concern over the quality and future of education nationally, prompting a variety of debates about future educational directions. While Camden's educational environment was perhaps among the worst settings in the country, dissatisfaction with educational performance in many states and cities was widespread during this time. As a result, a number of theoretical perspectives were available to help with the formulation of a new strategy for educational improvement.

Relevant Literature in Planning Educational Reform Strategies

During the 1990s, increasing concern developed over the quality of American education. In 1996, a public opinion poll identified education as a major policy concern among American citizens, and as a result education became a major political campaign focus.[23] Since publication of "A Nation at Risk" in 1983, which highlighted educational shortcomings among US students in relation to other nations, several subsequent publications reporting class and racial biases in the provisions for equality education were released. Progressive concerns over school performance developed as a result throughout the country.[24] In addition, pressures from the business community were being placed on government representatives for fears related to an unskilled workforce relative to the future needs of the country. Technological advances had occurred rapidly, and many skills were becoming obsolete while others were increasingly in demand.[25] These pressures stimulated a significant amount of interest in alternative options for traditional public education.

In 1991, President Bush promoted development of break-the-mold schools while President Clinton subsequently endorsed charter schools during his tenure. In 1997, Congress allocated more than $51 million for

---

[23] Michael Mintrom and Sandra Vergari, "Education reform and accountability issues in an intergovernmental context," Publius: The Journal of Federalism 27, no. 2 (1997): 143–66.

[24] James H. Lytle, "Reforming urban education: A review of recent reports and legislation," The Urban Review 22, no. 3 (1990): 199–220.

[25] Mintrom and Vergari, 1997.

charter school development. The US Department of Education likewise announced plans to create a target number of three thousand charter schools within the next five years.[26] Though the American School Act in 1994 provided mechanisms by which federal grants could be allocated for charter school development and support, these subsequent political efforts reflected a progressive perspective in favor of educational change. Underlying this change was a belief that decentralization and market competition were needed to advance innovation and school-based performance.[27]

Among the concepts prevalent at the time was school-based management, which embraced decentralization and encouraged greater self-management among individual schools. Industries, which typically benefited from such an approach, included environments where the work was considered complex, tasks were best accomplished in teams, daily uncertainty existed, and environments rapidly changed.[28] Educational environments were thus well suited for these school-based management considerations. Advocates of greater decentralization believed educational performance would flourish as schools gained autonomy away from centralized bureaucracy. Without the burden of district or state regulations, schools could develop teaching methods, curriculums, and learning practices that were more innovative while also developing strategies to use resources more efficiently.[29]

---

[26] Priscilla Wohlstetter and Noelle C. Griffin, Creating and Sustaining Learning Communities: Early Lessons from Charter Schools (US Department of Education, Office of Educational Research and Improvement, Educational Resources Information Center, 1997).

[27] Priscilla Wohlstetter, Richard Wenning, and Kerri L. Briggs, "Charter schools in the United States: The question of autonomy," Educational Policy 9, no. 4 (1995): 331–58.

[28] Priscilla Wohlstetter and Susan Albers Mohrman, School-based Management: Strategies for Success (ERIC Clearinghouse, 1993).

[29] Wohlstetter, Wennings, and Briggs, 1995.

Many proponents of decentralizing and self-governance also supported an increase in market competition among schools. Adopted after private school models and other capitalistic industries, market competition among schools for consumers (in this case students and parents) would drive performance.[30] From these viewpoints arose three trends in education during the 1990s. In addition to charter schools, which fostered decentralization, increased autonomy, and competition with public schools, voucher programs and open enrollment policies were also utilized. Open enrollment programs offered the least amount of change by simply enabling increased choice among educational consumers to go to schools outside their geographic areas. Voucher programs similarly allowed consumers to leave public schools that they disliked to attend private schools through the use of a payment voucher.[31] Each of these offered increased competition, which appealed to market-style education supporters.

In the educational debate, not everyone supported decentralization and a market-based approach. State and federal governments to an extent opposed these trends because of an increasing interest in learning outcomes. Over a series of several decades, state and federal funding of public school education increased. In 1993, local governments, which were traditionally responsibly for the bulk of funding, provided only 47.4 percent of revenues on average to schools. States provided 45.6 percent on average while the federal government provided 6.9 percent.[32] With increased funding comes increased accountability from recipients, and this need conflicted with progressive ideas concerning decentralization of schools. Both state and federal agencies wished to maintain some component of hierarchical control while insisting upon school performance accountability. Undoubtedly this led to federal and state legislations adopting state and national educational standards.[33]

---

[30] Wohlstetter and Griffin, 1997.

[31] Mintrom and Vergari, 1997.

[32] Ibid.

[33] Ibid.

With these social and political forces in place, open enrollment programs failed to provide the degree of change needed to truly encourage market-based competition among schools. Likewise, voucher programs failed as some were utilized to only facilitate access of low-income families to private schools, and court rulings prevented the use of such vouchers in religious-based schools.[34] However, charter schools flourished in some areas. The reason for inconsistencies of success seemed to result from variances in autonomy allotted charter schools within specific states. By 1997, twenty-six states had passed legislation permitting charter schools as part of their public school system. However the degree of autonomy and self-governance allowed for each school differed dramatically from state to state.[35] Presumably, the inability to be fully autonomous in all areas of organizational operations caused variations in learning outcomes and school performance measures.

The literature supported several factors that fostered success among charter schools. Studies that surveyed several charter schools in different states found four critical building blocks that helped determine improved educational performance. These included the adherence to a school mission, development of a school instructional program, a system of accountability, and strong school leadership. Among highly performing charter schools, these foundations were consistently in place.[36] In addition to these cornerstones, other environmental conditions enabled greater success when present. These conditions included a high degree of school autonomy and self-governance, the presence of supportive networks and organizations helping the school achieve its mission, and the involvement of supportive parents. All of these factors allowed the development of high-quality learning cultures, which resulted in increased student performance.[37] To a great extent, many of these aspects were incorporated into the LEAP model and strategy.

---

[34] Ibid.

[35] Wohlstetter, Wenning, and Briggs, 1995.

[36] Wohlstetter and Griffin, 1997.

[37] Ibid.

Educational resources were also addressed in the literature in relation to urban education and student learning. Interestingly, some researchers found that resources alone failed to predict school or student performance. However, the authors acknowledged that at some level resources are necessary to allow students the needed tools to perform.[38] The lack of correlation between resources and student learning outcomes was felt to be more of a reflection of policy decision making and its inherent complexities. In other words, policies which failed to utilize resources effectively and efficiently would result in poor outcomes regardless of resource allocation.[39] Other researchers, however, identified four key resources that were not only necessary but also required decentralization for school success. These resources included power, knowledge, information, and rewards.[40] Distribution of these resources throughout the school system among all stakeholders fostered increased collaboration and teamwork. Likewise, decentralizing the control of these factors encouraged greater engagement and commitment from all participants in the educational process.[41]

Among these four key resources was a system of rewards. Merit reward systems can be of particular interest in recruiting and retaining educators. At the same time, reward systems serve as a means of accountability and performance enhancement. Despite this, teacher reward systems routinely face barriers to implementation, according to the literature. The presence of multiple stakeholders in the processes, value differences between educators and the community, and a resistance to change among teachers can all serve to hinder the adoption of pay-for-performance systems.[42]

---

[38] Eric A. Hanushek, "Assessing the effects of school resources on student performance: An update," Educational evaluation and policy analysis 19, no. 2 (1997): 141–64.

[39] Ibid.

[40] Wohlstetter and Mohrman, 1993.

[41] Ibid.

[42] Ibid.

Because of this, and a shortage of educators in urban environments in particular, schools had resisted its implementation. Among urban school districts in thirty-nine major cities in the United States in 1995, 76.9 percent of urban schools allowed noncertified teachers to teach classrooms, while many facilitated tracks allowing teacher aides to teach while pursuing licensure.[43] Implementing pay-for-performance programs would likely be met with resistance and would further hinder teacher recruitment to these areas of serious need.

Despite these concerns, the literature supported pay-for-performance systems and accountability programs to enhance school performance and student learning outcomes.[44] Group rewards for educators based on positive performance promoted collaboration and teamwork. Individual rewards for performance encouraged high utilization of resources available to teachers. And both of these served to align school system goals with individual teacher goals while increasing engagement and leadership abilities.[45] Despite potential resistance, the benefits of merit reward systems appeared to outweigh concerns over reduced recruitment opportunities. A pay-for-performance system, in addition to providing a focus on self-governance and decentralization, also addressed concerns about accountability measures.[46] Such a system for teacher compensation thus appeared favorable in comparison to tenured-based pay or uniform salary allotments.

The literature review supported the majority of the issues considered in the development of the educational strategies associated with the LEAP case study. Concepts of school mission, decentralization, self-governance, autonomy, accountability, leadership, collaborative partnerships, pay-for-performance systems, and external support networks form a core part

---

[43] Segun C. Eubanks, "The Urban Teacher Challenge: A Report on Teacher Recruitment and Demand in Selected Great City Schools" (1996).

[44] Wohlstetter and Griffin, 1997.

[45] Wohlstetter and Mohrman, 1993.

[46] Ibid.

of many of the planned actions and decisions made in moving forward with the project. These concepts were well supported in the research at the time of inception, and research continues to guide effective change as the project matures and progresses. However, the literature lacked a holistic model incorporating comprehensive services to support the children and their families. A hypothesis was developed that assumed the development of such services as well as a focus on student instruction would significantly encourage student graduation and college enrollment. In the subsequent section, a detailed account of these strategies related to these specific areas would be described to highlight how theory was put into practice, resulting in the success of the LEAP case study.

IV. Strategy Formulation and Methodology

With an appreciation and understanding of the widespread deficiencies within Camden concerning social, economic, and educational systems, and with a working knowledge of the educational literature at the time, efforts were made to devise effective strategies and methodologies to remedy the needs of the Camden community. Numerous resources were accessed in the pursuit of this initiative. The process by which organization, planning, and implementation proceeded was conducted in a fluent but stepwise fashion. This enabled a steady progress toward defined goals of enhanced educational opportunities and outcomes as well as community empowerment.

As a foundational consideration, a significant and notable legislative development occurred prior to the creation of the LEAP Initiative. This event served as both a catalyst and a facilitator of subsequent efforts of reform. In 1985, a legal case was filed in New Jersey challenging the constitutionality of the state's Public School Education Act of 1975. The case stated that the state's methods of educational funding resulted in marked disparities, violating the state's requirement of a thorough and efficient education opportunity for all state residents. Though the case was repeatedly reviewed in relation to legislative efforts to remedy the problem, *Abbott v. Burke* highlighted the significant deficiencies in educational opportunity in many areas in the state, which included Camden.[47] These areas became known as Abbott districts, which eventually totaled thirty-one school regions throughout the state. Not only did the case prompt state legislative actions, but it also brought significant social and political attention to the educational problems within the state. As a result, *Abbott v. Burke* provided fertile ground upon which change could be considered, and it facilitated the efforts made as part of the LEAP Initiative.[48]

In 1993, New Jersey Governor Jim Florio created the Management Audit Review Commission, a seven-member body challenged with identifying areas of inefficiencies and waste in public operations and systems. In response to the Abbott rulings, the commission was also instructed to study issues and solutions relevant to the designated Abbott districts.[49] With Camden being one of these districts, the opportunity to access important public and government resources for the purpose of improving Camden's situation was provided. Thus the environment and climate in 1993 offered an ideal setting for the development of strategies and methods targeting educational and community reform in Camden.

While LEAP Academy first opened its doors in September of 1997, strategy formulation began much earlier, in 1993. During this four-year period, key components of LEAP's mission, objectives, and principles were defined. Likewise, key areas of stakeholder development, resource acquisition, operational considerations, and staff and student policies were considered and formalized. This section provides detailed descriptions of

---

[47] Education Law Center, "The history of Abbott v. Burke," 2013. Retrieved from http://www.edlawcenter.org/cases/abbott-v-burke/abbott-history.html.

[48] Ibid.

[49] Steven A. Clark, "Performance auditing: a public-private partnership," *Public Productivity & Management Review* (1993): 431–36.

the methods by which these areas were contemplated and determined. A thorough understanding of these efforts and reasons behind them provide a better foundation for interpreting subsequent results and for considering future implementation of similar models.

Mission Management

The ability to successfully implement positive change demands a commitment to a well-defined mission and set of objectives. The effective management of a project's mission thus represents an important foundational activity upon which other achievements depend. Similarly, a vision for a project's direction and ultimate outcome drives participation, fosters collaboration and guides action while helping establish goals.[50]. The vision of the LEAP Initiative had its origins in 1993 as a result of key individuals sharing ideas and seeking to pursue a needed change for the Camden community. The outcomes of these events established not only a more refined guide for change but also eventually led to a collective focus that enhanced planning, strategy formation, and implementation.

The initial vision for LEAP originated in a meeting in 1993 between Governor Jim Florio, Dr. Gloria Bonilla-Santiago, and Dr. Walter Gordon. Dr. Gordon was the Rutgers-Camden University provost at the time. As a traditional academic, his vision was to engage local community stakeholders in educational processes while having local educational institutions contribute to host city development and enhancement. Dr. Bonilla-Santiago was vice chair of the Governor's Management Audit Review Commission and assistant professor of social work at Rutgers-Camden University. She expressed a vision of a partnership project between public education, higher education, and the community as part of a commitment to improving Camden's situation.

---

[50] Charles W. L. Hill and Gareth R. Jones, Strategic Management: An Integrated Approach (Boston: Houghton-Mifflin, 2007.

From this meeting came the planning dollars for the LEAP Initiative, and Governor Florio committed $1.5 million for the project's initial planning development.

Additional influences upon the creation of the LEAP Initiative are also attributed to the working group that was established to develop a strategic plan. Partnerships among parents, community leaders, higher education institutions, private foundations, business leaders, and public agencies are all recognized as potential resources within this framework that fosters academic success.[51] This perspective combined with awareness that New Jersey's urban school dilemmas reflected a systemic problem rather than simply a financial one. It encouraged a project that embraced innovation and accountability.

Initial guidance for strategy formulation for the LEAP project involved the use of an external facilitator and consultant. Dr. Joseph Fernandez, president and CEO of School Improvement Services Inc., previously held the positions of chancellor of the New York City and Miami-Dade public school systems prior to 1993. He helped coordinate and direct the initial efforts in ethnographic data collection to define comprehensive needs of the Camden educational system and community. These efforts include demographic study and review, literature review, direct observations, and focus groups, as well as in-depth stakeholder interviews. In addition, with Dr. Fernandez's direction, the LEAP working group was organized for the purpose of plan development.

The LEAP working group consisted of a wide variety of stakeholders within the Camden community in conjunction with a focus on collaboration and partnership. Members included parents, community leaders, Rutgers-Camden University staff and faculty, Camden teachers, Camden Board of Education administrators, representatives of Health and Human Services, local business leaders, and philanthropists and

---

[51] James Jennings, Evaluation Report for the Project LEAP Academy Charter School, Rutgers-Camden Centre for Strategic Urban Community Leadership, Camden, NJ, 1997.

clergy members. The group met routinely over a two-year period between 1993 and 1995 in the creation of a strategic plan for the LEAP project. Stakeholders considered for the working group involved a multilevel analysis. On the initial level, potential stakeholders were identified as supporting, opposing, or neutral in their perspective on the LEAP project. In the second tier, these individuals were then evaluated based on access to resources, involvement in resource networks, and the advantages and disadvantages they might bring to the group. Subsequent to this review, members were targeted for enrollment, with the resultant number of participants being between ninety and one hundred in total.[52]

The working group, in conjunction with Dr. Fernandez as a consultant, devised a LEAP strategic plan. The resultant document "Camden Counts" was completed in 1995, and reflected a variety of steps to be performed as a means to create a LEAP Academy charter school that met the needs of students, parents, and the community. These steps included research and program design, commitment building, planning, resource development, operational design, and ongoing documentation and evaluation.[53] Among these, mission management primarily involved research, program design, and commitment building among stakeholders. These activities determined community needs, evidence-based success strategies, a unified vision, and a committed group of stakeholders in an effort to facilitate effective and efficient efforts.

Among the earliest tasks of the LEAP working group was the establishment of a guidance system by which all activities could be held accountable and measured. This system was based upon three important components, which included a mission statement, uniformly held beliefs by the group, and a set of guiding principles. Once these were established, all future actions and decisions were considered with this guidance

---

[52] Jennings, 1997.

[53] Center for Strategic Urban Community Leadership (CSUCL), Camden Counts: A strategic plan for the Project LEAP Academy (Camden, NJ: CSUCL, 1995).

system in place.[54] As a result, the group quickly developed a focused and collaborative culture, which allowed strategic planning development to align well with the project's vision and to proceed efficiently in accomplishing the group's goals.

The approved mission statement for the LEAP working group was "to enhance opportunities for the children and families of Camden through the collaborative design, implementation, and integration of education, health, and human service programs and through community development."[55] This mission statement was congruent and supported by the underlying beliefs identified as important by the group. Foundational assumptions included a belief that all children can learn, can excel in an environment of challenging academics with high expectations, and can benefit from adult role models in the process. In addition, beliefs also supported a proactive, integrated approach to education that met academic needs as well as the needs of the family and community.[56]

With this in mind, collaboration and cooperation were key ingredients to success, and all stakeholders, including public and private institutions, had a responsibility to improve the quality of life within the community.[57] The mission statement and foundational beliefs established were further supported by guiding principles identified by the LEAP working group. The principles identified included access for students to high-quality education, abilities to have family needs met within the community, and provisions for access to health and human services for community individuals. Likewise, students were to be empowered to be self-sufficient, strive to reach their potential, and enjoy an environment that prepares them for success.[58]

---

[54] Ibid.

[55] Ibid.

[56] Ibid.

[57] James E. Austin, The Collaboration Challenge: How nonprofits and businesses succeed through strategic alliances (San Francisco: Jossey-Bass, 2010).

[58] CSUCL, 1995.

Based on these established components, the guidance system utilized by the LEAP working group expanded the traditional scope of educational improvement strategies to include the entire community as well as the community's needs. Thus the mission statement, beliefs, and principles adopted uniformly embraced collaboration, participation, and responsibility in a more comprehensive fashion in considering a strategic plan for the project. The unified nature of these components, combined with an insistence on accountability, demanded all other efforts of plan development adhere to a focused vision. Mission management was thus accomplished through the creation of this guidance system and facilitated efficient achievement of the LEAP Initiative's objectives.

Stakeholder and Partnership Alliances

Both literature support and mission management stressed the importance of collaboration and strategic partnerships in developing the plan for the LEAP Project. A variety of stakeholders were considered in the development of the strategic plan, and their participation involved all aspects of the planning process. Four main categories of stakeholders represented summarized the various partnerships and alliances pursued. These groups included government and public sectors, parents and community sectors, private entities, and Rutgers University. Each stakeholder was evaluated in terms of resource support, networking potential, and access facilitation. Likewise, opportunities to be involved in decision making, strategy formulation, policy formation, active support, and program leadership were provided. As a result of this focus, the LEAP Project gained significant momentum and strength, which ultimately allowed it to attain its primary objectives.

Not unlike traditional public education, involvement of government and public networks proved to be crucial to the advancement of the initiatives of the project. As indicated by the literature, charter schools were being touted as an alternative to traditional education, however, since educational performance and academic outcomes were being questioned on a national stage.[59] This was particularly evident in Camden and within Abbott districts throughout the state of New Jersey. Given the perfect climate in which to gain public support for charter school development, government partnerships were pursued to gain support. Through interactions with state senator Jack Ewing, who headed the Senate Education Committee, a legislative bill in support of charter schools within the state was introduced. As a result, New Jersey became the twentieth state to approve public alternatives to traditional K-12 education through the Charter School Act, paving the way for the LEAP Academy.[60]

The LEAP Project enjoyed political circumstances at not only state government levels but at federal levels as well. During the presidency of George H. W. Bush, a federal mandate was passed that encouraged public authorities to commit funds toward economic development projects within their host cities.[61] Simultaneously, Governor Florio was pushing a job creation and business development plan for Camden. As a result of these influences, the Delaware River Port Authority (DRPA) was well positioned to provide partnership support to the project. Peter Burke, vice chair of the DRPA, as a representative for the governor, understood that business development in Camden needed an educated workforce. This need fueled support for the LEAP Project, while the federal mandate provided a means by which funds could be provided. The partnership aligned needs of the community and the state, as well as the federal government.

In 1993, the DRPA provided $1.5 million in grant funds for the

---

[59] Chester E. Finn, Bruno V. Manno, and Gregg Vanourek (2001), Charter Schools in Action: Renewing Public Education (Princeton, NJ: Princeton University Press).

[60] Donna Leusner, (1993), "Whitman Signs Bill, Rings Opening Bell on Charter Schools," Action on Trenton, January 12, 1997.

[61] John Kincaid, "Developments in Federal-State Relations, 1992–93." The Book of the States: 1994–95 (1994): 576–86.

LEAP Project. In addition, David Murphy, who was the economic development director of DRPA, served as a liaison to the project and oversaw disbursement of funds and helped guide budgets. His extensive knowledge in capital projects provided a tremendous amount of expertise, which helped allocate resources effectively. Murphy likewise assisted with faculty search, negotiation of contracts, and construction projects. The end result allowed the goals of the DRPA and the LEAP Academy to become well aligned, which resulted in a collaborative effort and formation of community partnerships. Prior to the LEAP Project, the DRPA had never participated in any significant community-based project and was not viewed as a community resource.

While charter schools were favored by many wanting educational reform, others perceived charter schools as a competitive drain of financial resources. Though initially supportive, the Camden Board of Education over time developed an adversarial position in relation to the LEAP Project. A shift in support occurred in part as changes in directorship developed over time, but the primary source of contention was the public use of funds for charter schools that otherwise would have gone to traditional public systems.[62] Unlike the LEAP Project, which focused on strategic alliances, traditional public school systems had less autonomy to consider such options by comparison. While long-range benefits to the public education system were anticipated through enhancement of the Camden community through the LEAP Project, short-term perceptions of competition hindered the partnership relation.

Another key network for partnership identified included parents and community leaders within Camden. In an effort to create a truly collaborative alliance, focus groups were conducted with a number of parents of Camden students and with a variety of neighborhood representatives throughout the city. The information gained from these focus groups provided insights about additional needs of the community

---

[62] Thomas Martello, (1995), "Teachers OK Charter School Plan," Courier Post, December 19, 1995.

while also identifying individuals who would be willing to serve as members of the LEAP Project effort. Some parents and community leaders were selected to participate in the LEAP working group. As a result, involvement of this network in information analyses and decision making enhanced school-wide participation and community support over time. In addition, these actions helped identify potential leaders who could help guide and direct the project toward its mission and vision.

In addition to gaining information about educational needs and identifying additional community resources, focus groups also identified many community needs within Camden. From this information, a Parents Academy was created, which served to train parents on how they could participate as leaders within the community and within the LEAP Academy system. This training provided a means by which capacity building occurred among parents and community members, and it enhanced individuals through measures facilitating personal growth. The alliance with parents and the Camden community thus involved their inclusion in the process of data collection, data analysis, decision making, and leadership, in addition to provisions for their needs through school-based services. The partnership was strengthened as a result of this reciprocal and bilateral relationship.

A similar approach to partnership alliance was performed with Rutgers Camden University to a degree. Students of the university were invited to participate in the LEAP Academy through volunteerism and tutoring opportunities, which could serve as educational opportunities for them within their fields of study. In addition, specific departments within the university provided support as a means of civic engagement. The departments of nursing, public policy, law school, social work, business school, and education valued social justice, equity, and community excellence, and thus supported greater civic engagement as a result. Their involvement in centers of excellence associated with the LEAP Academy demonstrated an attitude of collaboration, common goals, and a focus on the greater good.[63] Other traditional academic departments, however, were more resistant, as their focus was primarily on research and academic study. Traditional approaches to higher education academics were identified as an obstacle to partnership in this regard.

These same struggles in developing a strong allegiance between the LEAP project and Rutgers Camden University occurred politically as well as academically. On a positive note, Roger Dennis took over as provost for the university and perceived Rutgers Camden as having a responsibility as an anchor for the local community. As a result, he leveraged a great deal of support for the LEAP Academy through the university's board of governors. However, the board of governors later demonstrated resistance by delaying the filing of the LEAP Academy's charter, stating the university's role was to provide higher education rather than K-12 educational support. Given the political nature of these conflicts, influence in favor of the LEAP Academy was provided by New Jersey Senator Donald Di Francesco and Governor Christie Whitman upon request. As a result, the board of governors authorized the filing of the school's charter in 1996 and adopted a resolution defining a clear partnership with the LEAP Academy.

The initial alliance between Rutgers Camden University and the LEAP Academy stated that no more than 20 percent of the LEAP Academy Board of Trustees would consist of university representatives. Likewise, the LEAP Academy would be required to be financially independent of the university. However, the university was crucial in providing resources and support for the development of the LEAP Academy's Centers of Excellence, which facilitated community support and empowerment as well as educational success of the school. Leveraging political and university-related networks and resources to achieve a solid

---

[63] Gloria Bonilla-Santiago, "Responsible Civic Engagement: Supporting Sustainable Communities." Paper presented at the International Conference on Interdisciplinary Social Sciences, Monash University Centre, Prato, Tuscany, Italy, July 22–25, 2008.

alliance proved to be very valuable in achieving the objectives of the LEAP Project's mission.

The fourth network, which served as a partnership alliance group to the LEAP Project, involved the private and nonprofit sector. Early members representing this network included the Prudential Foundation, the Robert Wood Johnson Foundation, the Fund for New Jersey, and the Geraldine Dodge Foundation. The benefits of these private foundations were not simply provisions of financial resources but other nonmonetary resources as well. While the Prudential Foundation provided funds to establish the Parents Academy and mobile trailers, which housed many areas of the LEAP Academy in 1997, the Robert Wood Johnson Foundation provided planning and development assistance in the creation of the Health Center and provided student staffing. In addition, the Geraldine Dodge Foundation provided resources, which allowed ongoing funding for teacher trainings to be completed, of the LEAP Academy's progress over time.

In pursuing strategic alliances and partnerships among the various networks described, different challenges and recruitment tactics were realized during the strategic planning process. Overall, the ability to align the objectives and mission of the LEAP Project with other potential partners was readily achieved in most instances through open dialogue, collaboration, and negotiation. Areas of common interest and mutual desires were often present that facilitated the development of the partnership relationship. In some instances, however, competition over resources and different core philosophies concerning education and civic engagement caused resistance and obstacles to alliance formation. When possible, political and social capital were utilized to overcome these barriers. In other instances, the need for the partnership did not support use of significant resources to achieve this goal. In sum, the empowerment and success the LEAP Academy subsequently achieved was largely due to the development and strengthening of these strategic alliances.

Figure 2: Strategic Planning Areas

Operations Management

Operational excellence and functional infrastructure are necessary requirements for fulfilling organizational missions and visions. Thus a key component of strategic formulation for the LEAP Academy involved the determination of how resources would best be utilized to create the important foundational aspects needed for quality educational performance. In addition to securing and managing financial funding and assets toward operational goals, the development of governance structures, financial controls, leadership, and administrative procedures are needed to ensure a unified objective. While conceptual approaches to enhanced education and community support drive the mission and vision for the LEAP Academy, operational management is a priority to allow these goals to become a reality.

Among the first actions taken by the LEAP working group was to determine the type of governance structure the charter school would have in alignment with the project's mission. As previously noted, involvement of multiple stakeholders is an important objective for the LEAP Academy, since success hinges on community and parent participation and support. For this reason, any governance structure needed to include representation from a variety of stakeholder groups. Ultimately the group decided the LEAP Academy's Board of Trustees would be comprised of individuals not only from Rutgers University, which served as the primary partner in the LEAP Project, but also individuals from local businesses, parent groups, local philanthropists, and other educational backgrounds. The board of trustees now consists of seventeen members reflective of these different groups, allowing a broad perspective and vast array of expertise.

The board of trustees is charged with attending to macrolevel issues related to the LEAP Academy, leaving day-to-day management decisions to be handled by other governance entities. The range of activities managed by the board thus includes areas concerning accountability, efficiency, academic enhancement, and policy and resource development. As a result, functions involve financial and administrative, as well as operational aspects despite the board's perspective being predominantly broad in scope. For example, the board of trustees handles larger issues concerning facilities oversight, financial resource management, teacher union negotiations, school charter amendments and oversight, and future planning for growth and budgeting. In addition, the board provides strong leadership to guide other operational and management groups throughout the LEAP Academy organization.

A subgroup of the board of trustees with select financial expertise serves as the financial committee and is charged with maintaining fiscal stability and solvency of the organization. Routine responsibilities of the financial committee thus include the development of short-term and long-term financial goals, budgeting and forecasting, assessment of lease and purchase proposals, maintenance of banking and financial institutional relations, and strategies to optimize financial resource leveraging. The financial committee is also charged with reviewing and implementing corrective action plans devised by outside auditing firms, which are annually performed as a safeguard to ensure legitimate fiscal practices. This structure of financial operations provides both internal and external measures that facilitate efficiency of decisions while ensuring regulatory and legal compliance.

In addition to the board of trustees and the financial committee, a school management team serves LEAP Academy by handling daily operations for the school. Unlike the board of trustees, its responsibilities include fiscal, administrative, and operational implementation, and the team's focus is more microlevel in comparison. Key members of the team include the chief academic officer, chief financial and operations officer, and the director of curriculum development. In addition, principals of the various lower, middle, and upper school grades comprise the remaining members of the management team. Despite a lack of direct representation of various stakeholder groups within the school management team, input via the board of trustees on macrolevel concepts directs team actions and decisions, as do informal inputs on a daily basis through student and community interactions.

Fiscal responsibilities of the school management team include instructional oversight, internal operational and accounting controls, and budgeting controls. Specific policies to prevent theft and misuse or loss of funds are developed as an administrative and financial objective of the team, as are the routine preparation of financial statements for the school. In addition, policies that demand legal compliance with the board of trustees' various budgets are maintained to similarly carry out the intended strategies serving the school's overall mission. The governance structure in place, between the board of trustees, the board committees, and the school management team, allows effective leadership oversight of operations while enabling daily attention to important policies and procedures. In addition, feedback between these various structures and external sources enables a system of checks and balances to ensure overall congruence in operations.

LEAP Academy was originally incorporated as a nonprofit organization in 1997 and is recognized as a 501(c)3 organization. In addition, LEAP Academy received its original charter from the state to serve as a publicly funded charter school in 1997. Since that time, the school's charter has been renewed and expanded three times, with the current charter active through 2015. While the original charter established a primary school with grades kindergarten through fifth grade, a grade phase growth model was devised that added one grade each year to accommodate advancing students and school growth. In 2001, this provided a path to the creation of the LEAP Academy high school, and in 2009 the STEM (Science, Technology, Engineering, and Mathematics) High School program was added. This model of growth, expansion, and charter renewal has served the school well in managing resources efficiently while progressively serving the needs of the community, the state, and the school's primary mission.

From an infrastructural standpoint, the LEAP Academy has managed operational growth and expansion carefully since its inception. From 1997 through 1999, the school serviced 324 elementary children through the use of temporary modular housing. Financial resources at the time were utilized to establish more crucial areas of staffing, curricular development, and fiscal stability of the school. However, since then, financial support has been acquired from strategic partners to develop more permanent state-of-the-art facilities for education in a progressive and well-planned fashion. A combination of donations, grants, and creative financing strategies have allowed the LEAP Academy campus to expand into five independent buildings along Cooper Street in Camden that now serve over thirteen hundred students at various primary and secondary grade levels. In addition, preschool and early development services, as well as community resource centers, are housed within these operational facilities.

The original Cooper Street building was acquired through direct financial support from the Delaware River Port Authority (DRPA), enabling a $7.5 million renovation project to proceed in 1999. In 2005, the second campus structure was purchased through financing that involved bond purchases through the DRPA, which were secured by Rutgers University, allowing lower interest rates. In 2012, the STEM High School and Elementary Program buildings were financed through creative strategies involving the Reinvestment Fund and Chase financial institutions. And the fifth building utilized for the Early Learning Research Academy (ELRA) was secured through a grant gift from the James Knight Foundation with Rutgers University, which owns the building. Through planned phased strategies, the board of trustees has provided leadership in developing the infrastructure needed for the school's educational mission. At the same time, this expansion has occurred while maintaining fiscal stability and solvency. A pipeline from cradle to college is available to children in Cooper Street at LEAP.

The infrastructure attained since the inception of the LEAP Academy has fostered the ability to meet school objectives and missions. This combined with financial goals and administrative policies and procedures have been a strong part of operations management. Rutgers University provides several areas of support for the LEAP Academy not only in leadership and financial areas but also in other performance areas.

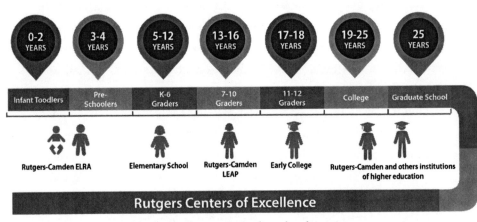

Figure 3: A focus on pipeline development—
The Rutgers/LEAP pipeline to college

For example, the Rutgers Community Leadership Center (CLC) provides oversight and support to LEAP Academy, allowing the Centers of Excellence to serve as a foundation for the LEAP Academy's mission to provide students and their families support for lifelong educational learning. CLC support represents a major channel through which Rutgers

University provides additional resources. The College Access Center, Human and Health Services Center, the Law Clinic, the Parents Academy, and the Early Childhood Program are just a few of these centers where Rutgers University is able to support ongoing school operations. Thus the interrelation between the organizational structure, the governance structure, facilities infrastructure, and operational components all complement the LEAP Academy's overall objectives.

A final component of operations management involves the acquisition, compensation, and the professional development of the educational curriculum and staff. Inherently the board of trustees has served to participate in these efforts, since these represent core needs of the school and its mission. Likewise, these issues represent important operational concerns for the academic success of students, the overall performance of the school, and the satisfaction of the educational staff employed. Given the importance of this specific area in relation to the school's overall performance strategies, this area will be considered separately to better detail how professional educational development of the LEAP Academy was pursued.

Table 1: Strategies to guide professional development at LEAP

Observe deficiency—Topics to improve professional development

Aligning and Implementing curriculum

- Curriculum alignment and instructional material selection
- Curriculum implementation
- Curriculum replacement
- Data of student assessments

Collaborative structure

- Partnership with scientists and mathematicians in the industry and university

- Professional development
- Instructional team / study groups

Examining teaching and learning

- Action research
- CASE discussion
- Examining student work, thinking, and scoring assessments
- Lessons / study time
- Review of data
- Instructional teams

Immersion entrepreneurs

- Immersion in inquiry in science and problem solving in mathematics
- Immersion into the world of science and mathematics

Practice teaching

- Coaching
- Demonstration lessons
- Mentoring

Additional strategies

- Developing program and learning communities
- Technology for professional development
- Institute, courses, and seminars

Performance Based Compensation System

Early in the educational system development for LEAP Academy, a strong effort was made to implement a systematic structure that rewarded professional educators based on measures of accountability. During the initial discussions among members of the LEAP working group, the national climate concerning the future of primary and secondary education at the time influenced thought significantly. Past strategies to augment educational performance of schools had predominantly involved changes in governance, changes in inputs, and changes in process. Efforts to improve management within specific schools, to hire more teachers, or to require changes in professional standards were isolated in nature and had offered little improvement in educational outcomes.[64] In order to meet the evolving demands of the community's educational needs, these approaches were deemed to be insufficient by the group.

A shift was occurring throughout the nation at the time in terms of educational expectations. For one, declining resources for educational funding were being experienced in many public school systems despite increasing student enrollments and increases in labor service costs. In addition, schools were progressively being asked to do more. Entitlements in educational and support services for disabled children were mandated by legislation, and some traditional parental responsibilities in low-income regions were being transferred from home to school settings.[65] These issues were naturally relevant to Camden's community. A perspective that better resource utilization efficiency was needed given this atmosphere was pervasive nationally, and performance outcomes were increasingly being monitored in relation to the needs of the nation embracing a global economy. As a result, a desire for educational accountability for resources invested was already evident throughout the United States.[66]

In order for schools to embrace these changes, a systematic strategy had to be considered as opposed to a site-based strategy. From a systems perspective, compensation must somehow be linked to educational outcomes instead of being based on longevity, educational degrees, tenure, and other nonperformance measures. Shifts in curriculums that met community and national needs, enhanced student engagement, and higher student achievement needed to be incentivized through compensation

---

[64] (Ladd 1996)

[65] Ibid.

[66] Ibid.

programs to ensure resources being invested were providing the results desired. Many experts during this time suggested combinations of skill-based pay, competency-based pay, and group performance rewards as a means to reach these targets.[67]. Based on such recommendations, the LEAP working group began devising a performance based compensation system for its teachers.

In order to pursue these goals, compensation programs would need to consider different areas of the educational process. This included not only student achievements but also how education instruction was implemented and the contexts in which education was provided. In order to evaluate implementation, a variety of strategies were considered important, which included focus groups involving teachers, stakeholder surveys, and observational techniques. In addition, contextual aspects of school size, school climate, and student demographics were deemed to be relevant. These core areas continue to define the basic foundation of ongoing evaluation and assessment of educational performance at LEAP Academy and serve as the means by which instructional improvement and program evaluations occur. In addition, these perspectives are used to devise current accountability measures by which evidence-based practices guide professional development and curricular changes.

The first performance-based compensation system for teachers was instituted at LEAP Academy in 1999. The board of trustees approved the initial version of the program, which school leaders subsequently implemented. This system focuses on three areas of performance evaluation that link teachers' pay to the instructional mission of the school. These areas of teacher performance include direct classroom observations of teachers, student achievement scores, and an assessment of professional leadership. This initial version was less structured and detailed compared to later versions, since the performance-based compensation system (PBCS) underwent several revisions over time. Regardless, the initial implementation served to acclimate teachers to

---

[67] (Mohrman, Mohrman and Odden 1996).

such a system, which has since been refined to better serve all the needs of all stakeholders involved.

The most significant changes in the PBCS occurred in 2007 after a three-year negotiation process with the New Jersey Education Association, the largest teachers' union in the state. In 2004, a majority of LEAP Academy teachers voted to join the union, and the PBCS remained a topic of bargaining for a prolonged period of time. The board of trustees played an integral role in the negotiation process, and LEAP Academy administrative leaders persistently defended the program as a means to ensure quality teaching skills and student performance. Ultimately an agreement was reached in 2007, and the LEAP School PBCS remains the only pay-for-performance program in a unionized school throughout New Jersey. As part of the agreement, teachers receive a guaranteed annual 1.67 percent salary increase and have the opportunity to receive an additional 3.33 percent salary increase based on performance criteria. This represents the most recent foundation, upon which the PBCS currently exists.

While the prolonged negotiations with the union could have strained relations between LEAP Academy teachers and administration, the compromise was used as an opportunity to redesign and improve the merit pay system. Focus groups were held with teachers to allow ongoing feedback about the merits of the system and potential areas of improvement. Issues concerning fairness of evaluations as well as professional support were included in these discussions, resulting in a collaborative effort to enhance the PBCS. Because of the inclusion of teachers in the feedback and evaluation process, teacher support for the program progressively increased. The process and framework developed during this time established shared dialogues and a constructive collaboration, which has persisted between teachers and administration since. As a result, the PBCS continues to represent an innovative and creative structure with a common goal for quality educational outcomes.

LEAP Academy's PBCS was developed using the framework for

teaching effectiveness devised by Charlotte Danielson. Danielson's framework consists of four domains in which teacher responsibilities are evaluated. These domains include planning and preparation, classroom environment, instruction, and professional responsibilities.[68] LEAP Academy teacher evaluations encompass these framework areas in their evaluation domains of "teacher effectiveness" and "leadership-professional contributions." In addition, LEAP Academy teacher evaluations also address a third domain involving "student achievement." This format was designed through collaboration among administrators and educators as a means to pursue the primary mission and objectives of the LEAP Project.[69] Likewise, by using Danielson's framework, a transparent and public account of performance became evident, demonstrating the high standards of practice by which the LEAP Academy measured its educational quality outcomes.[70]

Part of this process naturally involved the development of professional learning opportunities for teachers so they could advance their knowledge and skills and align their goals with the mission of the school. A focus was placed on teaching and learning improvements in addition to specific certifications and course completions. Where possible, stand-alone professional workshops and similar development programs were avoided. Instead, learning opportunities have been developed through a school professional development program where teachers gain knowledge and skills during regular educational activities and through real-time coaching and mentoring at the school site. These structures provide greater opportunities for interaction and evidence-based learning for educators.

---

[68] Charlotte Danielson, *Enhancing professional practice: A framework for teaching* (Alexandria, VA: ASCD, 2007).

[69] Jessica Griffin and Cheryl Pruce, *LEAP Academy University Charter School's Performance-Based Compensation Program* (Washington DC: Center for Educator Compensation Reform, 2013).

[70] Danielson, 2007.

In order to develop effective alignment between teacher goals and LEAP Academy's mission, the category of leadership and professional contributions are considered important. Teachers who demonstrate activities and behaviors that further the mission of the school deserve support, and the PBCS is a means by which these behaviors can be further incentivized. Leadership is evaluated through an assessment of four key domains involving teacher activities. These include a functional domain where teachers demonstrate specific leadership skills and problem-solving abilities, as well as a programmatic domain involving curricula, instructional methods and learning strategies. Other domains involve a contextual and interpersonal domain, which examines enhancement of the overall school's culture, and an academic achievement domain, which pertains to approaches to standardized and local assessment education. By rewarding teachers for behaviors in these areas, which advance school objectives, greater collaboration toward improved educational performance occurs.

In an effort to be objective and consistent in the evaluation process, a detailed rubric has been devised by which numerical scores for each of the three domains are obtained. The teacher effectiveness domain and the leadership/professional domain each receive "in-action" scores where direct observations are made by evaluators. Likewise, teachers receive "in-reflection" scores from evaluator-teacher conferences, which evaluate the prior observations. During the "in-reflection" conferences, teachers provide additional information and evidence supporting their performance to augment their total evaluation scores.[71] The student achievement domain, in contrast, does not have these scoring components but instead assesses student performance based on national/state standards and on local achievement standards. If standards for student assessments are not met, teachers can still earn points as part of their total score by showing improvements in both national/state and local categories of performance by the students.[72]

---

[71] Griffin and Pruce, 2013.

[72] Ibid.

The number of points potentially earned by a teacher totals 100 annually, which is comprised of 48 maximum teacher effectiveness points, 24 maximum leadership-professional points and 28 student achievement points. For the teacher effectiveness and leadership-professionalism domains, new teachers receive five evaluations through the school year, while tenured teachers receive four annually. An average of these scores serves as the final points received for these two domains. The third domain, of student achievement, is then added to these averages to determine the final annual score upon which performance-based salary increases are determined.[73] In addition to these standard components of the PBCS, teachers also have opportunities to receive one-time performance bonuses. Teachers can earn a fixed bonus amount as part of a group performance incentive if grade-level performances for students meet a specific standard. Also teachers can earn an exemplary leadership performance bonus for participation in projects or activities beyond the scope of their regularly duties that advance grade, school, building, or district level goals and mission.[74]

The purpose of the PBCS was to fairly reward teachers for their performance and educational outcomes while seeking to align organizational and professional goals. In addition to the compensation model developed, other structures have been created as part of this model to further these objectives. Specifically, professional development support for teachers has been established through a variety of efforts in conjunction with the PBCS. For example, each teacher receives an individual professional improvement plan developed in collaboration with the teacher and based on the strengths and weaknesses noted during PBCS observations.[75] Additionally, a number of resources are provided for professional development through in-house training sessions, mentoring programs with master teachers, observational feedback opportunities,

---

[73] Ibid.

[74] Ibid.

[75] Ibid.

and videotape analysis of teacher instruction.[76] These programs are encompassed within the PBCS and are believed to demonstrate more clearly its purpose of improving educational outcomes and performance while simultaneously enhancing teacher development.

The PBCS at LEAP Academy represents a commitment to accountability and performance while pursuing the core mission and objectives defined by the LEAP Project working group. In order to meet external expectations of resource utilization and student educational outcomes, performance needs to be linked to teacher compensation. However, at the same time, adequate support for teachers needs to be provided in order to meet performance goals. LEAP Academy continues to find ways to accomplish both tasks in its compensation model. Through professional development support and inclusion of teachers in the development process of the model, individual and organizational objectives have become well aligned. While the model has undergone periodic revisions and will likely continue to do so, the foundational concepts of the PBCS provided here outline the basic strategies employed in creating a desirable teacher compensation model for the school.

Student Empowerment

Strategies focusing on student empowerment and their specific needs were believed to be central components toward the LEAP Project's success. However to appreciate student needs, a clear picture of the academic and social environments surrounding children in the Camden area was required. Solutions to resolve the longstanding academic problems associated with public education in Camden demanded an in-depth perspective that went beyond the school's climate and curriculums and extended into extracurricular activities and into the community at large. Failure to consider larger perspectives was believed by the working group to not only limit the potential success of the

---

[76] Ibid.

LEAP Academy but to actually prevent the school from achieving its mission and vision.

In the late 1990s, Camden's educational system was essentially broken and ineffective. Less than half of all students passed standard state examinations in reading, and approximately half were categorized as functionally illiterate. The dropout rate among students in the area averaged 50 percent, and few incentives encouraged students to persevere in their studies.[77] With less than 30 percent of the community holding a high school degree or higher, academic role models were nonexistent for many children. And with only 5 percent of Camden adults having a college degree, many students perceived college as being unattainable. Few examples existed within the community that fostered a vision of higher education and career success, and as a result, the incentive and desire to continue in school was limited.[78]

In addition to a lack of promotion for educational success within the Camden community, other socioeconomic factors further hindered student abilities to excel academically. More than two-thirds of the Camden community was single parents when the LEAP Project began, and the unemployment rate of the region was three times the national average. The average per capita income in Camden was only $10,000, which reflected these unemployment figures as well as the large number of families living below the poverty line.[79] More than 85 percent of students qualified for free lunch programs; and due to declining property values, dwindling residential and commercial populations, and lowered educational funding, many schools were struggling to provide these meals.[80] Housing was also inadequate, with a quarter of the public housing units being unsuitable for living based on minimal standards. A waiting list of homeless families seeking housing was ever-present. In

---

[77] Casey, 2001.

[78] Kozol, 2012.

[79] Casey, 2001.

[80] Kozol, 2012.

addition, less than one in five Camden residents had health insurance at the time, posing additional stressors for children and families.[81] With basic needs being unmet, students would be less likely to invest strong efforts in school and in learning.

Given this scenario for Camden students, strategies needed to be devised to counter these overwhelming educational, social, and economic problems. Though funding for LEAP Academy was being secured, the ability to serve the needs of all the students in Camden was beyond the scope of the project. As a result, a lottery system was devised to allow an equitable system by which students could gain admission to the LEAP Academy without prequalifiers. Members of the working group hoped to establish a cornerstone of change within the community, which would foster both local growth of the LEAP Academy system as well as community-wide changes that fostered better educational opportunities.

In an effort to encourage student recruitment into the lottery, the Parents Academy (as part of the LEAP Academy's Centers of Excellence) trained parents to recruit families and students and to identify interest in college preparation. This strategy was instrumental in the student recruitment process. A college education was promised to every family that enrolled a student in the LEAP Academy program, and parents in return were expected to work with the LEAP Academy to support their children's education. New buildings, resources, a uniform, and a new culture of learning were likewise promised along with a college access center for student development. Resources were thus focused on LEAP Academy itself and on strategies for student empowerment believed to be most effective over the long term.

Educational challenges identified in empowering students to achieve academic objectives involved refocusing attention on learning, building their self-esteem and confidence, and transforming their expectations of failure into success while altering external influences. Negative environmental problems could not be eliminated, but efforts to improve

---

[81] Casey, 2001.

them while offering other constructive environments and role models for life success were possible. As a result, these ideas served as the primary objectives in student empowerment strategies.

The overall strategy for student empowerment was best described as a holistic approach. By acknowledging the needs of students as the focus of the institution, and by continually focusing on students' success as a means to college enrollment, schools were to serve as primary resources to address both curricular and extracurricular needs. The LEAP Academy's holistic approach thus identifies academic-based strategies as well as social and community-based strategies in meeting student needs. From an academic perspective, structures and expectations have been established to foster student success in the classroom and beyond.

The LEAP experience involves a range of educational "best practices" that prepare students to reach acceptable levels of student achievement and success. LEAP students are expected to function effectively in and contribute to a world of new ideas; think independently, critically, and creatively; be lifelong learners; view themselves as important, contributing members of a community; hope for continual improvement of that community; and play a role in that advancement. Guiding principles established for student empowerment can be identified within the school's pedagogical framework, which addresses high expectations, a holistic learning environment, integrated and active learning, a positive attitude, and varied assessments.

In conjunction with the high academic expectations implicit in the New Jersey Core Content Curriculum Standards and those of national professional organizations, LEAP students are expected to learn as well as and as the best students in the world. In the United States, low academic expectations for urban students and the inadequacy of resources allocated to urban schools have resulted in poor educational environments and achievement results. However, examples of urban schools exist where faculty and students' families have managed to establish and maintain high expectations, culminating in higher performance results. The curriculum, support structure, and organization of LEAP Academy create and support such high expectations of student achievement.

The students attending LEAP Academy represent a highly diverse, multilingual, mobile population. Because children need to have their physical, emotional, and social needs met as a prerequisite to achieving their maximum potential, proactive treatment and intervention programs in school-based health and social service centers are necessary. The providers of these services develop personalized, informal, and egalitarian relationships with children and families; and such provisions foster holistic support and development, fostering optimal growth and achievement socially as well as academically. Student empowerment thus requires attention to the child in a holistic manner in order to attain the objectives desired. From a social and community perspective, involvement and support have highlighted the integrated nature between schools and community while stressing the importance of how individual effort can make broader changes. By investing in a comprehensive strategy that focuses on microenvironments and macroenvironments, students learn to accept the high level of learning expectations promoted by the LEAP Academy while also envisioning their purpose in the world at large.

Specific strategies involving academics that have been adopted by the LEAP Academy include the extension of a longer academic year and daily school schedules to accommodate extracurricular interests and academic needs, increased access to college information and preparation, opportunities for athletic advancement, access to tutoring support, and a dedication in maintaining small classroom sizes. These strategies have social benefits as well as academic ones. Statistically, the majority of teenage pregnancies occur between the hours of 1:00 p.m. and 3:00 p.m. when many students are home alone while their parents are at work. Extension of school hours into the late afternoon and early evening thus provides increased opportunities for learning while protecting children from potentially risky situations.[82] Likewise, information about tertiary educational opportunities naturally raises academic expectations within the school and provides opportunities for hopes and dreams beyond their childhood. Students also participate in health and wellness programs as part of their extended-day activities to ensure a healthy body and mind. Each of these strategies demonstrates the holistic perspective of the LEAP Academy toward student empowerment.

Adoption of smaller classroom sizes also aligns well with the mission of the LEAP Academy and with student empowerment. As a philosophy, the LEAP Academy seeks to develop a desire for lifelong learning among students. In order to accomplish this, students are placed in educational environments that foster independent, critical, and creative thinking. Camden offers great diversity in its community, with over 90 percent of the population being comprised of ethnic minorities.[83] Embracing this aspect of the community offers a chance for students to not only express their unique perspectives and creativities but also to learn skills of cooperation and collaboration with peers from varied backgrounds. Smaller classroom sizes allow such interactions while encouraging self-inquiry, exploration, and positive learning attitudes. By rewarding such atmospheres for learning, students adopt constructive learning habits and practices, which will last a lifetime.

Assessments also play a significant role in student empowerment strategies at the LEAP Academy. Standardized assessments are routinely administered not only due to requirements of the state but to demonstrate the expectation that all LEAP Academy students should attain these educational standards. These assessments are combined with classroom evaluations and other educational performance indicators, which allow students to receive feedback about their progress on a regular basis. Also, other authentic measures of learning are provided that encourage

---

[82] Gloria Bonilla-Santiago, PhD, "One drop-out in four is still too many," *Huffington Post Blog*, 13 June, 2013.

[83] Casey, 2001.

self-assessment and self-adjustments in learning techniques. All students are expected to achieve success within their learning environments at the LEAP Academy, and students as well as teachers work together to meet these expectations. By placing student needs as well as student outcomes at the center of the LEAP Academy's student empowerment strategies, opportunities to make corrective improvements are continuously present, enabling progressive advances in performance.

From a curriculum perspective, integrated learning has been identified as important for student learning and success. Core curriculums routinely stress mathematics, science, and technology as cornerstones for academic success, and the ability to integrate different concepts within these disciplines among other curricula offers new educational opportunities. Innovation and creativity become enhanced through the integration of different knowledge sources, and this subsequently strengthens independent and critical thinking abilities. To a great extent, this same strategy provided the vision for LEAP Academy's STEM High School, which offers advanced opportunities in science, technology, engineering, and mathematics for qualified students. Developed in 2010, the STEM High School encourages project-based learning through specialized academic curricula, which demand concept integration. The same holistic approach to student needs is exemplified here in the approach to education. By encouraging the consideration of multiple disciplines in devising solutions to educational problems, students learn to expand their perspectives and develop new ways of knowledge application.

Student empowerment involves the integration of academic learning. A curricular focus on mathematics, science, and technology is important to align societal needs with student career opportunities as described. However, the ability to appreciate the natural connections among these subjects is critical for students to advance their knowledge in both depth and complexity. As a result, an emphasis will be placed not only on each of these curriculums but also on their interrelationships. In this way, students will be empowered to become advanced in their creative skills and have greater talents toward innovation and problem solving.

To a great extent, integrated learning can be enhanced by active learning. The ability to build knowledge and meaning through active learning experiences—such as inquiry, exploration, and peer interaction—is important. LEAP students should have the opportunity to manipulate tangible objects, interpret physical phenomena, and investigate practical problems. By interacting with a wide variety of people, students can develop personal motivation and be responsible in part for their own learning. Knowledge gained through such experiences endures, having personal meaning for the learner. Cooperative and collaborative opportunities provide the opportunity to develop their ability to function as members of a team. And building on different perspectives, students working together can build new knowledge and appreciate strengths that arise from a group with diverse backgrounds, experiences, and ideas. Participating in active learning environments can therefore serve to empower student success both within their current settings as well as within those of their future.

The culture of the school fosters creativity, originality, self-esteem, and a sense of wonder and excitement about learning. Developing a sense of worth is fostered through an environment of respect for the individual and his or her ideas. Individuals whose ideas are valued, whose feelings are identified and accepted, and who are treated with common human courtesy develop the sense that they are people worthy of respect. The school environment is safe for students to take risks and is a place where errors provide opportunities to learn.

Meeting the social needs of children in the Camden community has been identified as an important strategy for student empowerment in conjunction with the ability to meet educational needs. These efforts have been discussed in the section regarding stakeholder management and acquisition of partner alliances; however, some aspects of these strategies relevant to student empowerment deserve further mention. Parental engagement and support were identified early by the working group as necessities in fostering student success. As a result, numerous centers of excellence and comprehensive services were developed to provide resources to parents and the community, which would in turn enhance student support for learning. By addressing social and community needs, the ability to comprehensively meet student needs was believed to be possible. This perspective not only provided a foundation for the LEAP Academy as a whole but also contributed to the success of student achievement.

Key centers of excellence, developed as a component of LEAP Academy, implemented specific strategies to enhance student empowerment. For example, the Center for College Access, developed in 2005, seeks to enhance college awareness and readiness through extracurricular efforts. Academic advisement, exam preparation, student ambassador programs, dual college placement, and early college services are just a few of the offerings of the center that serve to empower student success. Similarly, the Parents Academy teaches parents skills in leadership, parenting, college awareness, and educational advocacy, which furthers interests and advances in student academic outcomes. These centers target students and their immediate support systems to develop a vision of ongoing educational achievement and lifelong learning.

Other centers of excellence serve to reduce other distractions, which may hinder learning and educational success due to unmet social needs. The Family Support Center, for example, provides family educational services regarding health, nutrition, and social skills while also offering activities associated with healthier lifestyles. The Health Wellness Center helps fill the void in health coverage among students and their families by offering immunizations, preventative care, nutritional counseling, and basic treatments and referrals for medical conditions. The Health Wellness Center, in addition to meeting family needs, often increased school attendance when students would become ill. By immediately evaluating for health complaints, students were often able to return to school activities the same day. These extracurricular centers provide a means for students and their families to address needs early and effectively and thus prevent the development of extended problems that could interfere with student learning.

In summary, strategies for student empowerment have been comprehensive in scope and holistic in nature. At the heart of student empowerment is the belief that each student not only has academic potential but also is expected to fulfill his or her dreams. This message permeates each policy, process, and activity at the LEAP Academy. In an effort to provide students with the necessary tools to meet these expectations, academic and social/community-based strategies have been developed to accommodate a wide variety of student needs, with student outcomes driving further change. Some address specific learning techniques, curricula, and assessments while others focus on social resources and support. By pursuing a comprehensive and holistic approach to students and allowing outcomes to guide change, the LEAP Academy places student learning at the top of the school's priorities and objectives. This perspective is evident within the student empowerment strategies adopted.

Expansion and Institutionalization

In relation to expansion and institutionalization, a collaborative planning effort was designed to create a compelling vision and innovative approach to serve the educational needs of the Camden community. Although a variety of groups were involved in the planning process, Rutgers Camden University representatives played a leading role in formulating the first agreement with other stakeholders to ensure active and ongoing participation. The Community Leadership Center under Rutgers-Camden University led the effort ensuring all other stakeholders, such as the Delaware River Port Authority, Camden City administration, school district leaders, NGOs, and other anchor institutions as well as parents groups, were given an opportunity to serve. The working group appointed the first governance leadership group for the LEAP Academy to implement the school's charter, and each stakeholder involved in the LEAP Project received board representation according to level of involvement.

In terms of recruitment and retention, the strategy for a school leadership team was to recruit, attain, and train members a year prior to the school's opening. Areas to be considered in the training included the LEAP Project's philosophy, mission, operational plans, curriculum development strategies, and concepts regarding the training and recruitment of teachers. The role of the team was to develop the school culture and institute operations through a mission-driven focus. Organizational planning in terms of time, space, and personnel resource management was considered from a perspective of optimal student learning. The school organizational plan addressed issues common to urban schools such as master schedules, staff locations in the building, enrollment procedures, school operations, and finance.

Academic areas and the assignments of teacher teams were also considered in the organizational plan to ensure quality learning. A partnership with *Teach for America* was arranged by contractual agreement in order to recruit the best teachers, and the College of New Jersey, Rutgers University, and Rowan University also participated in the search. The implementation strategy for attaining instructors was to recruit a cadre of the youngest teachers possible with adequate experience. However, charter schools at that time attracted many inexperienced teachers and teachers without certifications. This combined with a paucity of teacher recruits meeting desired qualifications proved to be a challenge in the early years for the school. Because of a commitment to performance-based compensation, many educators required investment in training during the initial years or were released due to inadequate outcomes. Fortunately, the development of strong educational and curricular leadership at the LEAP Academy provided the school with the ability to persevere in this regard while staying steadfast in pursuing the LEAP Academy's mission.

Charter schools in particular have unique leadership challenges due to the nature of the schools' foundational aspects. However, the working group and board established two key positions that provided focused and effective leadership for the LEAP Academy. Charter schools are essentially school districts consisting of a single school. Responsibilities that are normally assigned to a school district's superintendent instead become assigned to an individual school. By identifying an Instructional principal and an administrative director, these dual aspects of the charter school's culture were better addressed.

In addition, the LEAP Academy was unique in being the first charter school in Camden. Because of the LEAP Academy's stark contrast to traditional Camden public schools, opposition was anticipated. This was expected, since comments criticizing the charter school's competition for state educational funds had already been verbalized by local public school officials. The leadership team sought to develop strategies to ensure stability and autonomy over the ensuing years. The first strategy was to market the LEAP Academy to students, parents, and community. Unlike traditional public schools, which safely assume students in their districts will attend, the LEAP Academy had no such guarantee. Second, the group sought to establish finance strategies for future facility development and growth. And third, through the Community Leadership Center at Rutgers, fund-raising strategies for the extracurricular programs (i.e., Centers of Excellence) and for LEAP Academy project expansion were developed. Fund raising was projected to account for as much as 20 percent of the overall budget.

In considering the ongoing financial stability of the LEAP Academy, the leadership group established the school as a nonprofit organization. This enabled the financial management to be secondary to the effective management of the school's primary mission. The group acknowledged the need for financial stability and sustainability. Finding a solid balance between educational revenues and operational expenses was essential in allowing the organization to thrive and grow over time. Ultimately this was a critical component to long-term success. Raising revenue, managing expenses, and monitoring cash flow were challenging endeavors, especially for the early leadership lacking business savvy. However, this limitation was eliminated through effective planning, team training, and the development of efficient and consolidated operational procedures. These structures combined with central managerial oversight became priorities in establishing financial stability. Because the LEAP Academy represents a different educational system model from traditional schools, goods and services normally networked throughout a school district had to be developed within a single school structure. While hierarchical structures may seem feasible in such a situation, open systems are preferable in allowing greater freedoms and in avoiding resource bottlenecks. Though implementation challenges existed in creating such a system, a progression toward this model was the goal in pursuing long-term financial sustainability and effective operational functions.

Traditionally public schools owned their own buildings and facilities, and very few utilized fund raising for capital expenditures. The strategies previously mentioned, including fund-raising efforts, demanded significant investments of time, which initially were provided by the LEAP Project leadership team. In addition to strategy development, the leadership team also assisted with human resource needs (recruitment of new teachers and staff), with governing board issues, with the creation of a working budget, and with establishing student transportation and related needs. Other activities in which the team participated initially included legal resolutions, Department of Education policy compliance, enrollment oversight, facility expansion search, and fund raising. Eventually these functions were overseen by the administrative director, but initially the LEAP Academy leadership group provided significant assistance.

The position of instructional principal, in contrast, was established to manage the day-to-day academic operations involving children, parents, and teachers. Both the director and the instructional principal served vital roles during the conception of the LEAP Academy. However, the board and leadership team anticipated the need for a political and social leader for the school, given the anticipated opposition for the public school arena. In addition, such a leader was deemed important in maintaining a focus on the project's mission and on student success. With this in mind, the founder of LEAP Academy and board chair took this leadership position. As a change agent and champion for the school's mission, the leadership role served to address tough problems and challenges, which required social and political capital to resolve. In essence, this leadership challenged the marginal status quo of education in Camden and initiated a public discourse on the need for educational opportunities for students in the community.

Expansion also had to be addressed from the standpoint of student numbers and acceptance. Having established a lottery system as a fair means by which student selection from the community could proceed, some measures needed to be taken in order to accommodate the long waiting list of students wishing to attend LEAP Academy. Already strategies to meet academic and social needs of Camden children had resulted in lengthening of the school day and of the school calendar; however, growth was also needed to accommodate greater student capacity. The expansion strategy chosen in line with financial and administrative abilities involved the addition of a single grade with each advancing year. In this way, upper level students at the LEAP Academy could proceed within the system without interruption while new students could be continually added. Likewise, as facilities and resources allowed, horizontal growth as well as vertical growth would be provided.

The expectation of success was created within the school's values and culture. The leadership process in developing these values and establishing such a culture involved several consistent approaches. These included identifying areas in need of change, targeting areas of stress and detrimental pressures that detracted from the school's mission, maintaining a persistent focus on priorities and important tasks, and utilizing leadership resources within the school to assist in making necessary changes. From leadership to financial systems to operational procedures to instructional and educational development, numerous strategies were devised and put into place in order to meet expectations and achieve effective implementation. The working group, and particularly the LEAP Project leadership team, provided large amounts of time and energy in ensuring these strategies were realized. While the efforts may have not been completely comprehensive in anticipating some challenges, the overall plan went a long way in avoiding potential pitfalls and established a solid foundation for ongoing growth and progress.

V. Results

LEAP Academy opened in 1997 and began serving a sizable population of students and families in the Camden area. The planning structure previously described in the earlier sections provided a guide for expansion and growth, and over the last decade, several metrics and data have been collected to provide an assessment of function and allow an assessment of the school's mission, vision, and objectives in relation to actual performance. While the data is not comprehensive in every aspect, the following provides details, which allow evaluations to be made and conclusions to be drawn. These results will serve as the basis for the subsequent discussion regarding the successes of the LEAP Academy Project as well as areas where future improvements may be made.

Student Performance Data

As noted in the educational environment descriptions for children living in Camden, baseline performance standards were notoriously low for the region compared to state standards. While grade point averages (GPAs) and other standardized test scores were tracked since 1997, the state of New Jersey altered the levels that defined student proficiency for grades five through eight in 2008 and for grades three through four in 2009. Therefore, data collected after these time periods provide the most relevance to student performance at LEAP Academy in relation to Camden, other charter schools, and the state. Likewise, performance data concerning graduation rates, college placement rates, college scholarship funding, and college credit acquisition will be provided for the last five years to demonstrate trends and a more recent snapshot of student performance.

The New Jersey Department of Education (DOE) routinely monitors student performance within public schools for students in third through eleventh grades. Language arts/literacy and mathematics proficiencies are assessed via the New Jersey Assessment of Skills and Knowledge (NJASK) examinations, and charter schools within the state are categorized within District Factor Group "R" (DFG-R) for comparison purposes. In addition, data is available for comparisons to statewide scores and to regional city scores in the Camden area. These provide the measures for comparison of LEAP Academy based on state achievement testing.

In the following graphic depictions, NJASK scores for eleventh-grade students at LEAP Academy are compared to eleventh-grade scores in language arts/literacy and mathematics in state schools, in state charter schools, and in Camden city schools. Based on the data, the LEAP Academy has consistently performed comparably to other state charter schools and well exceeded other Camden city schools. This has occurred despite drawing students from markedly disadvantaged environments. In comparing LEAP Academy student performance in these areas to state totals, the LEAP Academy students approximate state performance in language arts and literacy and attain approximately 80 percent of the state performance level in mathematics.

In examining similar data for eighth-grade students at LEAP Academy, performance trends show slightly lower performance in language arts/literacy and mathematics compared to DFG-R schools and state averages. But again, performance nearly doubles Camden city school performance data. The findings suggest a progressive trend in student academic proficiency in these areas, which improves over time for each student to eventually meet state and charter school standards by the time of graduation. Despite serving students from the same communities as Camden city schools, student performance based on state comparisons is dramatically enhanced at LEAP Academy.

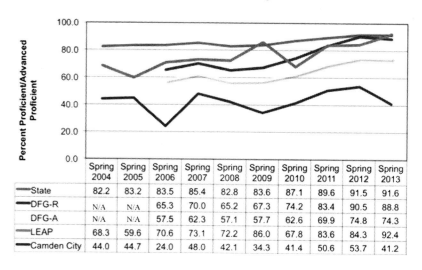

DISTRICT-DFG-STATE LONGITUDINAL TREND ANALYSIS
GRADE 11 - LANGUAGE ARTS/LITERACY – ALL STUDENTS
Spring 2004 to Spring 2013

	Spring 2004	Spring 2005	Spring 2006	Spring 2007	Spring 2008	Spring 2009	Spring 2010	Spring 2011	Spring 2012	Spring 2013
State	82.2	83.2	83.5	85.4	82.8	83.6	87.1	89.6	91.5	91.6
DFG-R	N/A	N/A	65.3	70.0	65.2	67.3	74.2	83.4	90.5	88.8
DFG-A	N/A	N/A	57.5	62.3	57.1	57.7	62.6	69.9	74.8	74.3
LEAP	68.3	59.6	70.6	73.1	72.2	86.0	67.8	83.6	84.3	92.4
Camden City	44.0	44.7	24.0	48.0	42.1	34.3	41.4	50.6	53.7	41.2

SOURCE: Spring HSPA11

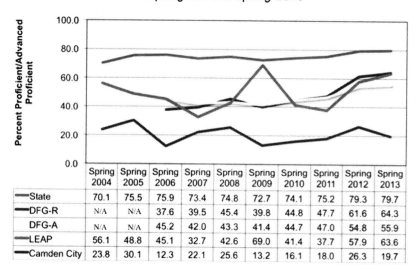

DISTRICT-DFG-STATE LONGITUDINAL TREND ANALYSIS
GRADE 11 – MATHEMATICS – ALL STUDENTS
Spring 2004 to Spring 2013

	Spring 2004	Spring 2005	Spring 2006	Spring 2007	Spring 2008	Spring 2009	Spring 2010	Spring 2011	Spring 2012	Spring 2013
State	70.1	75.5	75.9	73.4	74.8	72.7	74.1	75.2	79.3	79.7
DFG-R	N/A	N/A	37.6	39.5	45.4	39.8	44.8	47.7	61.6	64.3
DFG-A	N/A	N/A	45.2	42.0	43.3	41.4	44.7	47.0	54.8	55.9
LEAP	56.1	48.8	45.1	32.7	42.6	69.0	41.4	37.7	57.9	63.6
Camden City	23.8	30.1	12.3	22.1	25.6	13.2	16.1	18.0	26.3	19.7

SOURCE: Spring HSPA11

Similar trends in student performance can be identified in GPA metrics collected between 2006 and 2013. In the subsequent chart, cumulative GPAs rise progressively between 2006 and 2013, with a median initially around 2.5 gradually reaching an average around 3.0. These same improvements in cumulative GPA are also noted within individual grades beginning in ninth grade. These results suggest that not only are students progressively attaining higher grade point averages the longer they attend the LEAP Academy but also that the LEAP Academy itself is improving total student GPA performance year to year. These metrics demonstrate evidence of both individual student advancements as well as school advancements.

DISTRICT-GPA LONGITUDINAL TREND ANALYSIS
GRADES 9-12 and CUMULATIVE – ALL STUDENTS
2006 to 2013 By Grade

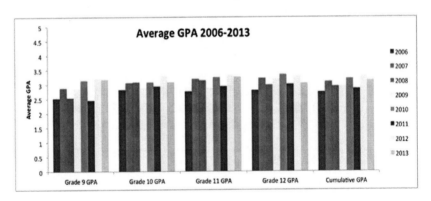

Other key student performance metrics routinely assessed involve high school completion rates, college placement rates, and college scholarship awards for students. Leap Academy graduation rates have consistently attained 100 percent for high school students since LEAP's first high school graduation in 2005, and college placement likewise has consistently reached 100 percent as well. For the 2012–13 academic years, LEAP Academy graduation rates can be compared to other schools throughout the region, which have shown less favorable results. The following graph depicts these metrics.

HIGH SCHOOL GRADUATION RATE 2012-2013

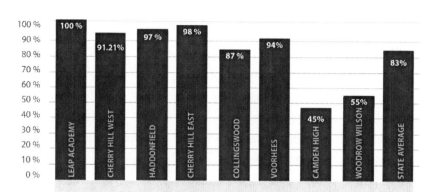

In assessing these statistics further, college placement into four-year versus two-year institutions is an important qualitative outcome further defining educational attainment and subsequent academic pursuits. Trends have progressively moved toward greater four-year college institutional placement over time for LEAP Academy graduates. Compared to 2010, when 65 percent of LEAP Academy graduates attended four-year colleges, this figure climbed to 89 percent in 2013. Likewise, student retention figures at college institutions for LEAP Academy graduates are high, with 80 percent of students remaining in college sixteen months or more after high school graduation.

Greater placement and retention within four-year colleges for LEAP Academy graduates result in part from better preparation for college studies. A measure that examines this aspect of student education involves the number of college credit courses in which students are enrolled at the LEAP Academy. In the graduating class of 2010, ten students were enrolled in college level courses. In the graduating class of 2014, twenty-four students are enrolled in college courses. Likewise, the amount of college scholarships received in total for each graduating class at LEAP Academy has progressively increased in recent years. The graduating class of 2010 earned $550,000 in tertiary education merit-based scholarships, and the graduating class of 2013 earned over $850,000 in similar awards. Both of these data sets support increasing preparedness for tertiary level educational success for students at the LEAP Academy.

In summary, the student performance metrics at LEAP Academy demonstrate positive gains in academic achievement based on regional-, district-, and state-based comparisons. The data demonstrates that, through the course of advancing grades, students attending LEAP Academy gain progressive proficiency in language arts, literacy, and mathematics. Also, cumulative annual trends among grades at the school demonstrate progressive improvements in GPAs, high school graduation rates, college placement rates, scholarship awards, and college preparation. Based on these metrics, student performance at LEAP Academy is exceeding regional school comparisons and matching average state and charter school performance throughout New Jersey. Given the surrounding environment involving Camden, these statistics provide evidence that LEAP Academy is progressing well toward specific student-oriented objectives and goals.

Student learning is personalized, and learning is competency based at LEAP Academy. Student learning takes place throughout the day, and students act as protagonists of their learning using intentional approaches to meet their varied educational needs. These structures combined with transparent systems for formative and summative assessments contribute to student learning that, based on the metrics provided, support beneficial gains in achievement in multiple areas.

Teacher Performance Metrics

The initial performance reward system for instructional staff at the LEAP Academy was initiated in 1999, and since that time significant revisions have been made to enhance the program. The most comprehensive changes occurred after 2004, when LEAP Academy teachers voted to join the New Jersey Education Association (NJEA) union. Currently, teachers are rewarded based on their performance above and beyond an annual base salary. Domains upon which these rewards are based include overall teacher effectiveness, leadership and professional contributions to the school, and overall measures of student growth and achievement. These three areas are examined to assess teacher reward amounts and to also examine organizational performance.

Teacher effectiveness scores are based on an average of scores determined through several instructional observations involving planning and preparation by the teacher, classroom environment development, and quality of educational instruction. New teachers receive a minimum of five observations annually while tenured teachers receive a minimum of four observations. Leadership and professional development scores are also based on an average for the year, which assess several domains, such as functional leadership, contributions to colleague development, effects on school culture, and others. Student growth and achievement points are then added to the above averages to obtain a comprehensive teacher performance metric. Student achievement points are based on a variety of measures, including grades, state assessments, literacy evaluations, advanced placement materials, and other dynamic indicators.

Of the total 100 points possible, the teacher effectiveness score comprises 48 possible points, leadership and professional contributions comprise 24 possible points, and student growth and achievement domains comprise 28 possible points. The total number of points determines the additional salary awarded instructors annually. Likewise, the program has onetime bonuses, which can be earned for collective improvements in student growth and achievement among teachers, as well as for exemplary leadership in different areas of educational performance. A notable aspect of this performance-based reward system is the consistent involvement and participation of the instructors in the evaluation and observation processes throughout the year. Communication, collaboration, and resource support are integral parts of this process.

Metrics concerning teacher performance can best be demonstrated through student performance, since this is the primary focus of LEAP Academy's mission. This data has been provided under the section concerning student performance metrics, which showed marked improvements in graduations rates, college placement, and subsequent college retention. In addition, grade point averages and state testing measures showed progressive improvement over the course of several years as LEAP Academy has expanded to service greater numbers of students in the Camden area. However, while these metrics directly correlate with teacher performance and effectiveness, teacher performance metrics must also be examined from an organizational standpoint. High teacher turnover rates, falling tenure rates, reductions in advanced degrees, and poor salary rewards affect efficient resource utilization and thus undermine the school's mission and objectives.

Comparison data from 2009 to 2013 is provided in the chart below. Overall, teacher growth has increased from seventy full-time teachers in 2009 to ninety-three full-time instructors in 2013. The overall retention rate between these years ranges from 57 percent to 83 percent. The average retention rate of teachers is thus 72.7 percent with a turnover rate of 27.7 percent. Compared to an urban national average teacher turnover rate of 20 percent, LEAP Academy still has progress to make in this area. The National Education Association reports that on average 33 percent of all teachers leave their schools within three years, and 46 percent leave within five years.[84] While all urban areas are struggling to retain teachers to manage costs, Camden in particular has a history of having poor retention rates because of its disadvantaged community setting.[85]

---

[84] (Kopkowski, Why they leave 2008)

[85] Eubanks, 1996.

Table 2: LEAP teachers' salaries 2009–13

Year	Number of teachers employed full time	Retention rate	Average salary	Number of tenured teachers	Percentage of teachers with advanced degrees	Percent of teachers meeting highly qualified criteria
2009	70	80%	$45,189.00	22.8%	21.4%	100%
2010	68	57.35%	$47,486.00	32.3%	26.4%	100%
2011	65	75%	$49,309.00	36.9%	20.0%	100%
2012	82	71.95%	$50,279.00	28.0%	27.6%	100%
2013	93	70.97%	$50,627.00	25.8%	16.1%	100%

Another valuable teacher performance metric involves teacher salaries. On average, LEAP Academy teachers earned $50,627 annually during 2013.[86] This compares with the state average of $63,111 for New Jersey in 2013 for all teachers in the state and an average of $44,872 for beginning teachers. Given these statistics, it might be expected that teachers with advanced degrees and tenured instructors might be represented in fewer numbers at the LEAP Academy. In 2013, 16.1 percent of instructors had advanced teaching degrees, which dropped, from 21.4 percent in 2009 and 27.6 percent in 2012. Like many urban and impoverished communities, the use of teachers without advanced degrees is required in order to achieve educational goals. Likewise, the successful ability of LEAP Academy to maintain small teacher-to-student ratios demands higher numbers of instructors. These factors likely account for the lower-than-average salaries for LEAP Academy and a smaller percentage of teachers with advanced degrees.

While teacher retention rates and average salaries are below national and state averages, respectively, LEAP Academy has excelled in achieving

---

[86] (Association 2013)

student performance, suggesting positive teacher performance and effectiveness. A significant part of this success has been attributed to the professional development programs for teachers at LEAP Academy, which provide each instructor with a Professional Improvement Plan (PIP). Resources for skill development for instructors include the Professional Development Institute, which offers monthly in-house sessions; master teacher support through modeling, coteaching feedback, and lesson planning feedback; and constructive observational analysis of teaching and classroom structures. Expert video analysis of teaching skills is also provided.

While metrics regarding the benefits of these programs are not available, it may be that these programs enhance performance of teachers without advanced degrees. This in turn would lead to higher student achievement performance among teachers who traditionally earn lower salaries. However the development of greater instructional skills may also allow greater opportunities for employment elsewhere, facilitating higher teacher turnover rates. Data to elucidate these potential cause-and-effect relationships are not currently available through traditional teacher performance metrics.

Charter School Performance Metrics

In considering performance metrics related to LEAP Academy as a charter school organization, aspects of student growth, campus growth, and financial sustainability represent key areas for evaluation. Clearly student performance and achievement highlight the main objectives for the school; however, these metrics have been previously collected and reported separately within the section on student performance. In this section, data collected regarding organizational performance outside of student academic achievements will be considered only. While student performance and organizational performance cannot be completely separated, the distinction provides some ability to discern some areas in greater detail.

Student enrollment at the LEAP Academy has progressively increased since the school's inception in 1997. Between 1997 and 2003, the school grew between 10 percent and 16.6 percent annually, which was anticipated based on plans for the progression addition of additional grades over time, achieving a full infants program with pre-K through twelfth-grade educational pipeline. Between 2003 and 2007, the school continued to expand, though not as aggressively. During these years, student enrollment grew between 3 percent and 9.5 percent, mainly through increased class size and teacher acquisition. Between 2007 and 2012, further student enrollment increases were not possible due to facility and financial constraints limiting growth opportunities. Student enrollment was relatively static during these years. However, in 2012, with the opening of the STEM High School and Elementary Programs building, capacity was increased, which permitted a 40.5 percent increase in student enrollment.

Between 1997 and 2013, total student enrollment rose from 324 students to 1,320 students. Despite these increases, LEAP Academy has maintained a constant teacher-to-student ratio of 1:20 in all grades. The commitment to maintain optimal learning ratios has been evident when assessing staffing metrics over the years. In 2008, a total of ninety-three staff members were employed by the LEAP Academy, of which sixty-four were instructional staff. These figures increased to 123 and seventy-eight, respectively, by 2012, which accommodated the marked growth of total student enrollment associated with the campus expansion. This data suggests organizational growth has not come at the expense of the school's primary educational mission and strategies.

Physical expansion of the LEAP Academy has paralleled the growth of students since 1997. Since New Jersey charter schools do not receive funding for facilities, this growth resulted from dedicated efforts in creative financing and through partner alliances. Between 1997 and 1999, the school operated in temporary modular housing. In 1999, the initial Cooper Street building acquisition, along with a $7.5 million renovation project, was completed with financial support from the Delaware River Port Authority (DRPA). Then in 2005, a second building, near to the first building on Cooper Street, was constructed through grants and creative financing supported by the DRPA and Rutgers University. In 2012, the third building along Cooper Street was financed through new market credits and private loans, resulting in the opening of the STEM High School and the Elementary Program facilities. These advances in the size of the LEAP Academy campus provided the physical capacity for growth, which has been the foundation of advances in student academic performance.

While student performance and growth combined with facility and operational expansion was of primary importance for meeting LEAP Academy goals and objectives, maintaining financial solvency and sustainability was a necessity in order to provide needed resources. With this in mind, the phased advancement in campus and student growth reflected a commitment of the organization to adhere to sound financial strategies as previously outlined. Between 2008 and 2012, total revenues collected by LEAP Academy grew from approximately $9.1 million to nearly $12.7 million. The majority of these revenues were awarded through local levies, which allocated funds to the school based on local and state shares and on student enrollment figures. However, charter schools receive only 90 percent of the per pupil public school revenues, which resulted in lower revenues than would have traditionally been received by public educational structures. Despite these challenges, combined campus and student growth resulted in revenue growth over time.

Between 2008 and 2010, organizational expenditures were consistently less than revenues, resulting in a net surplus at the end of each fiscal year. However, large capital outlays in 2011 due to campus expansion, and subsequent increases in instructional salaries due to teacher acquisitions, resulted in transient annual deficits for 2011 and 2012. Despite these recent expenditure increases, the overall fund balance for LEAP Academy at the end of 2012 was over $1.2 million, which exceeds the school's initial fund balance in 2008. This data supports the presence of conservative approaches to capital outlays and expansion aimed in maintaining sound financial stability for the organization. While various financial strategies have been utilized to support growth through loans, grants, and government bonds, these have been combined with capital investments from the school, demonstrating low-risk tactics overall.

In summary, the organizational performance metrics of LEAP Academy demonstrate progressive advancements in student enrollment, facility expansion, and staff acquisition since the beginning of the school. As a result, LEAP Academy has been able to serve increasing numbers of students while maintaining stable teacher-to-student ratios and providing better physical environments and quality education. Over fifteen years, the student population has nearly quadrupled, as has the educational campus. However, this rapid growth has been supported effectively through phased and conservative financial strategies providing consistent stability and solvency for the school.

Camden Educational District Impact

As referenced in the strategic development discussions, the LEAP Academy Project hoped to have a positive influence on the educational environment in Camden City Schools. By being a comprehensive educational plan engaging parents, community leaders and other community stakeholders, a collaborative model that embraced public school districts and their needs within the community was desired. During the initial years after LEAP Academy began, communications between LEAP Academy and the Camden Board of Education were open; however, no efforts toward change within public school domains occurred. Subsequently interactions became increasingly distant due to a perception that LEAP Academy and Camden schools existed in a competitive relationship for local and state funding and for other resources such as teachers and administrators. Despite personal efforts by LEAP Academy founders and members to change this perception, a collaborative relationship did not evolve.

LEAP Academy did change the educational discourse, however, and created a paradigm shift in the dialogue concerning the way public schools should treat children in impoverished communities. By changing the conditions and expectations, LEAP Academy became one the first and larger successful charter schools in the city and state, paving the way for other charter schools. This is supported by the number of charter schools opening in the last five years in the region and by the thousands of children who have transferred out of the Camden school system. This negative sentiment of Camden schools toward LEAP Academy was directed at other charter schools as well. Opportunities for the public school district to provide physical sites for the development of other private charter school systems in Camden were consistently rejected, despite state approval. Empty school buildings, which were not being utilized, were requested for purchase by outside charter school organizations. However, the public school district refused to negotiate access to these resources.[87] Thus while financial challenges persisted and students remained underserved in the area, the public school system retained a limited perspective focused on traditional models. Despite long-standing evidence of these failures, the public school system in Camden remained isolated in its efforts, which have continually proved unsuccessful.

Longitudinal assessments of student performance have failed to demonstrate significant improvements in Camden City schools over the last decade. The graduation rate for Camden High School in 2012–13 was only 45 percent, while the graduation rate at Woodrow Wilson High School in the city was only 55 percent. These statistics have changed very little since 1997 when LEAP Academy opened. In the meantime, graduation rates for LEAP have remained at 100 percent. The New Jersey state average among high schools shows a graduation rate of 83 percent. Therefore, it remains evident that Camden City high schools have continued to underperform despite a local example that improvements are possible through different educational and organizational strategies.

---

[87] (Mooney 2013)

HIGH SCHOOL GRADUATION RATE 2012-2013

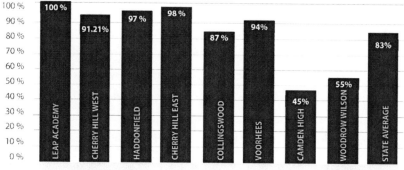

In terms of standardized test performance among students in Camden public school districts, state scores have also consistently demonstrated poor results. Proficiency among third-grade students in language arts in 2012 was attained by less than 25 percent of students, while less than 40 percent attained mathematics proficiency by state standards. Among eleventh-graders during this same year, approximately 54 percent attained language arts proficiency, while 26 percent attained proficiency in mathematics. These performance results have been relatively consistent over many years without any significant signs of improvement.

In addition to the low performance results in student academics and graduation rates, Camden public schools have also struggled financially in attaining needed resources and staffing. As an Abbott district, Camden City schools receive additional monies from the state to offset the higher poverty rates within the city and the lower tax base. On average, Camden public schools spend over $23,000 per student annually compared to the state average of $18,000 per year.[88] Charter schools in the state do not receive Abbot funding and yet produce better results consistently. However, this additional spending has done little to aid students in their academic growth or in their ability to stay in school to completion. These substandard

---

[88] (Vernon 2013)

results serve to create obstacles in recruiting talented instructors and in encouraging student effort. In contrast, the LEAP Academy has achieved reasonable results in teacher recruitment and significant results in student performance in the same community environment.

On June 25, 2013, New Jersey Governor Chris Christie announced the state takeover of the Camden public school system due to severe underperformance. The state of New Jersey has taken over three other school districts for similar reasons since 1995, with Camden now being the fourth. Unfortunately, the other three school districts have not demonstrated significant improvements in student academic performance since that time.[89] Therefore, mixed opinions exist regarding the outcome of this takeover over the long haul. Interestingly, one of the possible outcomes may be an increase in the number of privatized and public charter schools permitted in the City of Camden.[90] While this possibility is unknown, as is the potential educational success this might bring, the presence of a collaborative relationship between LEAP Academy and the public school system could have explored this possibility earlier. Instead, competitive sentiments appeared to have prevailed, limiting this opportunity previously.

Community Impact

LEAP Academy was designed as part of a community development initiative for children and families to become effective participants in the learning process through civic participation aimed at empowering their own community. LEAP emerged as part of the independent schools' movement focused on efforts to socially and educationally empower impoverished and low-income communities. The community approach was concerned with building the necessary social capital to facilitate success among families and children in both education and life.

---

[89] (Calefati, NJ.Com 2013)

[90] Calefati, 2013.

One can argue that the majority of the schools where students have high academic performance, rely on the social capital of their students and families rather than on the internal capacity of the schools themselves. Children raised in affluent communities frequently have parents with strong education and high expectations. They benefit from private tutoring, recreational outlets, and college-related stories from friends and neighbors. These resources are rather scarce in many economically distressed cities such as Camden.

Providing education that strengthens the communities simultaneously offers reciprocal benefits. Building partnerships with universities and community organizations to provide support and services to families and children establishes a foundation for young people to succeed academically. Accountability is then shared by numerous stakeholders on academic outcomes rather than on the school alone. LEAP Academy has instituted a number of practices to help youths, teachers, staff, and parents understand what it means to be accountable toward the pursuit of quality education. Similarly, efforts have occurred to influence government and public agencies, institutions of higher education, and the business sector toward a greater understanding of their roles and responsibilities regarding educational accountability.

Through this framework, integration of educational concerns has occurred within the family and community of students. The school represents a hub for family services, gatherings, and community events. Families support each other and work in partnership with the school to ensure academic accountability and school excellence. Children are beacons of hope, and families have become the tools of change within their community. The integration of social support services into the school setting allows for family preservation, support, interventions, and problem-solving efforts.

In the context of school improvement in urban America, LEAP sought to create sustainable change in a poor city. The desired change focused on three challenges arising from the presence of structural inequalities in US society. First, a lack of preparation and quality of educational options exist in many students as a result of economically depressed neighborhoods and poor preparation for education during preschool years. Second, a lack of connection exists between schools and communities and contributes to a range of insufficiencies in human and supportive services. Third, a lack of information about resources and advocacy opportunities exist within these same areas. Each of these influenced the approach taken by LEAP in addressing community needs.

Through a holistic educational experience, efforts can move beyond the classroom and into the lives of families and the community. Through this strategy, LEAP became a community service hub where families and children received health, legal, and social services, as well as adult education. A spillover benefit of this strategy resulted in improved living conditions in Camden and an expansion of educational and economic opportunities for low-income and working-class residents in the city. While Camden remains an impoverished community comprised of ethnic minorities who have below-average education and below-average employment opportunities, approximately five thousand families have improved the community's quality of life through training, education, and employment. A holistic approach has served the community as a whole quite well when examined from the lens of LEAP Academy's services.

The most serious challenge to the community in Camden, however, remains. Crime indices for the city region are high for both violent crimes and for property crimes. And children continue to represent a significant proportion of the Camden population, which places them at significant risk. Such challenges represent both threats as well as opportunities. The LEAP community has fought against violence and crime by partnering with the city and university police. Likewise, the school community is very active in protecting the neighborhood and the surrounding school area. The Rutgers Camden University police patrol program is one of the most visible and active forces against crime in the region, and it partner with LEAP Academy to provide programs for children as well as parents in enhancing community safety and security. To complement these programs, the school operates character education campaigns programs for children and families, recently receiving a mayoral award for community safety. By being a catalyst, LEAP Academy has served to empower the community as a whole to make large strides to improve the overall environment.

Baseline requirements for attending LEAP Academy include several parental commitments as part of the Parent Commitment Contract. This contract is signed by all parents of LEAP Academy students, and the contract requires a dedicated commitment of forty hours of volunteer service at the school. In addition to this level of involvement, the LEAP Academy has trained over five thousand parents through the Parent Partner Training program, which also involves 100 percent of all parents who have a student enrolled at LEAP Academy. In addition, over three hundred parents have received certification to become trainers at the Parent Partner Training program as well. These programs and contracts establish a foundation of commitment and involvement of parents, which in turn affect the community in many positive ways.

Many positive effects from parental involvement at LEAP Academy are demonstrated through parent surveys. Between 60 percent and 65 percent of parents report significant improvements in their family's abilities to read, write, and perform mathematics as a result of increased educational involvement. Likewise, between 73 percent and 75 percent of parents report increased social and emotional skills in their children's interactions with adults and children outside of the school environment. Surveys also show 70.5 percent of parents report increased abilities to talk with their children about their personal problems, while 72.5 percent describe an increase in conversations concerning their children's future aspirations and careers. Each of these responses was based on parental exposure to and involvement with LEAP Academy.

LEAP Academy has invested heavily in the community in several ways. The largest financial investment involved a $40 million investment in capital buildings along Cooper Street. Additionally, the various Centers of Excellence and their associated programs have perhaps had the largest impact on the community of Camden. Statistics demonstrate that over one thousand members have been enrolled in the Health and Wellness Center, which provides health services to the uninsured and underinsured. Likewise, more than 210 undocumented immigrant families have increased their ability to read and write through the Health Education Literacy Project (HELP). Programs also serve to train individuals on community leadership; and since LEAP Academy opened, over one thousand community leaders have completed this leadership training.

Parents and individuals participating in these Centers of Excellence report several other secondary benefits related to the community outside the LEAP Academy or its programs. Of parents surveyed, more than half reported increased participation and volunteerism with community organizations and neighborhood groups. An increased ability to appreciate various family resources were reported by 57.3 percent, while 60.9 percent described the acquisition of enhanced self-advocacy skills. Educational programs through the Centers of Excellence also accounted for 50 percent of survey participants reporting improved job-seeking abilities and employment skills. And 52.8 percent reported enhanced decision-making abilities in all areas of their lives. Given this data, the community outreach programs demonstrate positive community impact in a wide variety of areas. Parental engagement in educational activities establishes a foundation of involvement, which serves to strengthen families while focusing priorities on academic achievement. However, additional support programs through LEAP Academy take it a step further by providing social support systems that increase chances for student, family, and community success.

Partnership Impact

The underlying premise for LEAP Academy's mission supports the need for involvement among many stakeholders within the community in order to provide students with the greatest academic opportunities. This premise was incorporated into the strategic plans in the school's development, and it has remained a central concept during the growth and advancement of the LEAP Academy since 1997. Numerous governors and their administrations have been involved in supporting the LEAP Charter school trajectory efforts, including Governors Jim Florio, Christie Whitman, Jim McGreevy, Jon Corzine, and, now, Chris Christie. The Rutgers Board of Governors and Delaware River Port Authority likewise played an important role in supporting the school's mission and accomplishments. Parents represent one of the most significant partners in this educational endeavor, and results related to increased parental engagement have been reported previously. This section will address ongoing support from other community partners since the school's inception as well as the reciprocal effects LEAP Academy has had on our partners and affiliates.

Rutgers University has been a cornerstone of support both during the formation of LEAP Academy and throughout its tenure as a charter school. Leadership support and the provision of resources from Rutgers were essential in establishing LEAP Academy; but since that time, a further strengthening of a partnership relationship has evolved. This relationship is noted in LEAP Academy's Centers of Excellence, which demonstrate mutual benefits to both the university and the charter school. For example, Rutgers students have ample opportunities for research, observation, tutoring, and learning through direct participation within the centers. Law students participate in providing community services through the law clinic while gaining valuable education and direction. The Health and Wellness Center offers similar opportunities for nursing students, students studying social work curricula, and medical students in the Robert Wood Johnson Medical School. A LEAP Educational Fellowship program is available for prospective education students who wish to experience hands-on education through student instruction at LEAP Academy. A Rutgers Camden Master's Program in Educational

Policy and Leadership was also created to develop new school leaders for LEAP Academy and other Camden schools. Opportunities thus exist for Rutgers students to expand their education through practical experiences, which not only provide skills and knowledge development but also likewise meet community needs.

LEAP Academy has emerged as an important resource for undergraduate and graduate students in college interested in urban learning issues as well. LEAP has been utilized for student internships and for various course requirements at Rutgers University. The benefits of a university–charter school partnership are reciprocal. Rutgers considers LEAP a strategic partner for building precollege pipelines for recruitment of minority students. LEAP also provides the university with valuable opportunities for experiential learning for students as well as research opportunities for faculty. LEAP students appreciate the proximity to a university campus and the ability to interact with university students and faculty. Teachers at LEAP also appreciate the accessible academic resources provided by the university.

This partnership holds several lessons for other institutions of higher education seeking to build stronger bridges and communication with strategic partners. The Rutgers/LEAP partnership through the solidarity of school and community exhibits innovative ways in educating students while providing support. Through restructuring, strengthening, and revamping undergraduate and graduate programs, students become better prepared to address real life problems and to attend higher educational institutions. This partnership also enhances opportunities for students to engage university faculty steering away from the ivory tower stigma that is so prevalent in higher education. Ultimately this has resulted in increased numbers of students enrolling in the university upon graduation from LEAP.

Finally, LEAP has been successful in cultivating funding and other resources, influencing other partners to work collaboratively with LEAP to improve the environment for families and children in the community. Public and private foundations have funded evidence-based programs, which have been successfully replicated in the local school district and region. The board's chairperson has also been involved in activities that promote collaboration with other potential partners regionally, nationally, and internationally. The LEAP Academy model has served to stimulate the interest of others who wish to enhance communities and educational systems. As a result, the success at LEAP helps to perpetuate ongoing partnership potential in time.

Since 1997, over one thousand members have been enrolled in the Health and Wellness Center at LEAP Academy. In addition to the partnership associated with Rutgers University, community partners such as Cooper Family Medicine have also provided support. The Robert Wood Johnson Foundation, as the biggest supporter, provided millions of dollars to support the Health Clinic at the school. The Fund for New Jersey, Geraldine Dodge Foundation, ATT Foundation, and Verizon Foundation also funded planning efforts for the Rutgers Centers of Excellence. As a result of the positive impacts on students, their families, and the community at large, partnership relationships for support have continued to expand during the course of LEAP Academy's existence.

Community partners have also been instrumental in the development and growth of the Early Learning Research Academy (ELRA), which provides education to children between birth and age five. In 2005, the John S. and James L. Knight Foundation provided a $1 million grant to support training and research related to early learning. And in 2007, the foundation funded a $2 million grant in capital support for a new ELRA building. This ELRA facility now serves 126 toddlers and preschoolers in a dual language capacity. During this same time, the New Jersey Economic Development Recovery Act program donated another $1 million toward the ELRA facility, while the Kresge Foundation funded a major effort in a community campaign to generate support for the ELRA project. This effort brought local banks, businesses, entrepreneurs, families, and other key stakeholders together in support of ELRA. Through these partnerships, as well as with the professional guidance and contributions of Rutgers

University, ELRA has flourished and become established as an important Early Learning Research Academy to promote quality early learning for minority children in the city and has become a strategy learning site for the city. As previously noted, the Prudential Insurance Company provided an initial grant to establish the Parent Academy at LEAP. Since that time, thousands of parents have participated in this training, and more than half of the parents at LEAP report an increase in community activism since their child attended the school. In 1999, the William Penn Foundation contributed another $330,000 toward the Parent Academy, and in 2004 awarded the LEAP Academy a grant for $693,000 for the Center for Strategic Urban Community Leadership (CSUCL). These partnerships have made a significant impact on the Camden area, with more than one thousand community leaders having been trained through the CSUCL. Resource opportunities have been identified for these community efforts, and programs have been well supported based on the positive intentions and results of the programs themselves.

In addition to direct improvements to the Camden community at large, there has been reciprocity of benefits enjoyed more directly in specific circumstances. In particular, this involves tertiary educational enrollment among LEAP Academy graduates. Between 2005 and 2010, a majority of students enrolled in local college centers. Specifically, 20 percent attended Rutgers University, 10 percent attended Rowan University, and 31 percent attended Camden County College. In 2010, 92 percent of the graduates from LEAP Academy enrolled in colleges within the state of New Jersey. These statistics demonstrate a direct return on investment for these institutions from student enrollment in addition to the more indirect community benefits described. Such benefits serve to strengthen partnership relations due to their reciprocal nature of benefit.

A final area, which exhibits increased support among community partners, involves scholarship and endowment support for students at LEAP Academy. In 1999, the Rutgers/LEAP Alfredo Santiago Endowed Scholarship was established, awarding students financial support after graduating from LEAP and attending Rutgers University. Later on this scholarship was expanded by a large donation by Vernon Hill, CEO of Commerce Bank, allowing students attending other colleges to also be eligible for endowment funds. Despite humble beginnings, the Alfredo Santiago Scholarship endowment fund has now grown to over $1.3 million with the assistance of numerous other partners who help sponsor a fund-raising gala each year. This scholarship program has helped dozens of students obtain the necessary financial resources to pursue higher educational attainment.

In several areas, LEAP Academy has enjoyed increasing relationships with community partners in the last fifteen years. These relationships have allowed significant advancement in community programs, essential infrastructures, and student opportunities. Both direct and indirect benefits have provided incentives for such partnerships to grow and expand, and a shared vision with mutually beneficial objectives has provided the foundation for continued efforts by all stakeholders toward educational and community progress in Camden. In these instances, collaboration and cooperation were able to flourish, yielding stronger partnership relations over time.

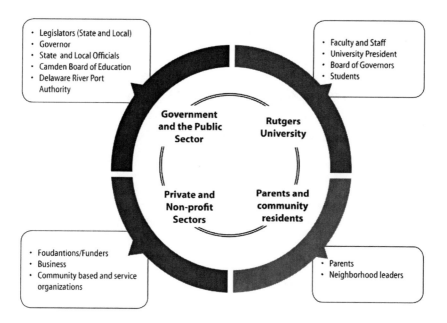

VI: Educational Lessons learned and Best Practices identified from the LEAP Model

From 1997 to present, LEAP Academy has made tremendous gains and established a strong educational foundation within the community of Camden. Despite numerous social, economic, and cultural barriers, the charter school has not only provided hundreds of children with a comprehensive education and access to tertiary educational opportunities, but it has also empowered them and their families as individuals. This holistic, comprehensive approach has resulted in advances within individuals, families, and the community demonstrating evidence that new perspectives and strategies are needed, particularly in communities such as Camden.

The challenges are formidable, and the degree of commitment required is significant in relation to improving educational systems. Regardless, the LEAP Model has provided many insights into many best practices, which can be upscale within other community-based educational models. When community resources are limited and the environment is antagonistic to student learning, implementing these practices is a means by which obstacles can be overcome. Likewise, these strategies and approaches are founded upon proven themes of engagement, empowerment, and accountability. Through these philosophies, students, families, and community stakeholders participate toward a common goal and vision. Combining this with evidence-based practices that have proven to be effective is essential for the future of education. The following are LEAP Academy's seven additional best practices under four factors that have supported our successful college efforts: (1) student factor, (2) teacher development, (3) organizational, and (4) stakeholders and alliances have been essential for the model. Each factor and best practice is described below.

Factors of LEAP Best Practices

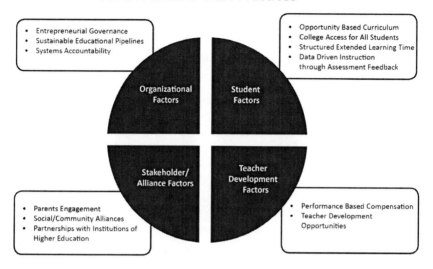

- Entrepreneurial Governance
- Sustainable Educational Pipelines
- Systems Accountability

- Opportunity Based Curriculum
- College Access for All Students
- Structured Extended Learning Time
- Data Driven Instruction
  through Assessment Feedback

Organizational Factors

Student Factors

Stakeholder/ Alliance Factors

Teacher Development Factors

- Parents Engagement
- Social/Community Alliances
- Partnerships with Institutions of Higher Education

- Performance Based Compensation
- Teacher Development Opportunities

Student Factors: Best Practices
Opportunity-Based Focus on Curriculum Structures

As educational systems advance, an important strategy must involve effective alignment between curricula and life opportunity. Periodically throughout history, advances in society have caused some occupations and knowledge to become relatively obsolete while opening the door for different sets of skills and insights. Curricula that focus only on standardized achievements from an academic standpoint without considering the needs of society poorly serve the long-term needs of students and their communities. Making school curricula relevant to modern-day and future needs allows greater opportunity for students to attain their life goals in career aspirations, economic attainment, and personal achievements. By focusing on student-centered approaches, LEAP raised the bar for all students to obtain the skills and knowledge needed for success and help close the gap between subgroups in achievement, resulting in higher rates of postsecondary readiness and attainment.

In 2009, LEAP Academy invested greatly in this direction with the development of a specialized high school focused on science, technology, engineering, and mathematics (STEM). An overall investment of $12.5 million permitted the expansion of the LEAP campus with a thirty-nine-thousand-square-foot building dedicated to these curricula. Courses in physics, chemistry, computing programs, and engineering were incorporated into regular course structures, and state-of-the-art equipment and practices were implemented as part of the learning process. These practices included project-based learning as well as a comprehensive fabrication lab, which encouraged conceptual creations and reality-based problem solving. Computer-aided design software, digital learning, Google Sketch-up, and many other design and mechanical tools are readily available to students as part of their education. Consequently, Leap students become engaged thinkers, ethical citizens, and entrepreneurial spirits.

By incorporating project-based learning with relevant concepts and subjects into modern environments, students gain practical knowledge and skills at an earlier age. Not only does this allow such abilities to advance more comprehensively over time, but this also prepares students better for college and careers where employment opportunities are most abundant. Consistently, students demonstrate higher levels of engagement, since problem-solving and creative exercises have greater relevance to real life. Likewise, they gain a better appreciation of their own individual interests, which helps guide subsequent decisions about future education and career.

The principles of learning are based on the mastery of course knowledge and on assessment and student tracking systems. Assessment is meaningful and provides positive leaving experiences for students. Different opportunities to support more time for those who need to learn are based on individual needs. College access and career readiness is stressed, which provides greater voice and choice for students. This is in alignment with National Curriculum Standards and the Partnership for Assessment of Readiness for College and Careers (PARCC), which is a consortium of eighteen states, plus the District of Columbia and the US Virgin Islands. This consortium works together to develop a common set of K-12 assessments in English and math focused on college readiness and career planning. These new K-12 assessments build a pathway toward college and career readiness by the end of high school, track students' progress toward this goal after third grade, and provide teachers with timely information regarding instruction. While the PARCC assessments will be ready for states to administer during the 2014–15 school year, LEAP has been pursuing these efforts this since 2005.

As a result, opportunity-based curriculum structures serve to enhance student engagement and empower students in their confidence and abilities. Ultimately these factors increase success rates not only in education but also in subsequent careers and life skills.

As will be highlighted in other best practices, student accountability is a part of these curriculum opportunities. Students enrolled in LEAP Academy through the educational lottery have the opportunity to enroll in the STEM High School only if certain criteria are met. These criteria include a grade point average of 3.0 or higher, proven proficiency in math and science, the successful completion of an admission exam, and a commitment to attend the STEM summer programs. By insisting upon these requirements, students learn to appreciate that the STEM curriculum is a privilege providing a unique opportunity. This combined with enhanced engagement and empowerment serves to encourage even greater commitment and success over time. As a result, students receive practical skills and knowledge needed for the real world as well as an appreciation for the education received.

College Access for All Students

More than 90 percent of the adults over age twenty-five years living in Camden lack a college education. As a result, many students lack role models for higher education and also adopt an attitude that presumes college is inaccessible. One of the most important best practices for LEAP

Academy has thus been to raise the levels of expectation concerning student enrollment in college after high school. This increased expectation has been accomplished in many ways, which center on greater access to college preparation and acceptance, instruction, curricula, role models, and assessment. For these reasons, college placement and enrollment has been consistently at 100 percent since LEAP Academy was able to provide educational services from kindergarten through twelfth grade.

The Center for College Access was established as one of LEAP's Centers of Excellence in 2005 as a means to raise college awareness and readiness. College access education begins in preschool as teachers and administrators consistently reinforce expectations for student enrollment in college among students and families. College Access creates a college culture through a pipeline from birth to completion of LEAP's programs. Academic organizations, student government associations, national honor societies, and leadership programs develop college level skills, while students are acclimated to other college-bound individuals. Academic advisement and coaching sessions are routinely performed for all students, again highlighting the need to consider career aspirations and related college pursuits. These efforts create the conditions and environments among students early, which demonstrate the expectation that each student will attend college and succeed in the process.

As students advance through higher levels of education at LEAP, additional access to college information and preparation are available. Students participate in dual enrollment opportunities where they attend high school courses in a college setting. This serves to expose students to college environments while also introducing them to college level courses. LEAP also has a student ambassador program where college students serve as mentors and role models for LEAP students. Through the Center for College Access, students also receive college entrance exam preparations, assistance with college applications, and student grants and financial aid information. LEAP students get individualized attention through time and effort from staff, and the students get an opportunity to tell their stories through their own voices and lenses in those college essays. College placement services are intentional, in addition to LEAP-sponsored college fairs and target interviews, which students are encouraged to attend.

The philosophy at LEAP Academy has been to immerse students in a culture that expects each student will attend tertiary educational pursuits upon completion of high school. This practice is essential in communities such as Camden, which offers little social capital to incentivize children in these directions. By establishing high levels of academic expectation, and by providing opportunities to gain knowledge, skills, and resources needed for college enrollment, students embrace the chance to pursue advanced education. College and higher learning is competency-based, which means students at LEAP demonstrate learning by mastering core competencies and bodies of knowledge through portfolio academies and field internships, rather than on a student's age and hours schedule in a classroom. These approaches have shown to be the means by which students can attain career aspirations and life desires, and as a result, students actively engage in college access activities. Including parents and family members into this process serves to strengthen these effects to an even greater degree. Based on LEAP's ability to achieve and maintain 100 percent college enrollment and high levels of college completion among its graduates, providing these college access support structures is deemed to be a clear best practice for primary and secondary educational systems.

Structured Extended Learning Time

Given the high risk social environments for children and youth in Camden, strategies were considered that offer some protections for unwanted behaviors through alternatives to traditional school structures. As noted, Camden's elevated high school dropout rates increase the likelihood of crime, unemployment, and social dependency among residents. In addition, illegal activities such as drug trafficking are common in the community, since legal avenues of employment are limited. Such environments offer temptations to youth in particular and do little to encourage academic performance, high school completion, and advanced career aspirations. Replacing these environments and conditions with more constructive ones was identified as important.

Over the course of time, the LEAP model has identified extended learning time as an important structure for students in changing environments and cultures for learning. Initially the school day was constructed to last from 8:00 a.m. until 4:00 p.m. for students, due to less than desirable academic performance, and these hours correlated better with work hours for parents. Extracurricular temptations for negative behaviors were reduced as a result of these scheduling strategies. For example, a sizable percentage of teen pregnancies occur between 1:00 p.m. and 3:00 p.m., when students are home without parental supervision. Extending school schedules eliminates these risks and replaces them with learning opportunities and positive environments. These results were promising and resulted in an even longer school day, from 8:00 a.m. to 5:30 p.m., as well as extension of the number of calendar school days from 180 to 200 annually.

While many schools have experimented with alternative schedules and extended day programs, the best practice identified in this situation involves scheduling time for student learning and instruction and to engage educators in reflection and planning. Extended time allows for educational activities in conjunction with parent and family schedules. Many school systems structure such programs around resources available for student busing, classroom availability, and/or instructor access. While these resources must be considered, optimal scheduling of such extended learning sessions relates mostly to parents and family needs when student goals are placed as a priority. Having realized this, LEAP Academy also offers a Learning Center Extended Learning Program for students to learn together. This program offers academic tutoring, homework assistance, and other extracurricular activities through 8:00 p.m. for students. As a result, students enjoy positive, structured environments while parents attend training programs and other responsibilities.

Through the creative use of field trips, educational fairs, and community service opportunities, the ability to extend scholastic and extracurricular time to LEAP students has been accomplished utilizing existing resources. All total, more than five hundred additional school hours have been provided annually to students through extended day learning. Learning at LEAP is personalized, since every adult and peer knows his or her child. This practice is designed with the student in mind so that a majority of their time is spent in constructive learning and encouraging climates, which promotes academic achievement and personal success.

Data-Driven Instruction through Assessment Feedback

The LEAP Academy, as part of its students-first strategies, notably invests significant efforts into ensuring student instruction and curricula provide optimal opportunities for students to excel in a comprehensive learning environment. In addition to establishing core curriculum content standards based on local, state, and national standards of achievement, LEAP Academy goes well beyond these efforts to develop, assess, refine, and reevaluate instructional methods and content regularly based on data instruction results. This commitment supports evidence-based practices, which demonstrate effectiveness not only for school-wide student advancement but for individual student success as well. In other words, data and its continual analysis are necessary in order to perpetually improve instruction for students, allowing them to be best prepared for ongoing learning and life achievement.

As a foundation, LEAP Academy's approach to student instruction involves complex and comprehensive considerations. While large concepts are targeted within each curricular domain, interdisciplinary applications are routinely taught to enhance a cohesive knowledge base and to foster innovative and creative skills in critical thinking and problem solving. In addition, through instruction regarding communication, social responsibility, and cultural and global awareness, learning is linked to the development of personal management skills. In addition, ongoing evaluations of individual student cultures and experiences are invited through a variety of learning activities, and real-world practical application of knowledge is promoted regularly. These strategies are combined with continual assessments of student knowledge through several measures, which include classroom performance tasks, collaboration leadership guidance, group participation projects, teacher-designed assessments, and local and state standardized achievement tests. Through these measures, students receive frequent opportunities for feedback with progressive ownership of their learning efforts. These strategies foster increasing levels of accountability among LEAP students within a culture of high learning expectations.

While these efforts encourage student feedback and multifaceted instruction, they also provide teachers opportunities to enhance instructional content within their classrooms. LEAP Academy has identified this process of lesson study to be critical in advancing instructional content and methods in optimizing student learning capacity. Through collaborative teacher and student interactions, teachers identify both strengths and weaknesses of current instructions, which in turn allow continual improvements. Areas involving literacy skills, communication, information gathering, information processing, critical thinking skills, and problem-solving abilities are frequently examined and refined through lesson study. In addition, by linking student performance to teacher compensation programs, additional incentives to enhance student instruction are evident.

In addition to classroom data assessments and feedback, a school-wide instructional team conducts evaluations on a regular basis. LEAP Academy performs comprehensive curricular audits, which assess instruction curriculum in relation to local, state, and national standards. Through this audit, curriculum evaluations are divided into four categories. These include: (1) intended, (2) enacted, (3) learned, and (4) assessed components, which offer multiple areas to improve current instruction opportunities. Intended curriculum refers to instructional materials and their alignment with desired educational objectives. Enacted curriculum relates to the actual curriculum taught by teachers in the classroom as evidenced through direct observation. Learned curriculum examines student work through classroom activities and teacher-based assessments in comparison to educational goals. And finally, assessed curriculum correlates formal assessments at local and state levels to instructional objectives. Each of these areas of the audit offers a chance to correct or improve areas where underperformance may be present.

As evident in the student performance results previously reported, ongoing efforts to improve student instruction and curriculum are critically important for optimal learning environments. Without feedback from student performance at multiple levels, the implementation of effective strategies becomes limited and poorly guided. Likewise, unless direct objective data is obtained from multiple data points concerning instruction and curricula, key areas where improvement are needed may be ignored, neglected, or overlooked. Educational systems must utilize comprehensive data to guide effective changes. Only through such assessments can effective instructional methods and curricula be proven. As a result, LEAP Academy invests heavily in identifying such evidence-based practices to further its mission to enhance student learning through optimal instructional methods and curricula. These efforts have repeatedly demonstrated great success in enabling progressive advancement in student performance.

Teacher Development Factors: Best Practice Performance Based Compensation

LEAP Academy has maintained a commitment toward providing compensation incentives to teachers based on performance indicators. The LEAP Academy mission of being student-focused places student performance as a priority, and, therefore, incentive structures were deemed important in many aspects to ensure the entire organization was pursuing this objective. In particular, aligning teacher preparation, training, certification, and instruction, as well as classroom strategies with improving student performance goals was the most important aspect related to this goal. Certainly student empowerment and accountability efforts remain imperative to the school's mission, but educational instruction and professional guidance must utilize effective and efficient methods of teaching to this end as well. This remains a philosophy and strategy of the LEAP model.

Initial performance-based compensation guidelines established in 1999 were subsequently enhanced and developed over time. As educational research provided guidance, LEAP's performance-based compensation changed. Currently the LEAP performance model is built on the Danielson Framework, which is utilized as a guide in this regard to determine compensation based on variables such as teacher effectiveness, leadership and professional development, and student achievement measures. In addition, individual and collective reward incentives are part of this structure, not only to promote efforts by each teacher in advancing his or her own personal achievements, but also to encourage collaborative efforts among all educators in achieving higher performance goals. In this way, innovative strategies that demonstrate effectiveness may be shared among all educators rather than being isolated within certain classrooms or departments. This framework and strategy for compensation was thus developed not only from research support but also in alignment with teacher input over a period of time and from organizational values and objectives.

As indicated in the results section, the performance-based compensation system can be examined from different perspectives. From a teacher perspective, the number of tenured teachers and the overall number of educators has grown progressively over time. In addition, retention rates among teachers have averaged around 70 percent over the last several years. Based on teacher surveys, the national average retention rate is 84.5 percent.[91] Assessment of this statistic, however, must take into account the environment in which LEAP Academy exists. Lower retention rates would be expected in a community such as Camden with high crime, limited resources, and low standards of living. Indeed the retention rate in Camden among teachers prior to LEAP Academy's presence was remarkably lower.

Teacher results also indicate the percentage of teachers with advanced master's and doctoral degrees continues to grow progressively. Additionally, 100 percent of teachers are identified as being highly qualified based on the federal definition of a highly qualified teacher. This is defined as a teacher who is fully certified and/or licensed by the state, holds at least a bachelor's degree from a four-year institution, and demonstrates competence in each core academic subject area in which the teacher teaches. As part of LEAP Academy's development programs, teachers attain high levels of competency from internal training and professional development. This has been found to be a best practice in improving the quality of instruction, although such skill development may provide incentives for teachers to leave to other schools in more affluent communities with higher salary structures. Because of this, performance-based compensation incentives for teachers cannot be viewed as an isolated best practices strategy but must be considered alongside student and community improvements.

The performance-based compensation system can also be examined from the standpoint of student performance and organizational objectives. Results indicate significant and progressive improvements in student performance on state and local standardized examinations, which cover mathematics and literacy areas. In addition, student graduation rates are 100 percent, along with 100 percent college acceptance rates with the addition of the teacher performance based incentives. Since these measures of student achievement, in addition to classroom performance

---

[91] (Statistics 2010)

measures, drive compensation, teachers invest greater energies into student instruction and learning. This incentive, combined with needed support structures, provides a strong recipe for student success. By providing support and pursuing realistic objectives, educators will maintain positive attitudes concerning efforts toward continued growth and improvements relative to compensation incentives. This is true at both individual and collective levels.

A final word concerning the performance-based compensation system for teachers and its use as a best practice involves its objective nature and the involvement of teachers in the evaluation process. The measures examined within the compensation system are based on objective assessments of teacher effectiveness, student performance, and professional development, rather than subjective assessments and opinions. Assessment metrics and observational practices have been refined over time for consistency and reliability. In addition, teacher feedback and involvement plays an important part in the process, allowing teachers to provide information and perspectives related to their performance assessments. This has provided mutual benefits for teachers and administrators in enhancing performance over time and in developing cooperative relationships with a common goal. In addition to the establishment of the performance-based compensation system, the structure and administration of the system through teacher inclusion and participation has also been defined as a best practice for institutional success.

Teacher Development Opportunities

As noted in the discussion of performance-based incentives for educators, the effort to encourage teacher advancement and satisfaction can be undermined when adequate support structures are not in place. Incentives mean little if teachers do not feel the ability exists to meet those incentives, or if the effort required far exceeds the reward attained. With this in mind, the LEAP model includes well-established systems for ongoing teacher training and development, which provide such support structures.

Several resources are made available to teachers to improve their skills, knowledge, and performance metrics, and individualized plans are created for each teacher regarding his or her professional development.

Strategies developed concerning teacher development have been the result of both literature review and experiential observations. Based upon the performance-based compensation metrics and observations, teachers are provided with a formal review of their strengths and areas of development. As a result, areas for improvement are identified, which can help individual teachers meet their own professional and personal goals while also progressively pursuing objectives of the LEAP Academy system. Also, given the cooperative and collaborative nature of these evaluations, open dialogues exist that provide opportunities for creative explorations of development strategies. Many of the existing teacher development practices have evolved from such conversations.

Three key strategies for development and support for teachers comprise the best practices identified by the LEAP model. The first involves direct observational techniques, which can be used to provide teachers with feedback and data by an instructional team. This information then serves as the basis for professional improvement plans for each individual teacher. An array of observational structures is currently in place. These include direct observations of classroom instruction and management over several sessions, from which specific feedback is provided to teachers. Likewise, similar observations and reviews of classroom artifacts, classroom designs, student assignments, and student assessments are performed providing additional data and information. If desired, videotaping of teacher instruction is performed with subsequent expert analysis, which yields additional information. Each of these objective measures helps identify strengths and development areas where specific strategies can be invoked to improve skills and abilities.

The second best practice concerning teacher development involves pairing teachers with master teachers for guidance and coaching as their peers review their work and provide feedback. Offerings for teacher development include modeling sessions, coteaching opportunities, and lesson planning support with master teachers, who also provide ongoing feedback and suggestions. These learning opportunities from experienced instructional experts not only help enhance skills and performance among LEAP teachers, but also contribute to the collaborative culture within the school. Likewise, these assessments by educational colleagues help validate other objective measures of assessment and feedback already received. As a result, each support structure reinforces the other in encouraging professional training and development.

Finally, formal teacher development opportunities for growth are also provided through the LEAP Academy's Professional Development Institute. Monthly in-house sessions are offered to teachers to advance their skills and knowledge in a variety of areas, and many of these sessions are conducted by master teachers or educational experts of the LEAP instructional team. Similar to master teacher coaching and individual professional improvement plans, teachers receive individual peer assessment feedback from their instructional team leaders and coaches. These formal sessions reinforce other areas of development and improvement. The overall focus of LEAP's developmental programs for teachers thus provides a consistent and accurate guide in advancing professional abilities. These efforts then add to teacher confidence, self-efficacy, personal satisfaction, and, eventually, student performance, which benefit everyone. The high rates of tenured teachers, the high percentage of those identified as highly qualified, and marked improvements in student performance support these strategies in teacher development as clearly a best practice.

As with other themes within the LEAP model, accountability and empowerment remain a focus with teacher development and advancement. Teachers are held accountable through objective measures of evaluation, observation, and feedback, which enable them to have autonomy in developing their own professional improvement plan. At the same time, empowerment for advance development is provided through the numerous structures in place to aid teachers toward these goals. The results have demonstrated that these efforts combined with compensation incentives offer great advantages and ultimately help the LEAP Academy achieve its overall mission, vision, and objectives.

Organizational Factors: Best Practices
Entrepreneurial Governance

One of the key strategies identified from the beginning of the LEAP Project, in addition to the engagement of multiple stakeholders, involved establishing a diverse governance structure focused on organizational mission, vision, and objectives. In contrast to other educational governance structures common to the traditional public sector, where school board members are elected by the citizens or appointed by the mayor, the decision in establishing LEAP Academy's school board was designed based on stakeholder appointment and representation. This difference has resulted in many changes unique to LEAP Academy, and has offered many advantages.

The governance board at LEAP oversees a variety of aspects of the school, including policies, instructional oversight, finance, operations, strategic planning, fund raising, hiring and firing, growth, and expansion. The diffuse nature of these areas of oversight naturally permit varying perspectives regarding which decisions and directions may be optimal in relation to educational goals. It became important, therefore, to ensure these different viewpoints were accommodated by ensuring each stakeholder had a voice within the governance structures. As a result, the board of trustees for LEAP Academy is a collection of partners with different interests, experiences, and areas of expertise. Not only does this enhance the thoroughness of considerations over educational matters, but it also enriches the creative and innovative nature of those decisions and solutions.

Members of the board of trustees currently include five parent representatives, who represent the interests of the parent community and the community at large. Other board members represent anchor institutions of higher education, various businesses, and community interests locally and throughout the state. Representatives from university institutions, senior living centers, property management firms, acquisition and merger groups, and telecommunications businesses are board member participants, providing unique viewpoints and knowledge regarding oversight on the school business operations and management. Other board members include physician representatives of Cooper Hospital in Camden, LEAP Academy alumni, professors from Rowan University, and several representatives from Rutgers University. In addition to professors from Rutgers, the chancellor and dean of off-campus programs are routinely included as board members as well.

By having representatives from the community, parents, alumni, local businesses, and higher educational institutions, LEAP's governance has adopted less of a political structure and more of an entrepreneurial culture. The diversity enjoyed among the board members serves to augment creative approaches to problems, since the governance culture remains open, flexible, and evidenced-based. Inclusion of higher learning institutional members routinely infuses research-based ideas while other members provide experiential and practical knowledge proven to be effective. All the while, other members maintain a focus on the LEAP Academy core mission, ensuring the needs of students are being met.

Many areas have served as examples of this entrepreneurial style of governance. Through LEAP Academy's expansion and growth over the last several years, ongoing needs for financial resources were present. Entrepreneurial creativity provided several directions and solutions, which made acquisition of these resources possible. Likewise, innovative solutions to performance-based incentive program dilemmas and community resource structure challenges evolved out of discussion and cooperation among various board members with different strengths and other assets. Rather than experiencing political posturing, the group enjoyed constructive collaboration resulting in proactive efforts and efficient use of governance synergies.

The use of entrepreneurial governance structures for educational systems has proven to be a best practice for the LEAP Academy model, and it is presumed to be effective for other educational systems as well. Just as health-care services and social needs vary from individual to individual and from community to community, so do educational needs. Traditional governance structures for most school boards lack a composition of members or an environment that promotes entrepreneurial collaboration and creativity. However, these ingredients are important in tailoring instructional practices, school operations, and resource acquisitions to meet the educational needs of the twenty-first century student population. By developing governance structures, which invite entrepreneurial and innovative solutions, optimal use of resources, and identification of more effective strategies, urban schools will evolve into better places for learning.

Sustainable Educational Pipelines

Governance at LEAP has focused on establishing and sustaining an educational pipeline from birth to college. The board has been committed to creating a system where children enter at a young age and are provided with the best quality of education, as well as the best experience to transition and succeed in college. Every child is accounted for through his or her journey along this pipeline. Preliminary data confirm that the longer a child stays in the LEAP pipeline, the better he or she performs academically.

This emphasis on a pipeline also incorporates families as LEAP provides enrollment preference to siblings and, therefore, parents become a part of this pipeline as well.

Systems of Accountability

Accountability is everyone's responsibility and requires time and effort to ensure that the focus is on children learning, while paying attention to assure that all aspects of the organization are working and in sync with producing results. The board's work is guided by constant review of data of student progress, as well as ongoing review of satisfaction levels and teacher competence. Special attention is provided by feedback data received from parents and students on an annual basis, as well as alumni surveys.

Stakeholder Alliance Factors: Best Practice
Parents' Engagement

The planning process for LEAP Academy set a strong foundation for sustaining parental engagement with the school. Structures were created to include parents in the governance structure of the school through membership in the board of trustees, as employees by leveraging employment in various positions, as volunteers through creation of a Parent Resource Center dedicated to leveraging parental participation in programs and activities, as learners through the creation of a Parents Academy with multiple programs, and as customers of structures created to provide services such as the Health Center. The high level of parental engagement is one of the most successful outcomes of the school. At LEAP, families are valued and cultivated through multiple avenues. LEAP embraces four principles for family engagement: (1) parents are encouraged to be introspective about their own parenting, (2) parents are encouraged to consider what roles they can play to improve the school and the community, (3) parents are trained to think about future possibilities and expectations for both their children and themselves, and (4) parents are encouraged to provide leadership for change that is beneficial to the school and the community. At LEAP, parents are critical to developing a student-centered culture. Parents are the biggest asset in our LEAP community. The school has become their community village, where they share meaning and power in support of their children.

Social/Community Alliances

LEAP's engagement for improving the outcomes for families and children extends to the community at large. LEAP has been able to capitalize on local partnerships as a strategy for growth, sustainability, and relevance. The social capital needed to support the school comes from the social and community alliances LEAP has made with the following organizations in Camden: the mayor and city council, the state aquarium, the National Science Institute, Corriel Research Institute, Cooper Hospital, the Delaware River Port Authority, the Martin Lockee River Sharks, Bright Horizons, Cramer Hill Community Development Corporation, Cooper Ferry Community Development Corporation, TD Bank, Wells Fargo Bank, PNC Bank, Beneficial, Republic Bank, and others that have contributed to our growth and development. The Reinvestment Fund group and RBC capital has been critical to LEAP's growth in facilities funding. Government officials from the state Department of Education, its Charter School office, and the Charter School Association have been instrumental in providing guidance and oversight to LEAP's growth and sustainability. Local legislative leaders and representatives at both the state and national level have been instrumental in advocating efforts to strengthen the charter school law and bringing resources to the charter movement locally. These partnerships have been instrumental in securing four new school buildings and attracting resources to sustain the school's programs. LEAP's work is also relevant to the larger efforts for community development in Camden. The school has established itself as an anchor institution for education and for community development.

Partnerships with Institutions of Higher Education

LEAP's alliances with institutions of higher education are paramount to its agenda for college readiness for all students. The board includes representation from each major college in the region (Rutgers, Rowan, and Camden County College), and students take college-level courses while still in high school. These partnerships also allow for fluid interaction between university faculties and LEAP's faculty and students around content work in core academic areas. As explained in previous sections, this is an important feature for sustaining the college placement rates that are at the core of LEAP's vision. In addition, LEAP is signing Memorandum Of Understanding with colleges and universities to ensure that its students are getting the necessary early college experience and training. These institutions of higher learning also allow LEAP to work in collaboration with the best faculty and research-based approaches and civic engagement programs that target college students to work with LEAP. The Jump Start program is an excellent example of how participants are receiving their early learning training and academic preparation. About two hundred college students from nearby institutions are engaged in working with the LEAP district in academic learning projects, courses, and internships for their undergraduate and graduate education programs. LEAP provides opportunities for graduate students returning from Peace Corps programs to teach as teacher fellows and gain experience in student teaching. LEAP partners with local colleges to allow for students to conduct their practice teaching by becoming teacher fellows at LEAP, enabling the school to recruit the best and most talented candidates for teachers. Rutgers University developed a unique program for LEAP teachers to become principals by developing a unique Master in Public Administration-Educational Policy and School Leadership Program. These programs provide the training for instructional school leaders to become principals, directors of charter schools, and school supervisors. All of LEAP's principals and school supervisors have graduated from this program, and all of them have come from within the ranks of LEAP Academy teachers. This is an important lesson for building leadership capacity that is sustainable within the LEAP organization. All LEAP Academy College Access staff are graduates of this program, and all have shown great capacity for growth as future leaders at LEAP. In the context of lessons from an inner city school, these partnerships are critical for a charter school to be successful.

Conclusion

The results from the Miracle on Cooper Street and the many lessons presented here suggest that at the end of the day the ultimate measure for all involved in this work is the number of children we have graduated who are managing to succeed in college and are able to break with the cycle of poverty and live productive and happy lives. The scaling-up lessons mentioned in the LEAP case study served as examples of what works for LEAP Academy. This is especially the case when growth is managed in a purposeful way. However, it is important to remember that the factors of success offered here are guidelines and best practices that have worked for us. Every school that approaches growth must do so with a focus on its own organization structure and culture as well as an understanding of the communities it works to serve and the state and local policy contexts in which it is nested.

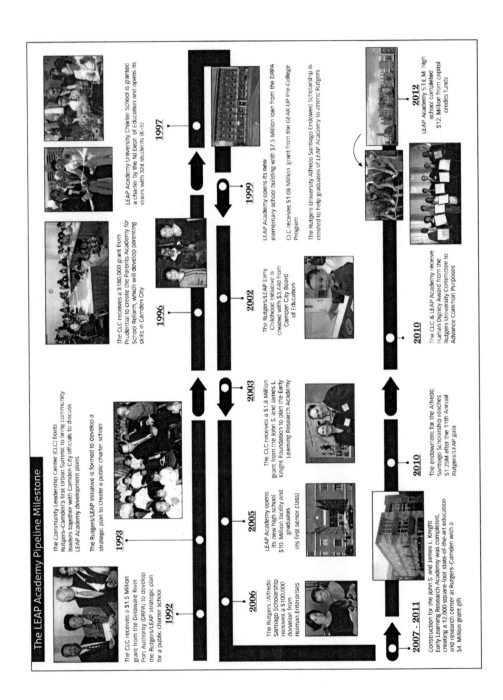

The LEAP Academy Pipeline Milestone

1992
The CLC receives a $1.5 Million grant from the Delaware River Port Authority (DRPA) to develop the Rutgers/LEAP strategic plan for a public charter school

1993
The Community Leadership Center (CLC) hosts Rutgers–Camden's first Urban Summit to bring community leaders together with Camden City officials to discuss LEAP Academy development plans

The Rutgers/LEAP initiative is formed to develop a strategic plan to create a public charter school

1996
The CLC receives a $180,000 grant from Prudential to create the Parents Academy for School Reform, which will develop parenting skills in Camden City

1997
LEAP Academy University Charter School is granted a charter by the NJ Dept. of Education and opens its doors with 324 students (K–5)

1999
LEAP Academy opens its new elementary school building with $7.5 Million loan from the DRPA

CLC receives $1.08 Million grant from the GEAR-UP Pre-College Program

The Rutgers University Alfredo Santiago Endowed Scholarship is created to help graduates of LEAP Academy to attend Rutgers

2002
The Rutgers/LEAP Early Childhood Initiative is created with $3,440 from Camden City Board of Education

2003
The CLC receives a $1.8 Million grant from the John S. and James L. Knight Foundation to plan the Early Learning Research Academy

2005
LEAP Academy opens its new high school $10. Million facility and graduates (its first senior class)

2006
The Rutgers /Alfredo Santiago Scholarship receives a $100,000 donation from Holman Enterprises

2007 - 2011
Construction for the John S. and James L. Knight Early Learning Research Academy was completed, creating a 12,000 square-foot state-of-the-art education and research center at Rutgers–Camden with a $4. Million grant gift

2010
The endowment for the Alfredo Santiago Scholarship reaches $1.25M after the 11th Annual Rutgers/LEAP gala

2010
The CLC & LEAP Academy receive Human Dignity Award from the Rutgers University Committee to Advance Common Purposes

2012
LEAP Academy S.T.E.M high school completed $12. Million from capital credits funds

EPILOGUE

LEAP is very much a work in progress. And where I once believed that there might be a conclusion to my work in education and a completion to my efforts at community transformation, I am now convinced that LEAP—despite its remarkable success and singular achievements—will always be an unfinished work in progress.

That's especially because at the epicenter of my work are the children—the poor, the disenfranchised, the disadvantaged and forgotten urban kids, and their families—who are locked in a cycle of poverty, with few opportunities to escape that cycle, with little chance to get a good education, and virtually no hope to find meaningful work and lead productive lives without a good education. I suspect that, when there is not a single child left who needs help to escape the cycle of poverty and achieve his or her full potential, maybe then my work will be done.

As it is, LEAP has helped hundreds if not thousands of children and their families break the cycle of poverty, with a 100 percent graduation rate since its first high school graduation in 2005 and a 100 percent acceptance rate into institutions of higher learning, a goal and achievement that is at the core of LEAP's mission and operation.

The book you have just read is very much a status report on the LEAP experience, from its earliest vision to opening in 1997, to its present day as one of the most remarkable charter school operations in America. I have opened five schools on Cooper Street in Camden—two high schools, two elementary schools, and an early learning research academy. One was a rehabilitated building, and four of them were new construction, all financed by bonds, loans, and private sources that have to be repaid, because charter schools in New Jersey receive no facilities money from the state or local school district.

With LEAP in the lead, Cooper Street, which had become a deteriorated and abandoned business thoroughfare, has been converted into a thriving education corridor, now boasting classroom buildings and residential halls of two universities and a community college, side by side with LEAP. Each of these institutions has new projects planned for Cooper Street. And, LEAP's proposed expansion is also rooted in Cooper Street, with an agreement to purchase a fully renovated twelve-story building that will house new schools, classrooms, and other ventures to support the LEAP education enterprise.

By 2018, LEAP's enrollment can grow to over eighteen hundred students, more than 15 percent of the entire Camden school-age population. The expectation is that this expansion of students will continue to grow at LEAP. The education pipeline I have created, from infancy through college, is also being extended, with LEAP alumni being organized and recruited to return to Camden and do whatever they can to support the mission of LEAP.

Great opportunities exist for LEAP as we look into the future to upscale our best practices and to support Camden public schools. In 2013, the State of New Jersey took over the Camden public schools, and we have begun discussions with the new, state-appointed Camden Schools superintendent, Paymon Rouhaniifard, at a time that he lay outs his vision for transforming the city's most troubled schools. We have been invited to provide a leadership role with the city's principal and assistant principal training program to build capacity for the district, and to partner with Camden schools that are struggling and need support. We have always wanted to support Camden's public schools and upscale our LEAP best practices, and now is a great opportunity and time to do so.

Our principal mission at LEAP now is formalizing and implementing the lessons learned and upscaling best practices that can be useful to others. Four factors make LEAP work different from any other school: (1) the student factor—students are the focus of our work; (2) the teacher factor—incentives for pay for performance,[92] partnerships with Teach for America, professional development as a priority, and teachers in instructional teams; (3) the operational factor—setting systems in place to provide support and hold people accountable; and (4) strategic alliances, particularly with anchor institutions, businesses, community interests, and parents.

I believe that LEAP, with its broad range of wraparound services in centers of excellence around the pipeline is a unique model for education reform. We are working to propagate the LEAP model through consultancy, in Ghana, West Africa; Puerto Rico and the Caribbean; Brazil; and Australia, as well as consulting in other states—New York and others.

In conclusion, It might be overly simplistic to say, but if there's one thing

---

[92] LEAP Academy Charter School, Performance Based Compensation Program:
http://www.leapacademycharter.org/Bulletin/LEAP%20pay-for%20performance%20plan.pdf

I've learned in my life experiences—from the beginning on that poor farm in Puerto Rico, through the dispiriting migrant worker camps to the mean streets of Camden, the struggle for academic acceptance and success, the treacherous world of politics and government in New Jersey, and the crowning achievement of creating LEAP as it is today—it's that dreams can come true. Certainly the conceptual American dream, as I have lived it—with hard work, perseverance, and dedication, regardless of a person's origin—is real and achievable.

So many of my visions and plans have become reality that at times I wonder why I am not as content or as satisfied with the results as I should be. I learned not to settle and to strive for excellence, so as soon as my hopes and dreams are realized, as soon as a project has been completed, I envision new and even greater challenges and bigger mountains to climb—certainly as those challenges pertain to the children of LEAP. I know that as long as I live, I will continue to dream for the children, to work for them, and, with every fiber of my being, to strive to make those dreams a reality.

ACKNOWLEDGMENTS

Many people influenced me in writing this book and contributed to the idea of telling the story of my life and the creation of LEAP, even before I decided that it was worth doing. Therefore, I must thank the inordinately large number of educators, parents, students, advocates, policy makers, philanthropists, academics, leaders of higher education, governors, legislators, social entrepreneurs, and mentors who have stood by me throughout this journey to support my dream and work. I also want to thank my family and friends from my kitchen cabinet, colleagues who made significant contributions to my life and work. Without them this book would not be a reality today. I hope this book is of use to them and others committed to community and school transformation.

The writing of the book was very challenging to me because it required much objectivity and transparency in telling my story and to be able to speak with freedom about my memoirs. It required sharing very personal experiences—representing tragedy and triumph in my trajectory—which was difficult and painful at times. If I have forgotten to mention acquaintances or important people who have supported my work, I ask for forgiveness ahead of time. Just know that you are all deeply valued, even if those names or experiences are not mentioned.

First and foremost, I want to thank the young people who inspired me to write this book, my amazing children at LEAP Academy, whom I love dearly. They are the most remarkable and resilient young people I have ever met. Their stories and mine are intertwined in mind and soul, and I see myself every day in them. This is a story of the American dream come true, a story of mostly poor immigrant parents who only want the best education for their children, and children who prove every day they have the potential to achieve at the highest level. I also want to thank the families, teachers, staff, and administrators of LEAP Academy, who work so hard to ensure that LEAP is producing excellent scholars. And, to the board of trustees, who contribute their time and efforts in ensuring that our students achieve, I thank you for your support and commitment to excellence.

I want to thank the original LEAP working group of stakeholders and partners that inspired the formation of this work: Dr. Joe Fernandez, the lead consultant to the LEAP planning project; Governor Jim Florio; Rutgers Camden Provost Walter Gordon; Rutgers President Frances Lawrence; Rutgers Camden Provost Roger Dennis; Rick Wright, chief of urban affairs for Governor Florio; Paul Drayton, Delaware River Port Authority executive director; state senator Jack Ewing; Governor Christie Todd Whitman; state assemblyman John Rocco; Governor Jim McGreevy; US representative Rob Andrews; Melanie Schultz; state senator Donald Di Francesco; Alma Sarravia; and state senator Wynona Lipman, whose collective mentoring and guidance taught me everything I know today about public policy. At the local level, Camden Schools superintendent Roy Dawson, his teachers and staff, and the many parents,

children, and community members who came to build the "village"—
thank you for believing in my efforts. And, for the Rutgers Camden
faculty, staff and students, who spent countless hours in research and
conducting service learning courses, I thank you for your commitment
to the children of Camden.

My heartfelt thanks go to the most devoted and loving people I know
in my life—my parents, Don Pedro and Dona Lila; my partner, Mikele
Pastorello, who loves me and takes good care of me unconditionally;
and my most loyal "friends" ever, my dogs Tilin and Atachi, who have
sat quietly next to me for many hours waiting for me to finish the work.
Without their support and understanding, this book would have never
happened.

I do want to give special thanks to my good friends not included in the
book who have been directly instrumental in the process of its creation.
My two "editors," Fred Hillmann and Rona Parker, conducted interviews,
transcribed many interviews from tapes, and edited and shaped my
writing. They listened to my endless stories, and those of my family and
friends, and helped choose those that in retelling would paint the most
authentic picture of my life experiences. I am deeply indebted to their
assistance and support. One of the most profound treasures of this project
has been the gift of their friendship and advice throughout this creative
process, and I will be forever grateful to them for believing, encouraging,
and supporting me throughout the entire journey.

I am also deeply grateful to my staff from the Center for Community
Leadership at Rutgers, particularly Sonia Gonzalez, who has devoted
many hours in collecting photographic and ethnography research, and
Darleen Garcia, my graduate research assistant, for assisting with data
collection and analysis, and layout and formatting of the work. I cannot
express enough gratitude to Wanda Garcia, my associate director at the

Center, not only for her diligent effort in collecting information for the LEAP case study, but for all of her support and dedication to my work all these years. She has been at my side since the beginning. And to the rest of the center staff, some of whom have come and gone, I thank you for all you've done to move this work forward.

Finally, I am truly grateful to the Rutgers University Board of Governors, the succession of university presidents, provosts, deans, and department chairs who supported my innovative ideas and provided the freedom to enable me to do my research, fund raise, teach, and create new programs to support the LEAP social enterprise. The partnership of Rutgers and LEAP has been critical to creating the social enterprise, and is a prime reason for writing this book.

APPENDIX A

The Miracle on Cooper Street
Cast of Characters

Saul Alinsky (1909-1972): Community organizer and social policy thinker whose writings and ideas served as guiding principles throughout my academic and professional career. LEAP Academy charter schools could not have been established or flourished unless they were built on grassroots support through community education, involvement, activism, and empowerment.

U.S. Rep. Rob Andrews: Democratic congressman whose district includes Camden, NJ, one of the poorest and most dangerous cities in the United States. His early support led to the acquisition and transformation of an environmentally contaminated property forsaken by Greyhound Lines and symbolic of Camden's deterioration and abandonment, into a state-of-the art playground for LEAP Academy students.

Brenda Bacon: Chief of management and planning, a cabinet position in the administration of NJ Governor James J. Florio (1989–93). As a founding board member of LEAP Academy and a trusted adviser, her insights and political smarts were key to the establishment of a strong board of trustees, as well as navigating the whirlpools of Camden politics.

Marta Benavides: Salvadoran exile in the '60s and '70s. Mysterious social activist and sometime Central American "revolutionary" who plucked me from Cowtown, the market frequented and beloved by migrant workers, and became the dominant influence in my early education and thinking. She introduced me to books and learning, to key Latino activist figures, and to social theory, and guided my development as a proud Puerto Rican and community activist. I learned from her how to work for social justice and, ultimately, how to leave her in order to pursue my own dreams.

Alejandrina Bonilla: Grandmother, "Abuela Mama." Her story is a testament to the moral strength and fortitude of the Bonilla women and sets the background for the migration story of the Bonilla family from Puerto Rico to the mainland United States. Hers is a story of love and dignity in a traditional and historic culture.

Nuncia Bonilla: My mother. Strong-willed and staunchly family-oriented, she is very religious and unwavering in her adherence to Puerto Rican culture and lifestyle. I inherit "sagacidad," my steely resoluteness, from my mother. Our conflicts grew as my independence and singular pursuit of an education took root. When it was a choice between my education and my family, I chose education and left. For ten years I did not go back, until my Alfie took me home to ask for my hand in marriage.

"Don" Pedro Bonilla: My father. Under Operation Bootstrap, he was the first in the Bonilla family to come to the States to work in migrant camps in New Jersey and Florida as a crew leader and migrant worker organizer, navigating his way between protecting the workers and representing the farmers. From him I inherit my values and deep sense of fairness. Strong and silent, he doesn't exhibit the typical Latino machismo or chauvinism and chose me, his youngest daughter, to become his "right hand" in the migrant fields as translator and often as intermediary between farmers and migrants. My first lessons in organization and labor problems were learned from him, and my experience in reading the all-important road map for him as navigator on our annual migrant labor trips from New Jersey to Florida and back evolved into creating my own personal road map to set and reach my future in education and community activism.

Peter Burke: Treasurer of LEAP Academy. As Governor Florio's appointee to chair the Delaware River Port Authority, the first time I met him he delivered $1.5 million for planning the LEAP initiative. He says that now each time I see him I expect him to bring a million dollar check. He is the sound fiscal voice who advises that I cannot finance the LEAP structures of my dreams and then works as hard as he can to make it possible.

Governor William T. Cahill: Governor of New Jersey 1969–73. A member of Governor Florio's Management Audit Commission, who asked me to serve him coffee and later apologized, saying he thought I was an aide because I looked so young. I was young, but Governor Florio had confidence in me and appointed me cochair of this important committee with Stanley Van Ness, the first public advocate of New Jersey. That committee also included John Petillo, former chancellor of Seton Hall University and then president and CEO of Horizon Blue Cross and Blue Shield of New Jersey, and Lawrence Codey, then president and CEO of Public Service Electric and Gas Company.

Cesar Chavez: Leader of the Migrant Farm Workers Movement. My father was part of his movement, and I became a passionate educator/ advocate during a youth encampment in Tuscon, Arizona, financed by the

American Friends Service Committee, when I explained why we must not cross his picket line and learned I, too, could influence the achievement of social justice. With Cesar Chavez at the encampment was his best friend and labor organizer Dolores Huerta, who was instrumental in getting labor to support his efforts.

Eric Clark: My friend from the '70s and on. A Camden resident and one of Marta Benavidez's group, Eric gave me my first real introduction to the city that has become the center of my life. He gave me work as a tutor that sustained me when I had no other income. His ideals of pacifism continue to inspire me in my fights for social justice.

President Bill Clinton and Secretary of State Hillary Rodham Clinton: My inspirations to believe again in the political system. Their vision moved me to become an elected Clinton delegate to the 1994 Democratic Convention, become involved again in politics, and actively campaign for him. I was invited by Hillary Clinton to join her at the UN Fourth World Conference on Women in China in 1995 and was thrilled by her declaration that women's rights are human rights.

Roger Dennis: Chancellor of Rutgers Camden campus until 2007—the chancellor who promoted me to tenure, professor, and distinguished professor. He supported me for over ten years as a member of the university community and board member of LEAP. As a mentor and a good friend, he provided guidance and support to me during difficult times and good times, always with integrity and courage and a commitment that matched my own to make Rutgers Camden a partner with the local community.

NJ state senator and former governor Donald DiFrancesco: Member of the state's Commission on Women and Sex Discrimination. From his position as president of the senate, he was an important supporter of charter school legislation and an effective advocate for school reform. He became a valued adviser during my work for welfare rights for women, and as a Republican he was instrumental in gaining the support of Governor Christine Todd Whitman to enact the charter law.

NJ Assembly Speaker Joe Doria: Sponsor of the charter law. An academic, with a doctorate in education, whose support for education is steadfast. He is a good friend of children, and his support for LEAP Academy was evident from its earliest inception, both as an educator and a legislator. Joining Democrat Joe Doria as sponsors were Republican assemblyman John Rocco and Democratic senate president John Russo.

Paul Drayton: Executive director, Delaware River Port Authority. He was instrumental in providing $1.5 million to initiate LEAP Academy. His efforts convinced the DRPA board to support the purchase of the first building for our students, which began LEAP's impact on the transformation of Camden's Cooper Street. It was Paul who secured bonding for the second LEAP building, our first LEAP Academy Charter High School.

NJ state senator Jack Ewing: Father of the NJ charter school law. As chair of the Senate Education Committee and sponsor of the charter school law in the senate, no one had a greater role as it worked its way toward passage. With the change of administrations from Democratic Governor Florio to Republican Governor Whitman, it was Jack Ewing, a Republican from a wealthy suburban district, who was instrumental in continuing the bill's movement, diverting voucher advocacy and keeping the focus on charters.

Joseph A. Fernandez, EdD: LEAP education consultant. Armed with his academic credentials, along with his experience as chancellor of the New York City Public Schools, his guidance has been invaluable. He worked with our stakeholders' focus groups of parents, community, educators, and elected officials to help design the LEAP model and build the support that brought us success.

Governor Jim Florio: Governor of New Jersey 1989–93. As governor he was instrumental in funding the original research that ultimately led to the passage of the New Jersey charter school law. He long ago advised me that if I wanted to work for change and social justice—and I did not want to run for political office to do it—I should concentrate on policy. His words guided me, and when he became governor and appointed me to his transition team, I was ready, having studied and enacted policy as an applied scholar. He is a former boxer, and he characterizes me as a verbal pugilist.

Wanda Garcia: Associate director of the Center for Strategic Urban Community Leadership. Wanda was a student representative on the committee that interviewed me for my first position at Rutgers Camden and questioned me in Spanish to convince herself that I was a bona fide Latina. She became my first employee and has been with me for thirty years. She is as tough as I am, my best trusted friend and colleague, and was the maid of honor at my wedding. She is currently a PhD candidate.

Sonia Gonzalez: LEAP webmaster and graphic designer. The treasured young member of my family whose talents amazed me from the moment I met her on a trip back home to Puerto Rico, and she showed me the artwork she had been storing under her bed. Since coming to New Jersey for her degree at Rutgers, she has flourished as an artist, and I am so proud of her. Her gentle strength was my salvation after Alfie died, when she came to live with me. It was Sonia who resolutely steered me into purchasing Fifo, the shih tzu, who made me smile during those first months; today, I think Fifo's successors, my Atachi and Tilin, love her as much as they do me.

Walter Gordon: Chancellor of Rutgers Camden until 1997. The Rutgers chancellor who hired me, he is the person who challenged me to think differently about academia. We began our long-term relationship with his advice on how difficult it would be to get my PhD. He also believed that I should go into an administrative role in higher education, because as he honestly warned me, no one who looks like me had yet become a full professor at Rutgers. I believed, however, that I needed to be in a teaching role. He challenged every decision I made, but in time became one of my biggest supporters.

Lisa P. Jackson: U.S. Environmental Protection Agency. Former commissioner of NJ Department of Environmental Protection, she provided the clout to get a cleanup and removal of oil tanks from an abandoned Greyhound property that has become the playground for our first LEAP Academy charter school. Her action stands as an example of fighting the corporate establishment and forcing it to be held accountable for actions that have abused the urban landscape.

James Jennings, PhD: Professor of Urban and Environmental Policy and Planning, Tufts University. An urban sociologist, he has influenced my work and supported me throughout my career. He continues to encourage me to pursue my dreams, and it was he who supported my early research efforts through tenure. He has nominated me for many national awards, which I received. A true scholar and a great friend, he is a person whose research and writings on urban poor and community and community development are monumental.

Sidney Katz: Dean, Rutgers Camden campus. On the day I fled Camden, no longer able to face the reality of gang warfare that killed a teenager in my youth group; I sat next to Dean Katz on a train. His kindness prompted him to express concern about my distress, to give me his business card, and to encourage me to submit my resume for my first job at Rutgers as assistant director of academic foundations. He hired me, and our friendship grew through the years. I will always be grateful for the enormous support from him in my early efforts to recruit Latino and African American students into Rutgers, which has made the campus more diverse.

William Kornblum, PhD: My mentor and dissertation chair. Dr. Kornblum is professor of sociology at the City University of New York, where I received my PhD. He influenced me to become the professor that I am and was instrumental in influencing me to pursue my career in academia as a professor, rather than as an administrator. He supported me for tenure and for promotion at Rutgers, which honors me because he is one of the most knowledgeable people I know.

Francis Lawrence: President of Rutgers until 2002. During his presidency I was considered and granted early tenure at the time I was working with the Florio administration in an appointed position on the state's Management Audit Commission. I worked under President Lawrence to understand the university budgeting process to better represent and explain our fiscal position as the commission considered budget cuts, a delicate position for a nontenured faculty member. President Lawrence was instrumental in my promotion and then in getting LEAP approved by the board of governors as the first charter school affiliated with Rutgers, the State University. I received the Warren Sussman Award for Excellence in Teaching, the highest recognition from the president of the university, from President Lawrence.

NJ state senator Wynona Lipman: The first African American woman elected to the state's upper house. A Fulbright Scholar with a doctorate in philosophy, Senator Lipman, more than anyone, taught me the power of ideas and knowledge in getting things done in a political environment. While always treating people with class and elegance, she was morally tough and constant and could fix a recalcitrant legislative colleague with a steely gaze and tell him to do "the right thing," most often on behalf of women, minorities, children, and small businesses.

Richard McCormick: President of Rutgers until 2012. President McCormick was installed as the new president as the McGreevey administration came into office in New Jersey. The LEAP Academy Charter High School was in progress, and we needed the university credit ratings for a $10 million bond to build the school. President McCormick endorsed this proposal and led the discussions and approvals with the board of governors. He has continued to provide support and encouragement for my program initiatives at the university and at LEAP. Most recently, our LEAP program has benefited from his endorsement of the Center for Strategic Urban Community Leadership, which I established at Rutgers, and the Early Learning Research Academy, which is housed in the newest building on Cooper Street to be constructed by my efforts in the city of Camden.

Governor James McGreevey: Governor of New Jersey (2001–04). The governor appointed me to his transition team to provide advice on education matters and, during his administration, I was appointed to the Charter School Committee to strengthen the movement in the state. My relationship with the McGreevys was personal, as well as governmental. His former wife, Dina Matos, who was New Jersey's first lady, was a student of mine in a Newark leadership program.

Gabriella Morris: Former president, Prudential Foundation. In this position, she provided advice and leadership, as well as giving us the first grant to train parents to be leaders in transforming the local school district. After the charter school law was enacted, she initiated a charter school short-term loan program for charters that were struggling financially. We were the first charter to use this program, which provided us with the $2 million that enabled us to serve our first students in portable units until we were able to buy a building.

David Murphy: Delaware River Port Authority. A friend and adviser to LEAP, Dave in his leadership position at the DRPA was the owner representative to the first building purchased and financed by DRPA for LEAP. To this day, Dave continues to be involved in supporting my efforts as the owner representative to the STEM (Science, Technology, Engineering and Math) High School building, which is under construction, and as adviser and supporter to all buildings purchased by LEAP.

Mark Murphy: Former president, Fund for New Jersey. He was the first person to give me a planning grant for all my projects, including LEAP. He is more than a funder. He is a believer in my innovations and ideas and supported all my projects that promote social justice, including leadership development, women's issues, and LEAP Parents' Institute. His early endorsement validated my work to other funders and in turn brought them to the table to support my efforts in Camden.

Joe Nathan, PhD: Charter school pioneer. After studying his work in Minnesota, I was honored to be mentored by him in the movement and in the progression of the charter legislation from development to enactment. His commitment has brought him to New Jersey to provide professional support and endorsement. His training has benefited teachers and parents, and enhanced the success of LEAP.

Joseph Rodriguez: First Latino U.S. District Court judge in New Jersey. A colleague since he taught at Rutgers Camden Law School, he became a member of my board for Hispanic Affairs when I served as director. His friendship and support are of great value to me and the LEAP community.

Norma Rosa Agron: Coordinator of enrollment, LEAP Academy Charter School District. The first parent to be hired by me to organize parent involvement, she trained to become the school's first parent coordinator and finished her own schooling. In the tradition of Saul Alinsky, Norma went door to door gathering supporters and participants for focus groups and training sessions—all to advance LEAP. Norma's two sons are graduates of LEAP, and she is now the proud grandmother of a LEAP Academy student.

Vilma Ruiz: My first friend in Camden. Vilma invited me to live in the basement of her parents' home to learn about Camden. That was my home for six months, and during that time I became a part of the community. Vilma has remained a friend all these years. Her two sons are LEAP alumni, and her sister's children are also part of our student body.

Alma Saravia: Aide to NJ state senator Wynona Lipman and counsel to the State Commission on Sex Discrimination in the Statues. Her guidance throughout the LEAP charter school application process was undaunted. It was especially valuable when I was faced with a last-minute need to defend the establishment of LEAP to the Rutgers hierarchy. She advised me to bring my own lawyer and then arranged to have an education attorney from her firm accompany me to New Brunswick during critical LEAP-saving negotiations.

Alfredo Santiago: My Alfie. My first love and soul mate. When I got married in 1983, immersed in my doctorate and teaching career, I was in love, and that was all I needed. So I married him fast, and we lived a century of happiness in my mind before he died. He was so handsome and so intellectually dynamic. He supported all my projects and all my dreams and was my ethical compass. He held my hand on the train ride all the way into New York when I went to defend my dissertation. Alfie was the highest-ranking Latino in the Rutgers administration, and the morning before Thanksgiving 1996 we were going to spend the day cooking, but first he was going to his office in New Brunswick. At a time he never went to his office, on a day he was not supposed to be at work, on a corner moments from our home, he was hit by a drunk driver. He never came out of a coma and passed away just before New Year's Eve. He never saw the signing of the charter school legislation, which became law a few weeks later. He lives for the students he never knew through the Alfredo Santiago Scholarship Fund, which has grown to over $1.5 million.

Melanie Schulz: Executive director of the Joint Committee on Public Schools of the New Jersey Legislature. A perfect example of the government committee staffers who really run things in Trenton, Melanie's knowledge of the legislative process and the legislators themselves made her a key player in the passage of the charter school legislation.

Yvonne Vargas: A founding parent. Her hard work in the early days has borne fruit. Yvonne's two sons are graduates of LEAP. Her oldest now has his bachelor's degree from Rutgers, and her youngest is a Rutgers Camden student. Yvonne works with the early learning program and is continuing her education.

Governor Christine Todd Whitman: Governor of New Jersey 1993–2001. With the defeat of Governor Florio, the charter school legislation and LEAP Academy dreams were in jeopardy, until Senator Ewing, a friend of Governor Whitman, took up the fight. Governor Whitman signed the charter school law in January 1996 with me at her side. LEAP Academy Charter School was on its way, and Governor Whitman was a good friend and frequent visitor.

Rick Wright: Florio administration associate treasurer, director of economic development, chief of staff. Well before the charter law was envisioned, Rick advised and mentored me into placing the concept of community schools on Governor Florio's agenda. He understood and believed in the importance of my work and supported it by opening doors and making available the resources that would make it possible to successfully lead this important reform in education.

Annual Rutgers/LEAP gala, December 2004; Senator Jon Corzine US senator from New Jersey and former governor

James Edward "Jim" McGreevey, former governor of New Jersey Annual Rutgers/LEAP gala, December 2002

Geoffrey Canada Promised Neighborhoods Conference in New York City, New York Harlem Children's Zone, November 2009

Archer & Greiner Partner James H. Carll; U.S. Senator of New Jersey Robert Menendez; Rutgers Camden Campus Chancellor Wendell Pritchett; Gloria Bonilla-Santiago; former Rutgers president Richard Levis McCormick; Donna Frisby-Greenwood; Congressman Robert E. Andrews, First District of New Jersey; and Rochelle Hendricks, secretary of higher education (ELRA ground-breaking, November 2010)

Ground-breaking LEAP Academy University High School, October 2003

REFERENCES

Agron, Norma, interview by Fred Hillmann and Rona Parker. *Interview* (July 29, 2011).

Association, National Education. *N.A. State-by-State Salary Listing.* 2013.

Atenco, Julio, interview by Fred Hillmann and Rona Parker. "Interview." *LEAP Academy Graduating Class of 2011 Salutatorian.* (June 29, 2011).

Austin, James E. *The Collaboration Challenge: How Nonprofits and Businesses Succeed Through Strategic Alliances.* San Francisco, CA: Jossey-Bass, 2010.

Bacon, Brenda, interview by Fred Hillmann and Rona Parker. "Interview." *Chief of Management and Planning, a cabinet position in the administration of NJ Governor James J. Florio (1989 – 1993).* (July 8, 2011).

Bonilla-Santiago, Gloria, PhD. "One Drop-out in Four is still too Many." *Huffington Post Blog,* June 13, 2013.

—. "Responsible Civic Engagement: Supporting Sustainable Communities." *International Conference on Interdisciplinary Social Sciences, Monash University Centre.* Tuscany, Italy, 2008.

Burke, Peter, MBA, CPA, interview by Fred Hillmann and Rona Parker. "Interview." *Treasurer of LEAP Academy.* (June 13, 2011).

Calefati, Jessica. *NJ.com.* 2013. http://www.nj.com/camden/index. ssf/2013/06/state to seize control of camden.html.

—. *NJ.Com.* 2013. http://www.nj.com/camden/index.ssf/2013/06/state to seize control of camden.html.

Casey, Annie E. *A Path Forward for Camden.* Baltimore: The Annie E. Casey Foundation, 2001.

Center for Strategic Urban Community Leadership (CSUCL). *Camden Counts: A Strategic Plan for the Project LEAP Academy.* Camden, NJ: CSUCL, 1995.

Clark, Steven A. "Performance Auditing: A Public-Private Partnership." *Public Productivity & Management Review,* 1993: 431-436.

Danielson, Charlotte. *Enhancing Professional Practice: A Framework for Teaching.* Alexandria, VA: ASCD, 2007.

Dennis, Roger, PhD, interview by Fred Hillmann and Rona Parker. *Chancellor of Rutgers Camden campus until 2007.* (September 26, 2011).

Education Law Center. *Education Law Center.* October 3 2013. http:// www.edlawcenter.org/cases/abbott-v-burke/abbott-history.html.

Eubanks, Segun C. *The Urban Teacher Challenge: A Report on Teacher Recruitment and Demand in Selected Great City Schools.* Belmont, MA: Recruiting New Teachers, 1996.

Finn, Chester E., Bruno V. Manno, and Gregg Vanourek. *Charter Schools in Action: Renewing Public Education.* Princeton, NJ: Princeton University Press, 2001.

Florio, James J., interview by Fred Hillmann and Rona Parker. *Interview* (May 25, 2011).

Garcia, Wanda, interview by Fred Hillmann and Rona Parker. "Interview." *Associate Director of the Center for Strategic Urban Community Leadership.* (July 11, 2011).

Genova, Angelo, JD, interview by Fred Hillmann and Rona Parker. "Interview." *First Legal Counsel for LEAP Academy.* (August 3, 2011).

Gonzalez, Sonia, interview by Fred Hillmann and Rona Parker. "Interview." *LEAP Webmaster and Graphic Designer.* (July 11, 2011).

Gordon, Walter K, interview by Fred Hillmann and Rona Parker. "Interview." *Chancellor of Rutgers Camden until 1997.* (August 5, 2011).

Griffin, Jessica, and Cheryl Pruce. *LEAP Academy University Charter School's Performance-Based Compensation Program.* Washington, D. C.: Center for Educator Compensation Reform, 2013.

Hanushek, Eric A. "Assessing the Effects of School Resources on Student Performance: An Update." *Educational Evaluation and Policy Analysis* 19, no. 2 (1997): 141-164.

Hill, Charles W.L., and Gareth R. Jones. *Strategic Management: An Integrated Approach.* Boston, MA: Houghton-Mifflin Company, 2007.

Jennings, James. *Evaluation Report for the Project LEAP Academy Charter School.* Rutgers-Camden, Camden, NU: Center for Strategic Urban Community Leadership (CSUCL), 1997.

Kincaid, John. "Developments in Federal-State Relations: 1992-93." In *The Book of the States,* 576-586. Council of State Government (June 1992), 1994.

Kopkowski, Cynthia. "Why they leave." *National Education Association,* 2008.

—. "Why they leave." 2008.

Kozol, Jonathan. *Savage Inequalities: Children in America's Schools.* New York: Random House Digital, Inc., 2012.

Ladd, Helen F. *Holding schools accountable: Performance-based reform in education.* Edited by Helen F. Ladd. Washington, DC: Brookings Institution Press, 1996.

Lee, Barbara A. "Letter from Barbara A. Lee to Walter Gordon (Provost, Rutgers-Camden)." *Project LEAP.* New Brunswick, NJ, July 31, 1996.

Leusner, Donna. "Whitman Signs Bill, Rings Opening Bell on Charter Schools." *Action on Trenton,* January 12, 1997.

Lytle, James H. "Reforming Urban Education: A Review of Recent Reports and Legislation." *The Urban Review* 22, no. 3 (1990): 199-220.

Martello, Thomas. "Teachers OK Charter School Plan." *Courier Post,* December 19, 1995.

Mintrom, Michael, and Sandra Vergari. "Education Reform and Accountability Issues in an Intergovernmental Context." *Publius: The Journal of Federalism* 27, no. 2 (1997): 143-166.

Mintrom, Michaela, and Sandra Vergari. "Education Reform and Accountability Issues in an Intergovernmental Context." *Publius: The Journal of Federalism* 27, no. 2 (1997): 143-166.

Mohrman, Allan M, Susan A. Mohrman, and Allan R. Odden. "Aligning teacher compensation wtih systemic school reform: Skill-based and group-based performance rewards." *Educational Evaluation and Policy Analysis* 18, no. 1 (1996): 51-71.

Mohrman, Allan M., Susan Albers Mohrman and Alla R. Odden. "Aligning teacher compensation with systemic school reform: Skill-based pay and group-based performance rewards." *Educational Evaluation and Policy Analysis* 18, no. 1 (1996): 51-71.

Mooney, John. "Going one on one with new superintendent of Camden public schools." *NJ Spotlight*, 2013.

National Education Association. *N.A. State-by-State Listing.* 2013.

"Rutgers University Camden." *LEAP Academy Charter School: Performance Based Compensation Program.* Camden, NJ: http://www.leapacademycharter.org/Bulletin/LEAP%20pay-for%20performance%20plan.pdf, January 9, 2011.

Schulz, Melanie, interview by Fred Hillmann and Rona Parker. "Interview." *Executive Director of the Joint Committee on Public Schools of the NJ Legislature.* (August 23, 2011).

Seneca, Joseph J. "Letter from Josheph J. Seneca (University Vice

President for Academic Affairs) to Dr. Gloria Bonilla-Santiago."
Project LEAP. New Brunswick, NJ, October 25, 1996.

Statistics, National Center for Education. *Teacher Attrition and Mobility: results from the 2008-2009 Teacher Follow-up Survey (NCES 2010-353).* Washington, DC: U.S. Department of Education, 2010.

Vargas, Yvonne, interview by Fred Hillmann and Rona Parker. *Interview* (June 29, 2011).

Vasquez, Sylvia, interview by Fred Hillmann and Rona Parker. "Interview." *LEAP Academy LEAP Academy Graduating Class of 2011 Valedictorian.* (June 29, 2011).

Vernon, Elliott. *World Socialist.* 2013. https://www.wsws.org/en/articles/2013/03/30/camden30.html.

Wohlstetter, Priscilla, and Noelle C. Griffin. *Creating and Sustaining Learning Communities: Early lessons fom Charter Schools.* US Department of Education, Office of Educational Research and Improvement, Washington, D. C.: Educational Resources Information Center, 1997.

Wohlstetter, Priscilla, and Susan Albers Mohrman. *School-based Managment: Strategies for Success.* Washington, D. C.: ERIC Clearinghouse, 1993.

Wohlstetter, Priscilla, Richard Wenning, and Kerri L. Briggs. "Charter Schools in the United States: The Question of Autonomy." *Educational Policy* 9, no. 4 (1995): 331-358.

Wright, Rick, interview by Fred Hillmann and Rona Parker. "Interview." *Chief of Staff to Governor Florio, 1993-94.* (June 16, 2011).

CPSIA information can be obtained at www.ICGtesting.com
Printed in the USA
BVOW03s0816310315

393974BV00002B/5/P